TWO MONSOONS

TWO MONSOONS

Theon Wilkinson

with drawings by

Bill Smith

Duckworth

First published in 1976 by
Gerald Duckworth & Co. Ltd
The Old Piano Factory
43 Gloucester Crescent, London NW1

ISBN 0 7156 1015 5

Filmset by Specialised Offset Services Limited, Liverpool
and printed in Great Britain by
A. Wheaton & Company, Exeter

Never the lotus closes, never the wildfowl wake
But a soul goes out on the East wind that died for England's sake –
Man or woman or suckling; mother or bride or maid –
Because on the bones of the English, the English flag is stayed.

Miles Irving

To the souls 'on the East wind'
especially
Percy John Warren McClenaghan

Contents

Preface

The origin of this book is as follows. In 1972 I took my son on a sightseeing trip to India to mark his 21st birthday, retracing the steps of three generations of the family. One of the things that struck us on our visit was the appalling condition of many of the European cemeteries. A few of the cemeteries contained fascinating architectural monuments crumbling into total dilapidation; some tombs were damaged beyond repair, their stone used by local builders, their marble slabs removed for grinding curry-powder – or even reappearing as coffee-tables in the fashionable houses of Calcutta. Above all, we noted the obvious waste of acre upon acre of cemetery land, often in the centre of an overpopulated city.

I began to collect information on cemeteries and tried to enlist the support of the interested parties – the State, the Churches, the British High Commission, the local community and relatives. As I proceeded, the spirits of the past seemed to rise from their monuments, as it were, and to demand inclusion in a book. An abundance of curious material was revealed, and the book began to write itself.

Various themes have emerged in the writing, and the structure of the book is as follows. After an introductory chapter setting the scene, I begin in Chapter 2 with a panorama of personalities: some, the officials – Governor-Generals, Judges and Bishops – who strove to impose rules in which they believed upon a culture quite different from their own; others – traders, soldiers, doctors, missionaries – who reacted in their own ways to the ferment of ideas and lifestyles. Chapter 3 draws on the public records of young wives and their children and describes the extraordinary consequences for them of high mortality and the combination of mercenary and romantic motives in the marriage market. Chapter 4, on the Portuguese, Dutch, French and other Europeans, reminds one that if there had not been a British Raj there would have been some other form of foreign Raj. In Chapter 5, some interesting or amusing epitaphs and stories are collected for their own sake; and Chapter 6 discusses the causes of mortality as evidenced by the stones, from plagues and fevers to murders, sporting accidents and other sudden deaths peculiar to India.

It is my hope that these fragments from the past will give an insight into the life and death of Europeans in India in the last three centuries, and show the attempts that were made by some to bridge the cultural gap between East and West – attempts often visible in the architectural style of the monuments themselves. Much was taken by Europeans out of India, and this in turn influenced Europe; but much more than is commonly realised was put back in its place – morally, culturally and materially – as can be seen from the epitaphs.

Another aim of the book has been to further my long-term project – the preservation and restoration of a few of the historically important cemeteries, which are as much a part of India's heritage as Roman remains are of Britain's, and the return of most of the acres of decaying graveyards in city centres to the Indian State for use as parks or playgrounds, once the legible tablets have been removed to the nearest churchyard. Action is needed by a third party to break the existing deadlock between the State, which owns the land, and the Churches, who are responsible for its upkeep but have very inadequate financial resources. The Indian Christian community can hardly be expected to pay to maintain what was often an exclusively European graveyard. Ruin therefore proceeds apace, aided by vandals. For instance, the tablet on Rose Aylmer's grave has recently been destroyed; a falling tree has pulverised the tomb of Warren Hastings' first wife; and each year many important tombs and monuments collapse beyond repair. The best protector of cemeteries is superstition. The belief in ghosts remains strong in the neighbourhood of each old cemetery and restrains some would-be despoilers of the valuable stones, marble and wrought-iron – but not for long. Even the Burial Registers and Church records are being gradually eaten away by white ants.

Encouraged by the interest shown in the problem by Indians and British alike during my two further visits to India in 1974 and 1975, I have formed an association of Friends of European Cemeteries in India, Pakistan and Bangladesh, to exchange views and consider the best way of translating good intentions into deeds, and to compile a register of available information and a photographic record of interesting tombs. Anyone interested is welcome to join.

To return to the book. For simplicity, the whole sub-continent, including modern Bangladesh and Pakistan, is referred to as 'India', and 'England' is often used to cover the whole of the British Isles. I have not attempted to impose a rigid system on the chaotic spelling of Indian words and names; some are of one period, some of another, but once adopted, the same spelling is used consistently.

There is a glossary of the less common words at the end of the book. The epitaphs have been taken from many different sources (see Appendix B and bibliography). Sometimes there is an inevitable conflict of evidence over a date, word or phrase. In all cases I have taken the version that appears to me the most likely. In transcribing inscriptions I have tended to omit repetitive introductory phrases such as 'Sacred to the memory of' and sometimes a few lines or sentences.

The drawings by Bill Smith of tombs and monuments are based on actual graves in particular cemeteries (details are in the List of Illustrations), with some artistic licence allowed in the grouping. I think the drawings succeed admirably and am grateful for this enhancement of my text.

I have used several diaries or family papers which have never been quoted before. Thanks are due to the late Lt.Col. A.V.A. Mercer of Darjeeling and his nephew Lt.Col. A.E.E. Mercer in England for the loan of the following: the diary of Major-General T.W. Mercer, spanning the period between his joining the 46th (Bengal) Native Infantry in 1843 and his retirement as a Commissioner in the Punjab in 1877; *The Autobiography of an Old Soldier*, a privately printed account of thirty-six years' service with the 45th (Bengal) Native Infantry and later the 1st Goorkha Light Infantry, by Major-General J.S. Rawlins, 1843-79; and *Letters of a Servant of the Hon. John Company*, the privately edited and printed correspondence of Major-General J.S. Rawlins. I am grateful to Richard Langworthy for permission to quote from the letters of Stanhope Cary, a fascinating unbroken correspondence of over one hundred letters, written home while he was serving as a young subaltern and later as an Assistant Commissioner, between 1855 and 1862, during which period he was twice recommended for the V.C.; and Anthony Harris for letting me use the letters of David Inglis Money, Judge of the Appeal Court, Calcutta, written to his mother in England and his son William – for a time Private Secretary to Major-General James Outram at Lucknow – during the period 1857 to 1860.

I am grateful to friends who have lent me material, both papers and photographs, which I have used in one form or another in the book: Doris Andrews; Vincent Davies; Giles Eyre; John Hearsey; Katherine Manstead; Monica Morris, who gave me the notes made by her father Colonel W.A. Morris; Ian Murison; Louis Pinhey; Douglas Rivett-Carnac; and my sister Zoe Yalland. A number of libraries were most helpful, and I take this opportunity to thank personally Miss Joan Lancaster, the Director of the India Office Library and Records, along with Mrs. Mildred Archer and all the other staff there who have assisted me in so many ways over the last two years. Also Mr. A.K. Pallot, the Director-General of the Commonwealth War Graves Commission; Donald Simpson, the Librarian of the Royal Commonwealth Society; Colonel P.S. Newton, the Secretary of the Army Museums Ogilby Trust; Miss E.R. Talbot Rice of the National Army Museum; and Mr. L.W.L. Edwards of the Society of Genealogists. And I must add a special word of gratitude to Dennis Rowe for painstakingly drawing the map.

I am indebted to many friends and contacts in India for the assistance and hospitality I received during my three visits between 1972 and 1975, in particular to Sir Michael Walker, the British High Commissioner in New Delhi, Mr. J. James, the First Secretary, and his office staff – particularly Mr. D.C. Chauhan – who provided every facility for me to examine the relevant records; Colonel Lall of the United Services Institute Library, John Webster of the Library at the Christian Institute of Sikh Studies, Batala, and Miss D. Keswani of the National Archives, New Delhi; Maurice Shellim who provided a base for many of my researches in Calcutta, and Robert Wright who showed me round Bhowanipur Cemetery; Geoffrey Seager and William Oakley in Mirzapore, Archdeacon Harlan in Allahabad; the Hooker family in Benares; the Butterworth family in Dharmsala; Father Timothy in Amritsar, and others in Calcutta, Cawnpore, Delhi, Bombay, Madras and elsewhere who are too numerous to name, but without whom I would have missed much.

I am grateful to Messrs. Macmillan for permission to quote verse and prose by Rudyard Kipling; Messrs. Faber and Faber for extracts from *Old Soldier Sahib* by Frank Richards, London, 1936; and S.K. Chatterjee of Calcutta for extracts from *Old Calcutta Cameos* by B.V. Roy, Calcutta, 1946.

There have been many remarkable coincidences in the writing of this book which have spurred me on, not the least strange of which is that both my father-in-law, Captain P.J.W. McClenaghan M.C., and my publisher's father, Major W.C.S. Haycraft M.C. (and Bar), were officers in the same battalion of the same regiment (5/8th Punjab) and met similar violent deaths in peace-time within months of each other forty-six years ago. I am grateful to my publisher and his wife for their help and encouragement, and also to my editor, Emma Fisher, who has struggled with my untidy manuscript and rescued me from numerous solecisms. If any inaccuracies remain, they are my own.

T.C.W.

April 1976

Illustrations

INDIA

... at Bombay, September and October, those two Months which immediately follow the Rains, are very pernicious to the Health of the *Europeans*; in which two Moons more of them die, than generally in all the Year besides. For the excess of earthy Vapours after the Rains ferment the Air, and raise therein such a sultry Heat, that scarce any is able to withstand the Feverish Effect it has upon their Spirits, nor recover themselves from those Fevers and Fluxes into which it cast them ... Which common Fatality has created a Proverb among the English there, that *Two Mussouns are the age of man.*

(The Revd. James Ovington, 1690)

... the breaking up of the rains this season was attended with much fatal illness and a number of the European inhabitants of Calcutta were carried off; in the month of September alone there were seventy funerals.

(William Hickey, 1791)

1 Two Monsoons

Each year the monsoon winds of July and August bring the rains on which India's teeming population depends, but the early European travellers found them the very opposite of health-giving. The mortality rate was unbelievably high by modern standards. The sea voyage itself claimed a fair share of victims during the six or seven months it took to cover the 15,000 miles from an English port round the Cape to Madras, Calcutta or Bombay; and deadly fevers, contagions and other unknown causes of sudden death awaited the arrivals. Ovington in 1690 noted that 20 of the 24 who arrived with him in Bombay at the commencement of the annual rains, as well as the entire ship's company, had died before the rains ceased. Bombay had then scarcely 800 European inhabitants, but only 100 survived the seasonal fevers of 1692. India was a 'White Man's Grave' before that expression became fashionable in the new West African colonies of the late nineteenth century, when young men going to the Gold Coast used to be advised to make friends with the Baptist Mission, as they possessed 'a hearse with plumes'. There was no such luxury in the seventeenth-century Bombay, and it was probably more deadly than any of the West African stations.

After a series of deaths near Madras in 1833, the Surgeon requested the Commandant to let the dead be buried quietly without music or firing, as the almost daily repetition of the 'Dead March' had a depressing effect on the sick and dying. In Calcutta, in one year, out of a total European population of 1,200, over one third died between August and the end of December. Nor was this mortality confined to particular epidemic years. It was a regular annual occurrence: the survivors used to hold thanksgiving banquets towards the end of October to celebrate their deliverance.

Yet still they came: the traders, artisans, sailors, military adventurers, priests and physicians from Portugal, the Netherlands, England, France, Denmark, Greece, Italy and almost every country in Europe. The Portuguese came first, after their sailors had discovered the route round the Cape of Good Hope in 1498; and they had a century's start to build their trading posts around the coast of India before the Dutch and English formed Companies to compete with them for the wealth of the Indies. The French entered the scene a little later, in the second half of the seventeenth century, and the Danes too in this period began taking their share of the trade. In fact between the early 1600s and 1760 India was a fairground of Europeans of many nationalities establishing factories and settlements around the coast under the protection of the local Raja, to whom they paid tribute.

India was firmly ruled at the beginning of this period by a succession of four strong Moghul Emperors – Akbar, Jahangir, Shahjahan (builder of the Taj Mahal) and Aurangzeb – who consolidated their Empire over virtually the whole of the country. After Aurangzeb's death in 1707, however, the government fell into the hands of weak puppet-emperors who were unable to stem the tide of mounting Hindu reaction to their conquest. Anarchy spread. The European traders had to look more and more to themselves for protection, recruiting their own armies and turning factories into forts. It was the English reaction to the sacking of their fort at Calcutta in 1756 – the 'Black Hole' disaster – which led to the battle of Plassey and the establishment of the English, almost by accident, as landlords of 882 square miles of Bengal. Profitable trade depended on tranquillity, and the unsettled conditions in the districts bordering their trading posts gave the English, French and other Europeans a direct interest in extending their influence. Eventually, in the second half of the eighteenth century, it became clear that the power-vacuum caused by the collapse of the Moghul Empire would be filled by one or other of the European nations, and by 1800, while the French were preoccupied with their own internal revolution, the English East India Company supported by King's troops emerged as the paramount power. Thereafter India was, for all practical purposes, 'British India'. The other European nations only retained small trading enclaves, but 'John Company', the greatest capitalist corporation the world has ever seen, continued to spread its influence over the whole of India, defeating each fragmented province in turn – Bengal, Mysore, the Mahrattas, the Gurkhas, and finally the Sikhs – so that by the mid-nineteenth century the Company held undisputed sway over the whole of India. For a Company to rule an Empire was an anachronism, and after the traumatic events of the Indian Mutiny in 1857 the House of Commons assumed direct responsibility for the government of India, and continued to exercise this power with the aid of a handful of carefully selected administrators – the 'competition-wallahs' or the 'heaven-born', as the members of the Indian Civil Service were variously known; the 'incorruptibles', as later generations may learn to call them. They never numbered much more than 1,000 and, when the curtain was finally rung down on the British Raj in 1947, included in their ranks 400 Indians.

What, we may ask, brought these Westerners to this unhealthy country where sudden fevers took such a heavy toll, and what made them stay? The exciting prospects of huge fortunes to be made in India were enough to overcome their initial qualms, but the records of the early years of the East India Company bear out another saying that was common among the English, Dutch and Portuguese traders in Calcutta, that 'the kingdom of Bengal has a hundred gates open for entrance but not one for departure'. The city was nicknamed 'Golgotha' by sailors, and certainly few returned to Europe to enjoy their fortune. The lucky 'nabobs' who aroused the envy of their compatriots in London or Bristol, with their loud clothes and indiscriminate extravagance, were only a small proportion of those who set out so confidently to 'shake the pagoda tree' – as the expression was for bringing back a fortune from India (the 'pagoda' being equivalent to four rupees, or approximately one-third of a guinea). Their aim had been to seek a fortune and retire, not to stay and die; but the well-tenanted burial grounds in India testified to the many young men who 'drew a blank in the great Indian lottery'.

The proportion of those who escaped death and returned safely to their homeland has been put as low as one in seventy. This exaggerates the death rate, since some settled in Bengal permanently. Fryer, in the late seventeenth century, summed up the chances of survival in the East as follows:

For in Five hundred, One hundred survive not; of that One hundred, one quarter get no Estates; of those that do, it has not been recorded above One in Ten Years has seen his Country.

There is no denying the large fortunes amassed by the few who survived – often, even by the standard of those days, amassed by dubious means, as was stated in the Report of 1765, headed by Clive himself:

> ... that every spring of the Government was tainted with corruption; that principles of rapacity and oppression universally prevailed, and that every spark and sentiment of public spirit was lost and extinguished in the abandoned lust for universal wealth.

Many famous families in England and France rose to power as a result of Indian wealth. It was on the fortune he brought back from Madras that Thomas Pitt founded the great family which gave England two Prime Ministers. Starting as an 'interloper' – an unlicensed trader – he retired as Governor with immense riches, including the famous Pitt diamond. Another Governor of Madras who started as an 'interloper', Elihu Yale, founded the American University that bears his name, and two of his daughters bolstered up great landowning families by marrying a Devonshire and a North (who became the grandfather of a third Prime Minister, the great Lord North). Commerce and trade were still incompatible with 'gentility', as far as nabobs were concerned; but the social barrier could be crossed by means of such judicious marriages, and the next generation was then accepted in the closed ranks of the landed aristocracy. The attitude of the upper classes towards these Indian upstarts emerges clearly from contemporary accounts:

> It is an unnatural thing that persons who, had they remained in England, would have kept a shop or become county apothecaries, or at the best have been city merchants, should presume to stake their guineas, keep their mistresses and punish insults to their imagined honour in the manner of gentlefolks.

The feeling of outraged caste extended to the political field, where the nabobs were buying their way into Parliament and arousing great jealousy. Yet in spite of all the criticisms that could be levelled at these men for the way they acquired and spent their Indian wealth, England became the richer from the circulation of their new money. Universities, hospitals, botanical gardens and other cultural institutions had reason to be grateful for the interest taken in them by nabobs. Much new capital was injected into the rapidly expanding Industrial Revolution by millionaires like Farquhar. Many men of letters – from Addison to Thackeray – and many men

"The Kingdom of Bengal has a hundred gates open for entrance, but not one for departure."

in public life acknowledged their debt to the leisure that Indian wealth provided. So the allegations of corruption, rapacity and oppression can be mitigated by these contingent benefits. In the context of the enormous risks attendant on the long voyage to and from India and the years in a fever-ridden port, the moral perspective changes. For example, in the twenty-two years between 1755 and 1777, only two covenanted servants of the East India Company returned from Bombay with a fortune; and of these one, Henry Oxinden, was impeached, and the other, John Child, was later accused of fraud! Forbes writes of his own eighteen years in India, from 1763 to 1781, that of the original nineteen passengers that embarked with him from England 'seventeen died in India many years before my departure and for the last ten years I have been the only survivor'.

Early death was so common that there was constant reference to it in the literature of that time. Edward Terry comments on parents in England sending 'unruly spirits' – an expression meant to include both the black sheep and the illegitimate offspring of the aristocracy – out fortune-hunting, 'that they might make their graves in the sea or on the Indian shore'; and there are frequent references to the continual changing of characters on the oriental scene with the rise and demise of generations in a short space of time. Casual and matter-of-fact as the references often are, the cumulative evidence provided by contemporary journals, books and memoirs on the appalling risks confronting the European visitor to India up to the mid-nineteenth century and beyond, leaves one wondering, as Hilton Brown put it, 'at the courage that carried men – and the devotion that carried their wives – to the East of those lethal days'.

The average age of death of Europeans in India in the early colonial period, excluding infant and child mortality, was well under 30 for men and 25 for women, but these statistics do not reflect the meagre chances of survival during the first year or two in India. In some of the more unhealthy settlements the rate of mortality during the first year approached 50 per cent. In Batavia, in the East Indies, a consistent average of 50 per cent or more was maintained right into the nineteenth century. The comparatively healthier places, such as Madras, recorded 50 dead out of every 100 arrivals over a slightly longer time-span – of 30 Ensigns arriving there in 1775, only 16 were alive in 1780 – and five years was regarded as the acclimatisation period needed for the European visitor to become 'salted', or seasoned. Similar sickness and mortality was recorded in other tropical settlements throughout the world. Major Luke Smyth

O'Connor, comparing the mortality in Jamaica with that in the
Windward and Leeward Islands in the 1840s, wrote:

> I find Jamaica, with a sad reputation of being so fatal to
> Europeans, and even taking the 60th (Rifles), with the frightful
> mortality at the very onset, not more destructive of human life
> than the various colonies of the West Indies. Of 5,915 men
> scattered through the several stations in the latter, 823 died in
> three years, or one-seventh of the original force.

The difference lay in the means of checking these fevers in the West
Indies, where a two-hour march into the mountainous interior
reduced the temperature by as much as 40 degrees Fahrenheit and,
as Major O'Connor commented, 'the scorching heat of the plains is
exchanged for an exhilirating temperature and delicious
atmosphere, the salubrity of which is equal to any part of the world'.
The same could hardly be said of India, where the nearest hill-
stations were hundreds of miles away. It was generally accepted
that a European needed an iron constitution to survive a residence in
the plains of India.

Of course the mortality rate was high even in England at the
corresponding period, and outbreaks of cholera were quite common;
but the epidemic fevers which struck the overcrowded industrial
cities in nineteenth-century England were spasmodic, compared
with the Indian fevers, which were endemic and seasonal. The
London insurance companies regarded the chances of life in India as
very low, and 100 per cent worse than in England for a man before
the age of 50 – though after 50 the chances of the 'salted' Anglo-
Indian appeared better than those of the middle-aged Englishman,
who might succumb to the cold and winter damp. Nor must one lose
sight of the pitifully short life-span of most Indians and their
appallingly high infant mortality rate, even today. For example, the
Burial Register of the small community of Indian Christians in
Amritsar between 1944 and 1955 reveals that 65 of the 100 or so
burials were of infants under the age of three, a further 20 of persons
not yet thirty, and 10 of persons between the ages of 30 and 49; while
of the remaining 5 who died over the age of 50 only one reached
three-score years and ten. The local inhabitants were, to some
extent, resistant to diseases like malaria, typhoid and dysentery
through generations of natural built-in immunity, but their living
conditions and general under-nourishment exposed them to the
worst ravages of cholera, plague and other epidemics, once these
had caught hold in an overcrowded town.

Generation after generation of Englishmen echoed with hindsight the opinion that the Indian fortune was not worth the rigours of the climate. Sir Philip Francis, writing towards the end of the eighteenth century, when he was on the point of returning to England with a large fortune, exclaimed: 'No, not for that fortune would I spend the same two years again ... I would gladly accept two-thirds of the money if I could be up to the neck in the Thames.' And Macaulay, sixty years later, hating every minute of his time in India, listed over forty Latin and Greek authors he had read during thirteen months of his 'bitter exile' in a deliberate attempt to close his mind to oriental influences. 'There is no temptation of wealth or power, he wrote, 'which could induce me to go through it again.' In addition to other discomforts, the brain-distorting heat had to be endured in the most unsuitable clothes. The English (unlike the French, Portuguese and Danes) insisted on wearing the same heavy clothes 'whether stationed in the Torrid or the Frigid Zone, scorched in India or frost-bitten in Canada'.

The amazement felt by many at the motives that led ordinary Englishmen to face these hardships in India can be seen in the remark made in 1838 by the Hon. Emily Eden, the sister of the Governor-General:

> How people who might by economy and taking in washing and plain work have a comfortable back attic in the neighbourhood of Manchester Square, with a fire-place and a boarded floor, can come and march about India, I cannot guess.

Yet to many humble Englishmen, India offered an excitement not to be found at home, as expressed by Sir Alfred Lyall in his poem 'The Land of Regrets':

> Doth he curse Oriental romancing,
> And wish he had toiled all his day,
> At the Bar, or the Banks, or financing,
> And got damned in a common-place way?

It was the suddenness of death as much as its frequency that made an impact on Europeans living in India. Lady West, the wife of a Judge, noted in her diary on 22nd September 1825:

> We have just heard the melancholy news of the death of a poor young man here, a Mr. Bax, so sudden that he was dead before his friends knew that he was ill. He was to have dined with us today, and the bell tolling was the only way that we heard of it.

Another writer, Hadley, in a description of life in India in 1805, remarks:

> We have known two instances of dining with a gentleman [i.e. at mid-day] and being invited to his burial before supper time.

In face of this dramatic mortality, it was hardly surprising that the small community of Europeans adopted an 'eat-drink-and-be-merry' attitude which only created yet another source of death:

> Punch and sherbet, being always cheap, were the common drinks of the young military men – and pretty freely they were consumed, at all hours from morning to night. And to this slow poison it may be confidently asserted that a very large proportion of the annual mortality may be attributed.

While some found relief in alcohol, others experimented with hallucinatory drugs – such as datura, bhang (cannabis) and opium – which reputedly led to dropsy and other incurable diseases. There was an almost total ignorance of modern hygiene – of the importance of boiling water and milk, washing fruit and vegetables and avoiding extremes of temperature – and contemporary documents throw a lurid light on living habits:

> Having ate heartily of meats and drank a quantity of porter, they throw themselves on the bed undressed, the windows and doors open. A perfuse perspiration ensues which is often suddenly checked by a cold North-West wind. This brings on what is called a 'pucca fever' which will often terminate in death in six hours – particularly with people of a corpulent plethoric habit of body.

Some elementary precautions were taken over drinking water, the main source of infection. But this was perhaps more by accident than by design, for until almost the end of the nineteenth century medical men believed that most epidemics – cholera in particular – were airborne diseases. The abdar, or wine-bearer, always accompanied his master to dinner parties with his own private supply of cooled water and usually his own eating implements, thus unwittingly reducing the risks of contamination. Then there was the growing custom of tea-drinking, which required boiling water; and from the early nineteenth century soda-water became popular with various alcoholic beverages – each reducing the use of the local water supply. A local historian gives a vivid picture of the Calcutta water:

The European residents in Calcutta fought shy of using the river-water principally because of the unwholesomeness caused by the number of dead bodies floating in it and the filth thrown in. The arrangements at this time for the cremation of the Hindu dead bodies were primitive and extremely limited, and the poorer classes generally disposed of their dead by throwing the bodies into the river. Bishop Heber in his Journal, dated 1822, mentions dead bodies floating by as he was proceeding up the river by boat. Mr. Strachey in his report as Sanitary Commissioner for Bengal, so late as March, 1864, stated that: 'More than 5,000 corpses have been thrown from Calcutta into the river, which supplies the greater part of its inhabitants with water for all domestic purposes, and which for several miles is covered as thickly with shipping as almost any river in the world. 1,500 corpses have actually been thrown into the river in one year from the Government Hospitals alone!'

However, in spite of all these gradual and unconscious steps towards greater hygiene, the water-borne disease of cholera remained the chief single killer until comparatively modern times. In 1906, for example, it is recorded that an army battalion lost over 50 men in one month during the monsoon; and on another occasion 200 men and 4 officers were lost through cholera in 48 hours. In Agra cemetery there is a monument, typical of many, to the memory of 146 men of a Battalion of the Yorks and Lancs Regiment who died of cholera in the 1890s within two days of the appearance of the disease. Army officers' diaries recorded a similar picture in almost every cantonment on a frightening scale. For instance, Captain Mercer records:

The Cholera broke out at Ferozepore on 15th August (1856) and continued to rage till 20th Setpember during which time the following Europeans in the Station were hurried into the presence of their Creator:

Lieut. Taylor 45 Native Infantry
Mrs Ross, wife of Captain Ross, Assistant Commissioner

45 Men   ⎫
1 Woman   ⎬   of Artillery
3 Children ⎭

101 Men
1 Woman } of H.M. 70th Foot
26 Children

And several Subordinate Officers of the Magazine and Station Staff

Besides cholera, people died from typhoid, dysentery, small-pox, plague, malaria, heat-stroke, rabies and other contagions.

Disease and illness on such a scale provided a fertile field for doctors and surgeons who arrived in the Presidency towns of Calcutta, Madras and Bombay in increasing numbers. The normal medical fee was one gold *mohor* per visit – roughly equivalent to two guineas – a lot of money for those days; and soon the complaint was heard that 'you may ruin your fortune to preserve your life'. The methods of treatment were horrifying by modern standards, although they were merely based on the system of blood-letting and purging then prevalent in the West. A charge of one rupee for an ounce of salts and three rupees for an ounce of bark (quinine) added to the physicians' profit. Patients were cupped or leeches were applied until they fainted from loss of blood. Then they were blistered with red-hot irons, the treatment concluding with several strong – and very necessary – narcotic draughts. Another 'grand specific' was mercury, described enthusiastically by the surgeon on board H.M.S. *Caroline* during a voyage to India in 1805, as 'that astonishing medicine, the sheet-anchor in this [dysentery], as well as most other diseases of the country. It is hard to conceive how Europeans would manage if deprived of this wonderful drug, when it is considered how many thousands annually owe the preservation of their lives to its effect.' He then gave detailed instructions for taking this drug in conjunction with bleeding and purgatives – particularly as a cure for hepatitis:

1st. By bleeding to eighteen or twenty ounces ... particularly if the person is fresh from Europe.

2dly. By purgatives, especially calomel ones ...

3dly. As the above-mentioned are mere preliminaries, the grand specific must be applied to, as soon as the operation of the purgative medicines is over.

It may, and indeed ought to be used, both internally and externally. Internally say thus: Take four grains of Calomel [mercurous chloride] and one grain of Opium ... repeated every four hours ... using at the same time mercurial frictions on the thighs and arms etc to hasten the operation of the calomel ...

While these methods are pursuing, blisters (after evacuations) will of course be put to the side to relieve the pain ... never losing sight, however, of the principal object, the *saturating the system with mercury*.

It became a dramatic race between the doctor and the disease as to which would kill the patient first. The horrors of treatment were only alleviated by the reputed therapeutic value of claret, which was imbibed by patients in huge quantities whatever their complaint.

The hospitals, such as existed, enjoyed an unenviable reputation, and people only entered them when all else had failed. Strange rumours circulated of patients indulging in wild orgies and visiting the 'Black Town' at night. Hamilton, writing in the early eighteenth century – and medical practice advanced little over the following hundrd years – made the caustic comment:

> The Company has a pretty good Hospital at Calcutta where many go in to undergo the grievance of physic, but few come out to give account of its operation.

The *Bengal Gazette* of 1781 carried some amusing verses on doctors of which the following are a selection:

> Some doctors in India would make Plato smile
> If you fracture your skull they pronounce it the bile,
> And with terrific phiz and a stare most sagacious,
> Give a horse-ball of jalap and pills saponaceous.
> A sprain in your toe or an anguish shiver,
> The faculty here call a touch of the liver,
> And with ointment mèrcurii and pills calomelli,
> They reduce all the bones in your skin to a jelly.

When doctors and hospitals failed – as they so frequently did – burial followed within hours, because of the climate. Twelve hours was usually the most that elapsed between death and burial. There was a preference for night burials, perhaps for the heightened effect of the funeral cortege with the accompanying torch bearers, and also to avoid the heat of the day. One such night funeral is described in detail down to the last nail in the coffin: '1,500 nails@ Rs9/-; 100 cooleys to bear Dammers [torches]; 200 Dammers @ Rs7/- per 100.' Another explanation was as follows: 'All funeral processions are concealed as much as possible from the sight of the ladies, that the vivacity of their tempers may not be wounded.' As in England, ladies did not usually attend funerals. But the ladies were fully aware of the terrible toll of lives, as is shown in their diaries. Lady West wrote in hers, at Bombay, on 27th July 1826: 'These frequent sudden deaths make one tremble. The last year they have been quite awful.' And on an earlier occasion, 30th July 1823, again during the monsoon: 'Here people die one day and are buried the next. Their furniture is sold the third and they are forgotten the fourth ... O Lord! preserve my husband and me.' They both died in the monsoon of 1828.

The soldiery were so accustomed to the frequent burial parades that they adopted an almost jocular approach to the ceremony. On the way to the burial ground (known in soldier's slang as the 'Padre's godown') the band usually played the Dead March in *Saul*, breaking into rollicking comic songs on the return journey to the barracks. Thursday was a half-holiday in the garrison towns throughout India, and there was a standard light-hearted plea to any afflicted comrade struck down with fever – 'Please don't die on Wednesday night'. Rawlins records in his diary the death of five of his brother officers in 1851, one after another, of different maladies, and he dramatically describes the fifth officer's demise:

> ... but poor Moore's death at Cawnpore was much more sudden; he was playing billiards at 10 a.m., at 11 a.m. he was seized with cramps and nausea, dead at 1 p.m., and at 5 p.m. the same day we were taking him to the cemetery, playing the splendid but melancholy air, the 'Dead March in Saul', which grand piece of music I have heard on so many sad and painful occasions.

Elaborate arrangements were made for the rapid disposal of the unfortunate victims of these sudden fatal fevers, and when the Governor-General went on tour – as late as 1880 – spare coffins were carried on his train. At hill-stations, such as Mussoorie, where the ground was so rocky that it took two days to prepare a grave, there were always two spare graves dug ready for the next burial, and the practice has continued to this day.

With so many funerals taking place, the chaplains were busy. So much so that the duty had to be performed by young Company merchants deputising for them and drawing an allowance of £50 p.a. for their trouble. The chaplain's fees were high – 5 gold mohors for baptisms; 16 to 20 gold mohors for marriages; and from 2 to 10 gold mohors for burials, depending on the 'class'. The decision on whether a burial was in the first or second class was usually determined by the vestry in accordance with some rough line of social demarcation. In Madras, for instance, the vestry resolved: 'In burials, the rule shall be governed by this distinction; those who use the best pall (Europe black cloth) shall be considered in the first class, those who do not use the best pall shall be allotted to the second class.' The church, needless to say, kept a stock of both best and second-class palls for covering coffins and also hired out mourning palanquins. Religion and trade were not seen as incompatible in those days and several chaplains were able to make a reasonable fortune in a short time. Their salaries compared favourably with those of Senior Merchants in the East India Company. They were paid by the Company out of the revenues of the country, with the fees for birth, marriage and interment as private perquisites. The great majority of the chaplains and clergy of all denominations supplemented their income by the proceeds of the silk, tobacco and opium trade, making profits of over £1,000 in a year – a very large sum for those days. In addition they frequently took part in organising and speculating in lotteries, gambling at cards and the general amusements of the station; but although instances have been given of a chaplain expressing extreme irritability at the interruption of a good evening at cards ('Another d——d soldier to bury!'), the soldiers would have been the first to admit that he never flinched from duty. In many areas chaplains were scarce, and people often died without benefit of clergy. But the event was still always surrounded with its own pathetic ceremony, as can be seen in the following letter to his relatives on the death of Lieutenant Cary at Lullutpore in Central India in September 1862:

It took place last evening twenty minutes past seven o'clock ... and there was no clergyman within 76 miles, so he did not receive the last Sacrament before his death. He is to be buried this afternoon ... Just after his death my husband cut off a good portion of his hair which with his desk and other little things we will take care of until an opportunity occurs to send them home to you ... His coffin was made in our own house and the poor fellow laid in his last bed by my Husband, who did *all* for him. I merely mention this as his relations might like to know that in a foreign land all the last offices were performed by a friend and no native servant allowed to touch him.

The chaplains themselves were not immune from early death. The first English chaplain to visit India, in 1615, attached to Sir Thomas Roe's Royal mission to the Court of Akbar, the Moghul Emperor,

died a few months after arrival. A hundred years later the chaplaincy of Calcutta remained vacant for two years after Anderson died in 1710 and was then filled by three young chaplains who died in rapid succession. The year 1761 was known as the '*annus miserabilis*' for the church in Calcutta, as both chaplains were carried away in a terrible epidemic of cholera.

Apart from the chaplain's fees for burial and the extras for the pall and mourning palanquin, there was the cost of the grave itself. Here, once again, the niceties of social distinctions were taken into account. Officers' graves were in separate rows from those of non-commissioned ranks. For the 'civilians', as those who worked for the East India Company were known, the cost of the grave was about Rs.500 for the first ranks and Rs.300 for the second. The church historian refers to the two cemeteries of North and South Parks, 'disjoined merely by a broad road ... There is no difference between these two grounds, but in the expense of the monuments which denote that persons of large fortune are interred and vice versa.' The towering obelisks, pagodas and Grecian-style monuments reflected the relative wealth and position of those interred below. The custom was to open a subscription list towards the erection of a suitable memorial for each person that died; the bigger the subscription, the more ostentatious the monument. These constant contributions became a source of acute financial embarrassment to the less wealthy members of the community. The story is told of the manager of one jute mill near Calcutta inquiring of other mills whether their Company made any contribution to their assistants' funerals to relieve the pocket of their colleagues; and the reply from a dour Scottish manager: '*Our* assistants *never* die'.

Cemeteries were reserved exclusively for Europeans, apart from an occasional Indian Christian wife, such as the one recorded on a tomb in the Putligarh cemetery, Amritsar: 'Hannah Kaisroo, daughter of Diwan Kissim of Bhagul, loved wife of C. Andrew Esq., 1879, aged 23'. One General was so attached to his *beebee*, or mistress, that when on her death the chaplain refused to bury her in the consecrated ground of the European cemetery, he interred her in a neighbouring field and then built a church over the grave (see p. 118). Indian Christian cemeteries and European cemeteries are often found side-by-side but separate, and this 'apartheid' in death was maintained over much of the British India until the end of the Raj. Such separateness was derived not so much from any conscious racial policy as from the regulations of the East India Company which required that every English subject of the King be registered; hence all births, marriages and deaths of the King's subjects abroad had to be notified to the India Office in London. For administrative convenience, the cemeteries and Burial Registers for 'expatriates' tended to be kept separate from the 'native' Christians, and as late as 1934 there is correspondence within the Churches reminding chaplains that 'the Burial Register kept by us is for *Europeans only* and not for Indian Christians'.

With the expansion of trade into the interior of India, the progress of European influence was marked by the multiplication of cemeteries. Westward and north-westward from Calcutta, along the river Ganges, the main route for traffic was lined with cemeteries – Moorshedabad, Patna, Benares, Chunar, Mirzapore, Allahabad, Cawnpore and stretching to Lucknow, Delhi and then on to Ferozepore and Amritsar in the Punjab. The trades of undertaker, stone-mason and sculptor prospered. At first many of the ornamental stone memorials came from England, but soon the pressure of business led to local manufacture, stones being taken from the ruins of Hindu temples in old deserted cities – such as Gaur in the case of Bengal undertakers. The first undertaker to settle in Calcutta was a Mr. Oldham, who tried to popularise his morbid profession by exhorting people to buy their final plot in advance and urging them to erect conspicuous monuments 'to inspire martial enthusiasm, the flame of patriotism or the emulation of genius in the youthful breast'. 'It goes without saying,' wrote Busteed, the local historian, 'that Mr. Oldham amassed a fortune before he himself was laid, in 1788, in the Park Street cemetery, surrounded by numerous specimens of his own handicraft.' Oldham was a celebrated local character, and the *Bengal Gazette* published a poem in 1781 mocking the ineffectiveness of both doctors and clerics:

> In a very few days you're released from all cares –
> If the Padre's asleep, Mr. Oldham reads prayers.

Oldham not only arranged the burial and, on occasions, took the service, but provided all the 'coffin furniture', the mourning scarves and hats and other fashionable funeral accoutrements. The burying of a Nabob, as of his counterpart in England, was extremely lucrative – as is immortalised in one of the old songs in *Chambers' Journal*:

> Dukes, Lords I have buried and squires of fame,
>   And people of every degree.
> But of all the fine jobs that came in my way
>   A funeral like this for me.
>   This is the job,
>   That fills the fob,
> O! the burying a Nabob for me.

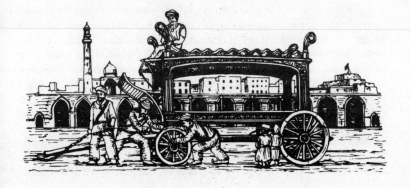

2 · The Social Spectrum

The impact of England on India produced many strange results. This chapter 'resurrects' from the cemeteries scattered around India some of the outstanding individuals in their various spheres of endeavour. Many great deeds were performed and many mistakes were made, but these Englishmen and women lived their lives full-bloodedly and were, in the end, as much influenced by India as they influenced it. There was a curious interaction between the two opposing cultures – the outward-looking, interventionist, innovating, impatient West and the inward-looking, fatalistic, changeless, mystic East.

In this review of selected tombs and monuments, I have preserved roughly the same order as the occupants followed in their lifetime under the strict 1841 rules of 'Precedence in the East Indies'. Life in those days was governed by such social distinctions. They continued to the grave, where the size and grandeur of the monument followed the same order of importance. After the Governor-General came the Governor of Bengal and the Governors of Madras, Bombay and Agra, in that order. The Chief Justice of Bengal and the Bishop of Calcutta came next, followed by their counterparts in Madras and Bombay. The Commander-in-Chief in India and Members of the Supreme Council – 'according to their situation therein' – followed with their exact counterparts in Madras and Bombay. The Puisne

Judges of the three Presidency towns followed and then –
surprisingly low down on the list – the Commander-in-Chief of Her
Majesty's naval forces; and so on down to 'civilians', the East India
Company servants. The civilians were categorised in six classes
according to their service in the East and equated with equivalent
ranks of army officers and clerics. The ladies took their places
according to the rank assigned to their husbands, with the exception
of ladies having precedence in England, 'who are to take place
according to their several ranks'.

But sometimes in this chapter logic has overtaken precedence. For
instance, missionaries follow Bishops, and military officers and
mercenaries follow Generals, instead of being relegated to the end.

Governor-Generals and Viceroys

Observance by the English of the social distinctions of seniority and
rank was reinforced by the oriental inclination to invest with
elaborate ceremonial those with power and authority. The
Governor-Generals, at the summit of Society and wielding a power
seldom equalled, lived like emperors, surrounded by a combination
of English and Indian pageantry. Gold and silver Chobdars, the
ceremonial mace-bearers, preceded the great Lord wherever he
went, while his wife entered discreetly through a side-door. (This
oriental protocol remained unchanged until after 1858, when the
Governor-General became the Viceroy to signify rule from England,
and Lady Canning became the first Vicereine.) The Governor-
General had state elephants, state umbrellas, state barges, and a
retinue to accompany him on state visits – sixty or seventy
elephants, three hundred camels and bullocks – that recalled the
splendours of Rome. The holders of this exalted post were usually
appointed from the ranks of the Scottish nobility and only one was
ever promoted from within the Indian Civil Service. They held a
unique position: their word was law over the millions of Indians on
the vast sub-continent, and any London criticism of their policy took
so long in transit as to be ineffective. It was said that their office
combined 'the irresponsibility of the Great Moghul with the
infallibility of the Pope'.

The first Governor-General to die on Indian soil was Lord
Cornwallis. Rawlins visited the place of his burial some forty years
later, when still a subaltern, and wrote:

The cemetery at Ghazepore contains the remains of Lord
Cornwallis, who died in 1805, and was twice Governor General of

India; the same Lord Cornwallis who so bravely defended Yorktown in 1781, and after the most obstinate resistance, was compelled to surrender it to the Americans and French. The Government erected a very handsome monument to his memory, which is well preserved and kept in order at the public expense.

This monument is still maintained in excellent condition by the Government of India through their Archaeological Department, a tribute to historical sense over-riding natural anti-imperialist sentiments. Cornwallis must be one of the most monumented men in the world. In India he was the object of ardent hero-worship; and statues, temples and memorials were erected to his honour in Bombay, Madras and several places in Bengal. His huge mausoleum reminded Bishop Heber (see p. 34) of an imitation Sybil's temple with pillars 'of the meanest Doric ... too slender for their height'. The cenotaph by Flaxman is of white marble, bearing on one side a medallion bust of Lord Cornwallis between the figures of a Brahmin and a Mussulman, and on the other, figures of a European and a Native soldier in atittudes of sorrow. These figures epitomised the career of a man who fought and ruled in three continents – he was also, for a time, Viceroy of Ireland – and his lengthy epitaph sets out his achievements in India:

Sacred to the memory of Charles, Marquess Cornwallis. Knight of the Most Noble Order of the Garter, General in His Majesty's Army, Governor-General and Commander in Chief in India ... His first administration, commencing in September 1786 and terminating in October 1793 was not less distinguished by the successful occupations of war and by the forbearance and moderation with which he dictated the terms of peace, than by the just and liberal principles which marked his internal government. He regulated the remuneration of the servants of the State on a scale calculated to ensure the purity of their conduct. He laid the foundations of a system of revenue which while it limited and defined the claims of government, was intended to confirm hereditary rights to the proprietors, and to give security to the cultivators of the soil. He framed a system of judicature which restrained within strict bounds the power of public functionaries and extended to the population of India the effective protection of laws adapted to usages and promulgated in their own language. Invited in December 1804 to resume the same important station, he did not hesitate, though in advanced age, to obey the call of his country. During the short term of his last administration he was occupied in forming a plan for the pacification of India which, having the sanction of high authority, was carried into effect by his successor. He died near this spot, where his remains are deposited, on the 5th day of October 1805, in the 67th year of his age. This monument erected by the British inhabitants of Calcutta attests their sense of those virtues which will live in the remembrance of grateful millions long after it shall have mouldered in the dust.

Cornwallis's regulation of 'the remuneration of the servants of the State on a scale calculated to ensure the purity of their conduct' was his greatest claim to fame, for, by providing proper salaries and forbidding private trading by civil servants, he laid the foundations of the Indian Civil Service. He was an exception to the general love of ostentation, and as he lay dying on the banks of the river Ganges, he instructed his staff to arrange a simple burial, 'for,' he is reported to have said, 'where the tree falls, there it should lie' – no doubt to spare his entourage the discomfort of boating the 600 miles back to Calcutta for a State funeral. An Officer of H.M.S. *Caroline*, berthed in Bengal at that time, takes up the story of the great man's burial, and records the thunderstorm which vested his tomb with an aura of superstition and accounts for much of the veneration still accorded to it by the local Hindu population:

His remains were interred without pomp or ceremony by the few attendants who composed his suite. At the moment of his interment a thunder-storm took place, the most tremendous that was ever recollected in this part of the country; and it seemed as if the very elements themselves expressed in loud accents their sorrow at this *ever to be lamented* event.

Other Viceroys to die in India were Lord Elgin and Lord Mayo. The former suffered a heart attack while on tour in the Upper Provinces and was carried to the hills, where he died on the 20th November 1863 after issuing a dramatic farewell message:

To his Colleagues in Council and to the Secretaries of the Supreme Government of India – he grieves that their joint labours should be so prematurely cut short.
                        Signed
                        Elgin and Kincardine.

His body lay in state in a large house near Dharmsala – since destroyed by earthquake – and he was buried in the churchyard of St. John's-in-the-Wilderness where there is an impressive monument to his memory among the pine trees and rhododendrons.

Lord Mayo was assassinated while visiting the Andaman Islands in 1872. An escaped Pathan convict stabbed him in the back twice, in spite of the special security precautions surrounding his tour of the settlement. Mayo is commemorated in a number of statues outside educational institutions which he founded in India, but his bones do not rest in Indian soil. His body was embalmed and conveyed back to Dublin at the request of his family. Ireland was evidently considered a good training ground for Viceroys of India, and Mayo had been Chief Secretary there, gaining experience of handling unruly 'natives'. The historial comparison ends there, and it was not without reason that Daniel O'Connell exclaimed: 'Oh that our skins were black!'

Other Governor-Generals and Viceroys who narrowly missed leaving their bones in India, dying prematurely of ill-health within a short time of their return to England, were Minto in 1814; Bentinck in 1839; Dalhousie in 1859 and Canning in 1862 – all victims of India's climate.

Vicereines

Lord Canning's wife pre-deceased him by a few months and the circumstances of her death were particularly poignant. Countess Charlotte Elisabeth Canning was a talented and artistic person with wide-ranging interests. At one time she was Lady of the Bedchamber to Her Majesty Queen Victoria; they corresponded regularly, and the Queen once wrote to her 'if it was not for the heat and the insects how much I would like to see India'. She landscaped the new Viceregal gardens at Barrackpore; she provided the inspirational designs for the sculptured angel over the Mutiny-memorial well at Cawnpore; she encouraged photography; she wrote and, above all, she sketched and painted. It was while indulging her love for painting flowers and rare orchids in the forests below Darjeeling in the Himalayas that she contracted what was then diagnosed as 'jungle fever' – virulent malaria. She was brought back to Calcutta as quickly as possible, the journey taking four days, and she died ten days later at the age of 44, on the 18th November 1861. Her body was borne that night on a gun carriage the eighteen miles to Barrackpore, the place she loved and which she continually strove to make more beautiful. The sad scene is vividly described by Lord Curzon:

In the breaking dawn of the next morning, while the full moon was setting in one quarter of the heavens and the first rays of the sun struggled up the Eastern sky and faintly flushed the silent stream, the body was carried down the terrace walk from Government House (Barrackpore) on the shoulders of twelve English soldiers, the ADC's holding the fringe of the pall. Lord Canning walked immediately after, the stricken figure of a doomed man.

Lord Canning never recovered from the blow. Theirs was a true love marriage, made in the teeth of parental opposition, as their families came from opposing political parties. He had fainted with shock four days earlier on first learning that she had an incurable illness and he became 'an old decrepit man from the day of her death'. He visited her grave every night after dark when he was at Barrackpore, and a lamp was kept burning there by which he used to read and re-read her papers, letters and diaries until he broke down altogether.

The public was deeply moved by these events and the local paper published an 'extraordinary' edition with black edging, with an obituary notice containing the comment:

Her sad death, just on the point of intended return, will cause deep grief; and the sudden and unexpected stroke will not tend to lessen the disinclination already felt among the governing class to tempt the climate of India which has been so fatal of late among our greatest men, and has not spared the best, the brightest and the dearest of their treasures.

The growing realisation that the rewards in India no longer outweighed the risks – at least as far as the 'governing class' were concerned – was reinforced by the premature deaths of Lord and Lady Canning, Lord Elgin and Lord and Lady Dalhousie, Lady Dalhousie dying of exhaustion from seasickness in sight of England where she was returning to recover her health. Three Governor-Generals and two of their ladies had died within the space of eight years.

Lady Canning's burial place was chosen with great care, under some beautiful casuarina trees by the river where she used to sit and paint. Her tomb was designed by her sister, Louisa Lady Waterford, and consisted of a catafalque and headstone, all of marble, inlaid with Moghul designs and standing within a large enclosure surrounded by iron railings in the shape of her monogrammed initials. Engraved upon the tomb was the husband's tribute:

Honours and praises written on a tomb are at best a vain glory; but that her charity, humility, meekness and watchful faith in her Saviour will, for that Saviour's sake, be accepted of God, and be to her a glory everlasting, is the firm trust of those who know her best, and most dearly loved her in life and who cherish the memory of her departed.

Sacred to the Memory of Charlotte Elisabeth, eldest daughter of Lord Stuart De Rothsay, wife of Charles John, Viscount and Earl Canning, first Viceroy of India. Born at Paris 31st March 1817. Died at Calcutta 18th November 1861.

But no sooner was the engraving completed than the following was added:

The above words were written on the 22nd November 1861 by Earl Canning who survived his wife but seven months. He left India on the 18th March, died in London on the 17th June aged 49 and was buried in Westminster Abbey on the 21st June 1862.

While Lady Canning's body continues to rest undisturbed in the garden at Barrackpore, the original monument above it deteriorated so rapidly from the heat and rains that it was removed first to St. Paul's Cathedral, Calcutta, and then to its present place in the north portico of St. John's Church, Calcutta, being replaced by a simpler replica with the same inscription. So Charlotte Canning sleeps alone beneath the shade of those beautiful trees with the sacred river of the Hindus flowing nearby; still in touch, as she would have wished, with the India that awoke in her an enhanced awareness of life. She is still remembered in modern India, partly for the Nurses' Home founded in memory of her outspoken support of Florence Nightingale; and partly – in a surprising way – for the sweetmeats she popularised at Viceregal parties, made of sugar-iced coconut, which are still known as 'Lady Cannings' and are sold in Calcutta to this day.

Mary, the first wife of Warren Hastings, should not be forgotten, even though her husband had not risen to the high office of Governor-General at the time of her death. She lies at Berhampore Cemetery in Bengal beside her infant daughter, in a grave which has recently been destroyed by a tree-fall:

In memory of Mrs Mary Hastings and her daughter Elizabeth

who died 11th July 1759 in the 2(?) year of her age this monument was erected by her husband Warren Hastings Esq., in due regard of her memory.

Governors

The Governor-Generals and Viceroys with their ladies completed their period of office more often than the Provincial Governors, but this was due more to chance than to anything else, for one reads in the 1860s of the Viceroy's French chef dying of cholera and the young wife of an Officer of the Bodyguards succumbing to the same disease. The Government Houses of Madras and Bombay had a sorry list of mortalities, as did the earlier Residencies of Bengal and the later Residencies of the 'Upper Provinces'.

Lord Pigot of Madras died of heat-stroke in 1777, perhaps exacerbated by his confinement as a prisoner of his Council on charges of misappropriation of funds, after he had allegedly amassed a fortune of over one million pounds by lending money to the local Raja at 2 per cent *per mensem* interest, an exorbitant rate even by today's standards. Two other Governors of Madras died of cholera: Sir Thomas Munro in 1827, one of the greatest Governors of all time; and Sir George Ward in 1860, after only a few weeks in office. Another Governor, Lord Hobart, died of typhoid in 1875: 'His sudden death was lamented as a general calamity ... immense and sorrowful crowds lined the funeral route from Government House to the Fort.' The inscriptions on his tomb eulogise the man and the ideals of the Indian Civil Service: '*Fortis vir sapiensque* ... without partiality and without hypocrisy.'

Bombay Presidency has much the same story to tell, particularly among the earlier founder-presidents of the factories that sprang up at Surat and Bombay. Humphrey Cooke, Sir Gervase Lucas, Sir Geoge Oxinden, Gerauld Aungier, Sir John Child and Bartholomew Harris are the names of the Governors during the last thirty-five years of the seventeenth century; they all died in office. Aungier, probably the greatest of them and the real founder of Bombay, was buried in an unknown grave in Surat in 1677 and hence has no epitaph; Sir George Oxinden, on the other hand, boasts one of the largest and most ostentatious mausoleums in India, which he shares with his brother Christopher, the 'most brotherly of brothers'. The structure is 40 feet high and 25 feet in diameter, with massive pillars supporting two cupolas which rise one above the other: round their interiors are galleries reached by a flight of steps. The epitaph on Christopher is entirely suitable for an exact merchant; written in

Latin in old English script, it expresses the usual sentiments in terms of profit and loss:

> Here he brought to a termination his undertakings and his life. He was able to enter in his accounts only days, not years, for death suddenly called him to a reckoning. Do you ask, O my masters, what profit you have gained, or what loss you have suffered? You have lost a servant, we a companion, he his life; but on the other side of the page he may write 'Death to me is a gain'.

His Governor-brother lies above him in the upper apartment with a grandiose epitaph in which he is magnificently described as '*Anglorum in India, Persia, Arabia, Praeses*'. Sir John Child was appointed Captain-General and Admiral of all the Company's forces by sea and land in northern India, and when he died in 1689 he was buried at Colaba Island, near Bombay, his tomb becoming a recognised mark for mariners. These were the early Governors; some had qualities of greatness, and insight into the building up of a new powerful trading-state; others merely pursued their own self-interest, and 'purloined the revenues ... accepted bribes ... manufactured title-deeds', according to the accepted standards of the time. An indignant chronicler of Bombay's history, writing in their defence at the end of the nineteenth century, points out that: 'Some men seem to begrudge them their very tombstones, as if they had enriched themselves at the expense of the nation, when in truth, it was they who enriched England', and the chronicler continues in stirring tones:

> The Americans are wise in their generation, and do not dive too deeply into Paul Jones, who first unfurled the flag of their freedom on the Atlantic Ocean. Let us follow their example. The men who built up the fabric of Bombay on Rs220/- – *per mensem* (£300 *per annum* at exchange of 2s.6d.) may well be excused when they occupied their leisure hours in making out invoices of pepper and cardamoms, or in looking over account sales of Golkonda diamonds. At all events the voice of calumny may be hushed for ever by the verdict, 'Died at their post'.

Other Bombay Governors to die at their post in the nineteenth century were Jonathan Duncan (p. 81), in 1811, after the longest governorship on record – sixteen years – leaving the epitaph 'He was a good man and just', and Robert Grant, in 1838, author of several hymns including the famous 'O worship the King'.

The early Governors in Bengal were men of a similar stamp, and from Job Charnock, the founder of Calcutta in the last decade of the seventeenth century, to Clive in 1757, there was a succession of men who died while holding the highest office in the Presidency – a composite Governor, Commander-in-Chief, Chief Justice, Port Trust Commissioner, Chairman of Chamber of Commerce and Head of Municipal Corporation, all rolled into one. There was Hedges who died in 1717, leaving an unusual instruction in his will that he should have no monument over his tomb; Frankland, a great-grandson of Oliver Cromwell, who assumed office in 1726 and died two years later; Stackhouse, whose death in 1741 was hastened by anxiety over being relieved from office because of a financial scandal; Forster who died in 1748 after less than two years in office; and Fytche who died in 1752 after only one month as Governor.

In the 'Upper Provinces' as they became formally administered – first under Chief-Commissioners, then under Lieutenant Governors and finally under fully-fledged Governors – there was a smaller but still significant premature mortality among the senior representatives of the Crown, although the reasons were now more often due to physical violence than to sickness. For example, Sir Henry Lawrence and his successor John Banks were both killed by shell burst at the siege of Lucknow in 1857 after holding their appointment for only a few weeks. Their two immediate predecessors also died at their post: John Colvin in 1857, 'worn out by the unceasing anxieties and labours of his charge', and James Thomason at Bareilly in 1853, the day he had been appointed Governor of Madras. Thomason was one of the greatest land-settlement officers, and 'there was hardly a place or a road in an area of 70,000 square miles, scarcely a clan or a tribe in a population of 30,000,000 with which he was not acquainted'. Sir Henry Durand was crushed to death in his elephant howdah in 1870 while going through the arch of a gateway at Tonk in the Punjab, where he had been Lieutenant Governor for only six months. The tradition continued down to the start of the twentieth century with John Woodburn, Governor of Bengal, falling ill on tour and dying in 1902. Michael Herbert Rudolph Knatchbull, the 14th Baronet and 5th Baron Brabourne, in 1939 had the dubious distinction of being the last British Governor in India to die in office. Brabourne had been Governor of Bombay for four years and Governor of Bengal for two, including a period as Viceroy and Acting Governor-General, and his death at the early age of 43 came as a shock to the British community.

The list of Governors who served India with a sense of dedication and duty, attempting to reconcile the Imperial role with the customs and way of life of those they ruled, is long; and these virtues are nowhere better exemplified than in the life of Sir Thomas Munro, the Governor of Madras already mentioned, who became a legend in his lifetime and a minor deity after his tragic death. Munro saw clearly in the 1820s that the time would come when England would withdraw from India, and worked to that end through the advancement of Indians. His advice to the Court of Directors of the East India Company in London deserves to be quoted in full as the ideal of 'colonial' government:

> Your rule is alien and it can never be popular. You have much to bring to your subjects, but you cannot look for more than passive gratitude. You are not here to turn India into England or Scotland. Work through, not in spite of, native systems and native ways, with a prejudice in their favour rather than against them; and when in the fulness of time your subjects can frame and maintain a worthy Government for themselves, get out and take the glory of the achievement and the sense of having done your duty as the chief reward for your exertions.

He was known in 'his' ceded districts as 'the Father-of-the-People' and many local ballads were composed in his honour, some still sung, while in several villages the eldest son was often named after him, 'Munrolappa'. A full-length portrait was hung in the *choultry*, or shrine, at Gooty, where he was first interred before being reburied at Madras, and stories are still told of how he had a presentiment of his death from cholera while on tour, 'seeing' a garland of flowers stretched across the valley. The first Lord Canning summed up his character thus: 'Europe never produced a more accomplished statesman nor India, so fertile in heroes, a more skilful soldier.' His epitaph at Madras makes it clear that this was no ordinary man:

> Near this stone are deposited the remains of Major-General Sir Thoms Munro, Bt. K.C.B., Governor of the Presidency of Fort St. George, who after 47 years of distinguished civil and military service, seven of which he passed at the head of that Government under which he first served as a cadet, was suddenly called from his labours on 6th July 1827 at a moment 'when', in the language of the honourable Court of Directors, 'he was on the point of returning to his native land in the enjoyment of well-earned honours from his Sovereign and from the Company having manifested a new proof of his zeal and devotion in retaining

CHARNOCK'S MAUSOLEUM

charge of the Government of Madras after he had intimated his wish to retire therefrom and at a period when the political state of India rendered the discharge of the duties of that high and honourable station "peculiarly arduous and important".' Aetat. 65. Sir Thomas Munro was from the earliest period of his career remarkable amongst other men. All those who were associated with him at the commencement of his service, many of whom have since become illustrious in the annals of India and of their country, yielded to him with common consent the pre-eminence which belonged to the ascendancy of his character.

Governors' Ladies

A search through the epitaph records in India reveals only a few wives of Governors, although there must be a considerable number 'concealed' in the cemeteries in the different Provinces. Perhaps the background role which most of them were content to play obscured their final resting-places from the glare of publicity to which their spouses were subjected. The earliest epitaph is of Mary Price, wife of a Governor in the seventeenth century, whose tomb at Surat picturesquely comments on her sudden death and translation to heaven: ' ... through the spotted veil of small-pox [she] rendered a pure and unspotted soul to God.'

The wife of Job Charnock, the founder of Calcutta, has a romantic story all her own. A Rajput Princess, she was snatched from the funeral pyre of her Hindu husband by Charnock when she was on the point of committing *suttee*. She was a young and beautiful girl of fifteen at the time, 'decked with her most pompous ornaments and arrayed in her finest drapery' to symbolise the end of her material existence. She bore Charnock several daughters, who married into English families of substance with no prejudice against their mixed racial origin. She died after the foundation of her husband's new city, and his sorrow was so great that, in the words of a contemporary, 'the public method he took of avowing his love was carried to an unusual though innocent excess. So long as he lived, he, on the anniversary of her death, sacrificed a Fowl in her Mausoleum.' This annual sacrifice was, almost certainly, an adaptation from the Hindu rites of the 'five saints of Bihar'; Bihar being the district from where she was rescued. She lies with her husband in the churchyard of St. John's, Calcutta, commemorated by an impressive mausoleum.

Two later Governors' wives, Lady Lawrence and Lady Fergusson, demand special notice. Honoria Lawrence, the wife of Sir Henry, of

Punjab and Lucknow fame, died at Mount Abu, in Rajputana, in 1854. Of Northern Irish stock, direct and unconventional, she refused to accept the luxurious standards of dress and behaviour that she found around her. Shortly before her death, she was planning to accompany her husband to camp and writes, with an uneasy conscience, of their excessive baggage, seeking to justify it to herself: 'Five elephants, twenty camels, six mules and very likely some cattle. This sounds a vast preparation, yet our camp is not a third of what most people would take – not a tenth, hardly a twentieth, of what the Governor-General or Commander-in-Chief requires.' She was always full of schemes for helping other people, particularly the families of the soldiers, and she and her husband were instrumental in founding schools for the orphans and children of British soldiers at Sanawar, in the Himalayas, near Simla. Later, a second school was founded at Mount Abu in her memory, and a third and fourth at Muree and Ootacamund in memory of her husband. The stained-glass window in the school chapel at Sanawar records her contribution, and beside it are memorials to her infant daughter who died nearby at Subathoo; to her eldest son who died at Simla in his early twenties; and to her hero husband who, after being critically injured during the siege of the Lucknow Residency in 1857, dictated his own epitaph: 'Put on my tomb only this – "Here lies Henry Lawrence who tried to do his duty. May God have mercy on him".' Thus four 'Lawrence' lives were given to India in the space of a few years.

Lady Fergusson died of cholera in Bombay in 1882, and as a result of her death – the last of many – Government House was finally abandoned as being too unhealthy. There were rumours of a curse on the place – originally a Franciscan friary built on the site of an old Hindu temple – but its situation in the middle of the 'island' of Bombay, close to a swamp and with coconut groves shutting out the sea breeze, was enough to justify the move. For generations there had been complaints about the air and water around the place, affected by the practice, described by Hamilton, of manuring the coco-palms with putrid fish – the bummelo, which when dried becomes the famous 'Bombay Duck':

They being laid to the Roots of the Trees, putrify, and cause a most unsavoury Smell; and in the Mornings there is generally seen a thick Fog among those Trees, that affects both the Brains and Lungs of Europeans, and breeds Consumption, Fevers and Fluxes.

In spite of the move, Government House retained its connection with disease, for after the fearful plague epidemic in 1896 – attributed by some loyal Brahmins to a punishment from the gods for the daubing of Queen Victoria's statue in the city – it was converted into a Plague Research Laboratory, which it is to this day.

Judges

The Judge was 'a tremendous dignitary!' according to Atkinson in 1860, 'right at the top of the social tree'. The Chief Justice of the Supreme Court of Bengal came first in the order of precedence, followed by his counterparts in Madras and Bombay and then by the Puisne Judges of the three Presidency towns and the Judges from the 'mofussil'. The importance attached to this order of precedence, particularly by the Memsahibs, is hard for us to imagine; but let the wife of a Bombay Judge, Sir Edward West, writing to a friend in England in 1824, speak for herself:

> The Society here is very formal, and the Ladies very self-sufficient and consequential, thinking of little but their fine Pearls and *local* rank ... From my being the first lady, Edward the second gentleman, we are terribly observed, and of course I doubt not pulled to pieces, but thank God we are still English.

The Judges appeared to suffer a heavier mortality than most other groups of men; a local historian, noting the frequency of death among the King's Judges in Western India, remarked caustically that 'there was a rot among them'. In Bombay and Surat at least seven Judges died between 1827 and 1831, three of these succumbing during the 1828 monsoon – Richard Orlando Bridgman, the Advocate General, aged 30; Sir Edward West, the Chief Justice, aged 46; and the Hon. Sir Charles Harcourt Chambers, the senior Puisne Judge, aged 39. This pattern was repeated over the whole of India, as the tombstones testify. The graveyards of Calcutta carry their proportion of Judges, many dying within a few years of each other – for instance Sir Robert Henry Blosset in 1823, Sir Christopher Fuller in 1824; both Chief Justices of the Supreme Court, one aged 47 and the other 50, at the height of their powers. The 'mofussil' towns also had their quota, as a visit to any of their cemeteries will prove; for example three Judges lie buried at Mirzapur who died within a few years of each other – Lind, who came out to India at the age of 16, in 1832 aged 34; Lochwood, who died at 44 on a river steamer after a few hours' illness (the river cruise being a common last-resort cure); and Currie who was 41. Perhaps the long hours 'penned up in that stifling enclosure (the court) from "rosy morn to stewy eve"', as described by Atkinson, imposed an additional strain on their health. Certainly the whole emphasis of the Raj, as soon as the sword had been sheathed, fell on the Courts – it was truly a 'Lawyers' Raj', and rewarded as such, the salary of a Judge in the early 1800s being between six and ten thousand pounds a year, a very considerable amount of money to ensure their immunity from bribes. Society complained that Judges were so absorbed with their official duties that one saw little of them; Atkinson commented that 'Our Judge' was

> saturated with appeals, criminal cases, decrees, circular orders and the like ... and when we do meet, the theme of discourse is so potently flavoured with law, we are overwhelmed with references to Act 95 of 17, Regulation 11 of 78, or some such frightful numbers which are about as intelligible to us as the hieroglyphics of Nineveh.

One Judge was so absorbed in his own weighty thoughts, or his brain so deadened by the humid heat of Bombay, that after hanging a particular man on Tuesday, he summoned him to appear the following Friday. The work involved a great deal of reading and translating of documents in a poor light, which ruined eyesight. David Money, a Judge of the Appeal Court in Calcutta, retired nearly blind in 1859 at the age of 52, in order to visit a famous occulist in Austria. He wrote to his son: 'That awful Suddur [Chief] Court! It blinded me the work! And I look back upon it as an unpleasant nightmare. It is such a luxury to be free from it and to be in Dear Old England again.'

They were giants in those days, both physically and mentally. Sir Edward West, the Chief Justice of the Supreme Court of Bombay, while fighting a losing battle for his life during the August monsoon of 1828, took 'three calomel powders a day, of I suppose 20 grains each and they cannot get the fever under', and he had 'an immense blister put on the back of his neck' – a body-racking cure, but all to no avail; he died that month and his wife Lucretia, who chronicled his treatment in her diary, died two months later. Blosset, the Chief Justice at Calcutta, had made his fortune at the Bar of England with the help of an inheritance, and after a profligate youth when 'it must be confessed that the ensnaring influence of the world, at his first entrance into public life, did for a season draw his heart from God,' he came out to India 'to promote the spiritual as well as the temporal welfare of the Hindus'. Such conscious idealism marked a new trend in Anglo-Indian relations and dates roughly from the 1820s – the beginning of Evangelical Christianity in India. In the manner of his predecessors, the great orientalists such as the Judge Sir William Jones, Blosset learnt Hindustani, Persian and Sanskrit, mastering them on his voyage out to India – a prodigious feat; but instead of using these languages as the key to understanding the philosophies, religions and customs of the East, he saw them as the instruments of change and conversion. Even on his death-bed, he implored 'the blessing of Heaven on the Hindu world – bring them to knowledge of the true religion and call them from darkness to light'. The earlier Judges did not parade their Christianity – at least not on their tombstones. Sir John Hyde's tomb of 1796 described him as 'a departed model of unexampled yet cautiously concealed charity'; and William Augustus Brooke's tomb at Benares bore sentiments of a religious broadmindedness seldom expressed in the latter half of the nineteenth century: 'His amiable character endeared him alike to the Hindoo, the Mussulman and the Christian inhabitants of this city.'

Perhaps the epitome of a Judge is expressed in this epitaph on William Leycester, a Senior Judge who died at Puri in Orissa in 1831 aged 57, after forty years in India:

He was upright as a judge, most affectionate as a husband, fond as a father and sincere as a friend. With a mind classically stored, his pursuits were elegant. The descendant of an ancient family, he evinced the British gentleman in every principle of his conduct, while imbued with the sacred truths of a revealed religion, lived and died a humble and confiding Christian.

Bishops

If there was a 'rot' of Judges, there was at the same period a 'wash' of Bishops, considering the number that met a watery grave. Reginald Heber, the second Bishop of Calcutta, famous as the writer of such popular hymns as 'Holy, holy, holy', 'From Greenland's icy mountains', 'The Son of God goes forth to war', and 'Brightest and best of the sons of the morning', met his death taking a cold plunge in a kind of covered bath provided as an annexe to the Judge's bungalow, in which he was staying during his visit to Trichinopoly in South India. The bath – described by one biographer as 'the destined agent of his removal to paradise' – was later railed off and a memorial stone erected:

> In memory of the devoted, accomplished, beloved and universally honoured servant of God, Reginald Heber, D.D., second Bishop of Calcutta and one of India's truest and most loving benefactors. This stone was erected ... at the expense of the Government on the margin of the bath in which he drowned while bathing on 3rd April, 1826.

There was a further memorial to him above his final resting place in the local church which concludes with the challenging words, 'Be ye also ready', and there are other memorials to the great man – only 42 when he died – at both Calcutta and Madras, sculptured by Chantrey. The following words in his epitaph summarise his achievements in India:

> He cheerfully resigned prospects of eminence at home in order to become the chief missionary of Christianity in the East: and ... in the short space of three years, visited the greater part of India, and conciliated the affections and veneration of men of every class of religion ...

Heber was a bridge-builder between men of different races and religions, and the journal he kept of his tours of Northern, Western and South India betrays as great an interest in all things Indian as in his ecclesiastical duties. Perhaps he had the feeling for the East ingrained in him through his family connections – his aunt married the greatest of all orientalists, Sir William Jones. This sympathy with Indians was reflected in Southey's 'Ode on the portrait of Heber' which contains the passage:

> Native believers wept for thankfulness
> When on their heads he laid his hallowing hands.

Contact between prelate and native was very unusual at this time. The East India Company, supported by a substantial majority of the House of Commons, discouraged the conversion of Hindus and Muslims – it might disturb the peace and interfere with trade – and confined their support of Christianity to the appointment of Chaplains for their own English servants; it was pressure from the Evangelicals, led by Wilberforce, that had led to the appointment of the first Bishop, Thomas Middleton, in 1814 with a salary of £5,000 p.a.

Bishop's Heber's successor, John James, also met a watery end, and his episcopate was tragically short. News travelled slowly, and over a year had elapsed by the time the report on Heber's death had reached England and James had been appointed and sailed the five-month voyage to Calcutta. His health at once began to give way, and he was sent on a river tour of the Upper Provinces in the hope that it would improve. When he had only gone a short way, it became clear that he was seriously ill, so the boat turned back and he was transferred to an ocean-going ship bound for Penang in the hope that the sea air might affect a cure. He died a few days later and was buried at sea on the 22nd of August, 1828, less than nine months after landing in India. News of his death did not reach Calcutta for eight weeks; such were the problems of communication. James was succeeded by John Turner, with a time lapse again of over a year. His episcopate in turn was cut short by a virulent fever contracted while he was touring Ceylon, and he died in July 1831.

The burden laid on this one English Bishop had proved too great. It was the largest geographical diocese of Christendom, extending at times to Australia, Cape Town, China, Penang and the borders of Afghanistan, and involved constant visitation of those areas within practical travelling distance – the Northern Provinces, Bombay, South India, Madras, Ceylon and Burma – during some of the hottest months of the year. Four Bishops, each appointed in their early forties, had died within the space of nine years: Middleton, the first, who died of sunstroke in 1822, followed by Heber in 1826, James in 1828 and Turner in 1831. In future it was decided to appoint separate Bishops of the other Presidencies and Provinces. Daniel Corrie was appointed to Madras, the first Company Chaplain to receive such elevation; the honour could hardly be withheld after he had preached funeral ovations over Heber, James and Turner and taken sole charge of the Indian Church during the gaps between appointments. Thomas Carr went to Bombay, followed by others at Colombo, Lahore, Lucknow and so on, all under a new 'Metropolitan' Bishop at Calcutta.

The first Metropolitan was Daniel Wilson, who took up his post in 1832 when he was 50, and defied the rigours of the climate for twenty-six years before he too was taken on a 'last resort' sea voyage, dying almost immediately after his return to Calcutta. He was a man of extraordinary energy, who visited Burma at the age of 78, touring the villages and living in houses of mats. No doubt his youthful training stood him in good stead. He came from a wealthy family, like all his Bishop predecessors in India, but his family was one of those thrown up by the Industrial Revolution, not county aristocracy as the others had been. His father was a silk manufacturer in London and at 14 he was apprenticed to a relation in the trade. His hours of work were from 6 a.m. to 8 p.m. – fourteen hours – and then he used to read Latin and Greek for two hours after supper. Though he escaped the virulent fevers in Calcutta, he was frequently in the presence of death, and the story is told of a Mrs. Ellerton, an aged lady who lived with him, sending for him when very ill to take leave of him and to give him some instructions regarding her coffin:

He promised compliance and then left her. During the night she rallied, and in the morning sent for him to countermand her directions. The Bishop informed her that it was too late for her to change. He had sent for the undertaker at once, as she wished, and the work was done!

The second Metropolitan was George Cotton, famous for founding the 'Bishop Cotton' schools at Simla, Nagpore and Bangalore to provide education for Anglo-Indians and the children of Europeans whose parents could not afford to send them to England. He played an important part in the transfer of St. Paul's School from Calcutta to Darjeeling, where it flourishes to this day. Under the shade of this school's chapel, looking out to the majestic Himalayan snow-range, rest the mortal remains of the last great Metropolitan of British India, Foss Westcott, who died after the close of the British Raj. Bishop Cotton, too, met death by drowning when in 1868, after consecrating a cemetery at Sylhet in Assam, he slipped on the gang-plank returning to his river boat after dark.

And the catalogue is amazingly not complete, as Bishop Robert Millman died of exhaustion in 1876 at Rawalpindi, after crossing one of the Punjab rivers by night; and, to cap it all, the *History of the Church of England in India* records with unconscious humour that:

During the Great War this Mission passed through deep waters, the Rev. A.L. Birkett, its senior missionary, being drowned when crossing one of the rivers in flood, and Miss Bull, who had been for years a household word in that part of India, being drowned while returning from furlough when the P. & O. steamship *Persia* was torpedoed off Crete … God buries His workmen, but carries on His work.

Missionaries

The renewal of the East India Company's charter in 1813, which
permitted the appointment of the first Bishop to the Indian Church,
also allowed British missionaries to enter and work in India under
licences issued by the Company. This is not to say that there was no
missionary activity before this date, but such as there was operated
illegally or through the Danish and Dutch settlements. The Baptist
missionaries were the first of the English Protestants to arrive in
India, and a party of four who arrived in Bengal in 1799 were
ordered to be deported immediately, the public excitement over
their reputed radical political opinions being inflamed by an
erroneous Press report describing them as 'Papists' and therefore in
league with the French revolutionaries. However, they escaped to
join William Carey at the Danish Settlement of Serampore just
outside Calcutta, where they established the Mission which was to
have such a powerful influence on the rising generation of Bengali
intelligentsia, through its printing press and the translation of
religious and other literature into Bengali. Yet, in spite of their good
works and sober living, they were subject to the same risks of
premature death as the other Europeans, and three of the original
six founder-members of the Serampore Mission were buried within
two years. The surviving three, representatives of a different social
stratum from the chaplains and bishops – Carey, a shoemaker;
Marshman, a weaver; Ward, a printer – were closely associated with
the slave emancipation movement gathering momentum in
England. They conceived it their duty to rescue the heathen from
sin, ignorance, false religion and oppressive social customs and
practices such as the Hindu caste system and the Muslim purdah
system for women. Christianity was seen as a liberating force in the
struggle against discrimination; the practices of suttee, thuggee and
infanticide were works of the devil to be rooted out in the name of
the Gospel. Their master-mind, Wilberforce, encouraged this point
of view and spoke out against these oriental religions
uncompromisingly; 'The Hindu divinities were absolute monsters
of lust, injustice, wickedness and cruelty. In short, their religious
system is one grand abomination,' he said in 1813. This was the
stirring of a new wind of intolerance over India which was to change
the whole nature of the British connection, and lead eventually to
the 1857 Mutiny, which filled so many graveyards.

　　All three – Carey, Marshman and Ward – saw this missionary
whirlwind gather force before they died at the Mission they had

founded, Ward (of cholera) in 1821, Carey in 1834 and Marshman in 1837. Carey's tombstone simply records his name, dates of birth and death, and the humble inscription, typical of the man: 'A wretched, poor and helpless worm, on thy kind arms I fall.' No mention is made of the extraordinary achievements of his life. This is the man who was the first advocate for mass education in India; who opened dozens of schools for Bengalis where they were taught in the vernacular; who for thirty years was Professor of Bengali and Sanskrit at the College of Fort William – paying his salary into the common Mission fund, so that the East India Company should indirectly finance the activities they opposed; the founder of the Agricultural and Horticultural Society of Bengal, with his Botanical Gardens at Serampore regarded as among the finest in the East; the translator of the Bible into six Indian languages and the entire New Testament into twenty-three more; the translator of Bengali epics; the publisher of the first Indian Newspaper in an Indian vernacular in 1818; the publisher of a monthly magazine, the *Friend of India*, which continued from 1818 to 1875 when it was amalgamated with *The Statesman*, still one of the leading papers. He came out to India fervently hoping to break the Hindu caste system, which he saw as another form of slavery, and to turn Hindu hearts to Christ; he scornfully castigated the compromisers: 'The Missions were sent out to exterminate heathenism in India, not to spread heathen nonsense all over Europe.' Yet by living in India and studying Indian literature he gradually became Indianised himself and underwent a cultural transformation, so that in the end he accepted the more tolerant philosophy that every man has a right to share in all good knowledge and truth, and in particular the revelation of truth through Jesus Christ.

It is difficult to imagine the extent to which missionaries were regarded by Company officials as troublemakers and ignorant fanatics. For several decades following 1800 they, along with Evangelical chaplains, were prohibited from any activity that might lead to the conversion of sepoys of the Company's Bengal Army. The East India Company was so firmly committed to preserving religious neutrality that it even allowed certain civil disabilities to be attached to Christian converts, who became classified under the law as 'apostates' from Hinduism and Islam and disqualified from rights of inheritance, remarriage to non-Christians, and employment in various government departments; disabilities not removed until the mid-nineteenth century. Yet from the 1820s and 1830s, Evangelical views gained ground; first among some of the Directors of the East India Company and Members of the House of Commons; then, in the 1840s, among a few of the senior administrators in the Company's service – the two Lawrences, Nicholson, Edwardes – until, by the 1850s, these views were shared by many officers both civil and military, all holding strong views about the need for spreading Christianity in the country, in opposition to the Company's declared policy of religious neutrality. Edwardes regarded the Mutiny as a punishment inflicted by Providence on the Company for its failure in this respect, and he said so so often that Canning in a moment of exasperation remarked of him that he was exactly the man that the prophet Mohammed would have been if the prophet had been born at Clapham instead of Mecca.

The missionaries were so dedicated, working selflessly in the most difficult circumstances, disregarding their personal comfort, and exposing themselves to the rigours of the climate, that not surprisingly there was a tremendous toll on their lives, often recorded not in the Establishment's cemeteries but on isolated graves in remote places. There is a sad little grave in Bhagalpur District recording the end of another high-minded missionary endeavour – to the Rev. Thomas Christian and Sarah, his wife, aged 31 and 24 respectively, attached to the Incorporated Society for the Protection of the Gospel in Foreign Parts; he died on the 16th December 1827 and she followed him four weeks later on the 11th of January – with these telling words: 'She, alike with him, fell a sacrifice to the climate of an unhealthy country.'

A percipient Scot, Alexander Duff, the pioneer Scottish missionary who first arrived in Calcutta in 1830, was quick to see that the regeneration of Indian society could not be accomplished by foreigners. 'Could Luther,' he asked, 'have become the reformer of Scotland?' and concluded: 'The real Reformers of Hindustan will be qualified Hindus.' Most Indians, including many converts, looked upon the missionary as 'a paid agent of a Religious Company', a view strengthened by the missions' paternalistic style of operation, which closely resembled that of the imperial regime, with power concentrated in the hands of a few Europeans who superintended the lives of their converts like fathers among their children. Western Christians too often failed to understand the subtly pervasive philosophy of Hinduism: 'We are *Hindu* Christians,' protested several high-caste converts in Bengal in 1870, and 'in having become Christians, we have not ceased to be Hindus.' This attitude was well understood by the Roman Church in its proselytising through the centuries, and the presence of fourteen million Christians in India today – the largest religious group after the Hindus and Mohammedans and more numerous than the Sikhs, Buddhists and

Jains – is mainly due to its efforts. But then the Roman Church had a long start. The Apostle Thomas is believed to have arrived in India in A.D. 52 and to have founded seven churches in Kerala before being martyred at Mylapore where his shrine stands today. The community thus founded has survived in good strength to this day under the umbrella of the 'Syrian' church. Another famous saint, Francis Xavier, arrived in India in the Middle of the sixteenth century, following in the wake of Vasco da Gama who had discovered the route round the Cape of Good Hope. Xavier made a great impact before he died at Goa, and while the Catholic faith made no doctrinal compromise, culturally an odd synthesis developed, with a general conformity to Indian ways of dress, food and social customs. There followed a series of Jesuit missionaries, of whom Roberto de Nobili was the most famous. He originated the 'accommodation theory', and attempted to attract high-caste Brahmins instead of the low caste 'untouchables' by claiming to be a Roman Brahmin, adopting the saffron robe of a sanyasi, putting sandal paste on his forehead and wearing the sacred thread. He was extraordinarily successful and converted a large number of Brahmin disciples who were allowed to retain their caste and its symbols. Who knows what would have happened if the British Protestant missionaries had adopted a similar stance, and identified the shepherd image of Christ with Krishna, accepting the Emperor Asoka's dictum of the fourth century B.C. that 'no religion has a monopoly of truth' – if they had realised that there was no spiritual vacuum in India and concentrated on the love, compassion and non-violence found so amply in Buddhism and Jainism? Generally they did not; yet there were men like C.F. Andrews who saw the spirit of Christ in Gandhi, as Gandhi and many Indians saw the manifestations of Christianity as part of the ultimate Hindu truth, and worked towards bridging the spiritual gap between the two communities. Andrews died in 1940 and is buried in Calcutta, having earned the epithet 'Deenandhu' for his compassionate service to the needy; and there are many other Christian missionaries buried in India who in their own way, according to their inner convictions, strove to bring a fuller life to the masses of India.

Generals

Religion did not concern the English in India too much in the eighteenth century, and when General Sir Eyre Coote died at Madras on the afternoon of the 27th of April 1783, frantic arrangements had to be made to clear St. Mary's Church – where the funeral was to be held the following day – of piles of rice, as a section of the church was being used as a warehouse. The General – three times Commander-in-chief, the decisive influence at Plassey, the hero of Wandewash and many other battles – is now belatedly regarded as one of the greatest commanders who ever lived, to be ranked with Marlborough and Wellington. Apart from his mastery of strategy and tactics, he was many years ahead of his time in showing genuine concern for the troops under his command. He mentioned Indian N.C.O.s and privates in his despatches eighty years before Napier, who is widely credited as being the first general to do so; and he was worshipped by his men almost as a deity, being called 'Coote Bahadur', Coote the brave. On his last journey he set off unwillingly in response to a personal plea from Warren Hastings to save Madras, complaining as he did so: 'I have one foot in the grave and one on the edge of it.' He suffered a stroke on the sea voyage between Calcutta and Madras, which took over a month because the ship had to dodge four French frigates, and he landed in a state of collapse. The only hope of his recovery lay in a dramatic new treatment, which his wife explained in a letter to his sister: 'The use of Electricity might arouse and restore him.' It would be interesting to know the details of this remedy, as it was not until the end of the eighteenth century that the existence of electric current was properly recognised. He died three days later and was laid to rest temporarily at St. Mary's Church. After nine months his body was exhumed, embarked on the *Belmount* bound for Plymouth, and after a seven months' voyage brought ashore in England with full military and naval honours and transported by slow stages to the parish church of Rockbourne in rural Hampshire. A memorial exists to him in nearby Fordingbridge, and another at the old India Office; there is a symbolic monument to him in Westminster Abbey by Thomas Banks complete with a winged Victory, an elephant, two weeping figures representing Mahratta and Hindu captives, and an inverted cornucopia the contents of which are falling into Britannia's shield.

Probably more Generals have campaigned over India during the last two hundred years than in any other country in the world and the graveyards are well stocked with them. Glimpses can only be given of one or two, but it should be remembered that India provided a very useful training ground for British Generals, with the North-West Frontier on a permanent war footing until modern times; there are few famous British Army officers who did not have 'Indian' experience at some stage of their career – from Wellington to Roberts, Kitchener, Wavell and Viscount Alexander.

The General most in the public eye, thanks to the massive 165-foot monument erected to his honour in the centre of Calcutta, is Sir David Ochterlony, victor of the Nepal wars, who died in Meerut in 1825. The inscription at the base of this extraordinary construction – in style part Syrian, part Turkish, part Egyptian – states: 'The people of India, native and European, to commemorate his services as a statesman and a soldier, have in grateful admiration, raised this column.' The monument is still known to the present generation of Calcuttans as 'Sahiba', and from the top there is a view extending 20 miles in all directions.

Another famous General who is commemorated by a column, though this time only 50 feet high, is Sir Robert Rollo Gillespie, who fell at the first assault on the Gurkha stronghold at Kalanga, near Dehra Dun. The capture of this small fort, defended by only 200 Gurkhas, entailed heavy casualties – '*killed,* 9 Officers and 62 men; *wounded*, 20 Officers and 649 men' – and in the highest traditions of chivalry two monuments were erected, one for the British and one for the Gurkha enemy, the latter recording the episode in which the General lost his life:

> On the highest point of the hill above this tomb stood the fort of Kalanga. After 2 assaults on 31 October and 27 November [1814] it was captured by the British troops on 30 November and completely razed to the ground. This is inscribed as a tribute of respect for our gallant adversary, Bulbudder, Commander of the fort and his brave Goorkhas ...

The General's personal memorial is at Meerut where a column rests on a square base with this curious inscription, the first three words being on a decorative scroll and the rest on the funeral urn in bas relief with the names of the battles out of order:

Vellore – Cornellis – Palimbang
Sir Robert Rollo Gillespie, K.C.B., Djoejocarta,* 31.10.1814, Kalanga

It is interesting to note that Gillespie's old Corps, the 8th King's Irish Hussars, had the column repaired in 1862 and it is still withstanding the ravages of time.

Then there were the Generals who lost their lives in the Mutiny, men like John Nicholson and Henry Havelock; the former with a

*The modern Jakarta, Indonesia.

charisma which caused the great Lord Roberts – once his staff officer – to remark that he impressed him more profoundly than any man he ever met; the other a strong Bible-reading leader whose troops were known as 'Havelock's Saints', whose father-in-law was Marshman the celebrated Baptist missionary of Serampore, and whose epitaph at Lucknow (where he died of dysentery during the end of the siege) records: 'It was the aim of his life to prove that the profession of a Christian is consistent with the fullest discharge of the duties of a soldier.' The two men were quite different; Nicholson in his thirties, sure of himself, a brilliant extrovert, the 'autocrat of all the Russias' as he was known; while Havelock at sixty was self-effacing, placing his strength in God and a muscular Christianity. Nicholson sought notoriety and dramatic effect from his actions, as when he wrote to his superior officer:

> Sir, I have the honour to inform you that I have shot a man dead who came to kill me.
> Your obedient servant, John Nicholson.

Havelock was content to counter public sneers by deeds: he was called 'an old fossil, dug up only fit to be turned into a pipe-clay', but won battle after battle to save the situation in the early months of the Indian Mutiny; at the news of his death flags flew at half-mast in New York – a rare honour for an English General. Havelock put all his faith in God; but Nicholson was turned into a god and deified. A Hindu cult to his name still exists in the Punjab. A tablet in St. George's church, Bannu, on the remote North-West Frontier where he served, describes his life and character in the form of an oriental panegyric:

> In affectionate memory of Brigadier General John Nicholson, C.B. once Deputy Commissioner of this District who at the siege of Delhi, led the storm, fell mortally wounded in the hour of victory and died 23 September 1857, aged 34; gifted in mind and body, he was brilliant in government as in arms; the snows of Ghuznee attest his youthful fortitude; the songs of the Punjab his manly deeds; the peace of this frontier his strong rule; the enemies of his country know how terrible he was in battle, and we his friends love to recall how gentle, generous and true he was.

However, many Generals at the time of the Mutiny were imbued neither with the spirit nor with the motivation of these two exceptional men. A number were old, infirm and gout-ridden, but as there was no compulsory retirement they generalled on until they died. Three key military centres – Meerut, Cawnpore and Dinapore – were under doddery old commanders who, when the Mutiny began, could not be expected to react with the vigour and speed required to stamp out the insurrection; a fault of the system rather than of individuals.

A long list could be made of Generals who died in India of natural causes after a life-time in the army without once returning to England: Sir John Horsford, at Cawnpore in 1817 at the age of 66, never having had a day's leave in 45 years' service; Sir John Withington Adams, at Agra in 1837 after 57 years' service; Sir Gabriel Martindell, at Buxar in 1831 after 58 years' unbroken service in India. Sir Gabriel was no angel and he left a large number of natural children by his several consorts. These were men who started their military career as boys of 12 or 13; having arrived in the East at this impressionable age they often became almost completely 'Indianised'. General Stuart went so far as to earn the sobriquet 'Hindoo' and was buried in the South Parks Cemetery, Calcutta, under a tomb embellished with Hindu temple motives (see page 84).

Socially Generals were very important personages and, as they took a lion's share of any prize money available, were often very rich. After the siege of Bhurtpore in 1825, for example, the Commander-in-Chief received about £60,000; Generals £6,000; down to Subalterns £238 and Privates £4. These differentials reflected the extreme stratification of society at that time and were even more marked in the case of native troops. The Sepoy received £2 and the valiant Jemedar – the Indian officer commanding thirty to a hundred men with similar responsibility to a Warrant Officer – received £12; this proportional share having more than trebled since the siege of Seringapatam in 1792 when Jemedars received *less* than Privates. The army was slowly changing as it expanded and depended more and more on the quality of the less senior military officers.

Military Officers

An officer joining the Company's army in the early nineteenth century said goodbye to his family in England knowing that there was only a slender chance that he would ever see them again. Statistics show that six out of every seven officers sent to India in the first quarter of that century never returned. Even if an officer escaped the deadly fevers and enemy bullets, he could seldom afford to come home on 'furlough' – leave on half pay – when he became entitled to it. This enforced separation, which subsequent generations succeeded in reducing bit by bit as communications improved with steamships, the overland route and the Suez Canal, resulted in the 'stranded' officers becoming 'Indianised'. Smoking a hookah became commonplace; adopting native customs and modes of dress, normal; keeping beebees socially acceptable, especially as officers below the rank of Major were strongly discouraged from marrying. Many officers, faced with the impossibility of getting out of debt before retirement, chose to stay in India, where at least they could afford to live on their meagre pension, often with an Indian lady as consort. The Mohammedan lady of Colonel T.D. Colyear had a Moghul-style mausoleum erected over her grave at their Simla home, the hill-station to which the Colonel had retired; when the property was sold in 1875 her body was exhumed and laid to rest in the European cemetery beside his grave and the mausoleum was demolished (see p. 151).

Non-Commissioned Officers and Privates who married 'native women' – the records made a distinction between the officer's 'lady' and the other ranks' 'native women' – had the alternative of taking their half-caste family back to England on retirement or being pensioned off to one of the Company's 'Invalid' Battalions established in some of the less unhealthy towns, like Chunar on the Ganges, where they could pass the remainder of their days in familiar surroundings. Many chose to stay, and the inscriptions on their graves tell their own story: 'Erected by his disconsolate housekeeper Rezia de Rozia who lived with him for many years' (Sergeant C. Edwards of the Invalids who died in 1809); or the more pathetically frank: 'Lucy, his woman, erected this tomb in memory of them' (Private Snape and infant son who died in 1808).

By the 1830s, however, this feeling of living in India and adapting oneself to it was being replaced by a new consciousness of English standards spread by the Evangelicals and fostered by the increasing number of English women. Everything Indian was now regarded as heathen, to be avoided if it could not be changed; so that by the second half of the nineteenth century, officers – now virtuously tucked up with their English wives – tended to live a circumscribed cantonment life, enjoying their recreation, clubs and dances with those of their own kind, and largely cut off from contact with the real India and the rising class of educated Indians aspiring to Western standards. Subalterns' letters home at this period depict the small world in which they lived and their preoccupation with sport and promotion. A young Ensign (Stanhope Cary) describes life at Barrackpore in 1855:

Occupation – Get up at half past four, parade from five to six, go to Mess where all the officers meet (at what is called Coffee shop) and drink a cup of coffee – home and dress and bathe by 9 – breakfast – ten to half past eleven private drill at home – two, tiffin at Mess – about half past five I go into the Park with my dogs after the jackals and dine at Mess at half past seven, play one rubber or game of billiards and retire to bed about ten o'clock – the next day and every day the same, the intervals being occupied in writing, reading and painting, yclept daubing.

Perhaps the routine was duller than in some cantonments owing to the presence of a Brigadier who was 'a fearful religious fanatic' and 'forbids balls, races, private theatricals and all amusements'. The same Ensign complains about the unfairness of the promotion system with its complicated rules which only the hand of death can adjust:

I got 7 Addiscombe [the Training College] fellows over my head that have not yet left England, because I did not go up for my examination a fortnight sooner than I did, it really is a great shame that the E.I. folks in Leadenhall Street dont warn you of these things ... not that these 7 fellows make any difference now, and perhaps they never will, but *if they live* they will be seriously in my way when 'line steps' begin to be of any service to me.

A father, David Inglis Money, writes to his aspiring son William in 1859 to remind him that hard work must be added to influence and patronage (the italics are his):

Work on, hard and perseveringly – never relax – Talbot (who has the ear of Lord Canning) may do something – Energy may have its reward – but in the long run from my experience, a *persevering constant* discharge of duty, whatever it be, with only fair ability brings a man to the highest honours – such competitors give all others the go by in the Race. A man who has only ability to show and seeks to climb without *hard* work will to a certainty fail.

It was a real scramble to the top; after J.S. Rawlins saved a brother officer from drowning, he recorded laconically:

... and the way he repaid me for saving his life, was by keeping me out of my promotion, for I was the senior Ensign for three years afterwards. He was a delicate youth, always took the

character of a female in our chirades and plays – poor fellow! he
died at Cawnpore in 1849, and made me a Lieutenant.

It was a long hard road for a Subaltern to secure promotion,
perhaps fifteen years' service, unless there was the prospect of action
against an enemy, which speeded the process and was therefore
welcomed by the younger officers such as Cary: 'Most probably I
go to Burmah next cold weather [1855] ... Hurra! it'll knock off
some of the old ones and save me purchase' – a passing reference to
the system of purchasing promotion, much cheaper for Company
officers than those in the British Army.

However, for a Private to secure promotion from the ranks was
almost unheard of, except as a summary appointment in the heat of
battle and then only to the dizzy heights of Ensign. This military
caste system was part of the social fabric of the time and not
resented, as can be seen in the proud epitaph on the tomb of Brevet
Ensign William Graham, who died at Monghyr in 1829, aged 86:

> William Graham came out to India a private in the Honourable
> Company's Army in 1766 and for his meritorious and gallant
> conduct was honoured with the Brevet of Ensign; frugal and
> judicious in the course of life, after retiring from active duties of
> his profession, he creditably educated his children and
> maintained his family and accumulated a very considerable
> fortune.

Out of the thousands of military officers' graves, in cantonment
cemeteries, city cemeteries, battlefield memorials or isolated by the
roadside, I have selected a few as a small cross-section of those who
went out from their home country over the last two hundred years,
with varied motives – some seeking adventure, glory and honour; a
few from personal necessity; others in answer to the calls of
patriotism or as twentieth-century conscripts – and never came
back.

Lt. D.C. Home, of the Bengal Engineers, won the first Victoria
Cross to be awarded in India. He was the second generation of the
family to be soldiering in India, his father being a Major-General of
the Bengal Army. The epitaph on his tomb near Aligarh
unemotionally states his achievement:

> In memory of Lieutenant Duncan Charles Home, Bengal
> Engineers, aged 29, who was killed by the explosion of a mine
> when engaged in destroying the Fort of Melagarh on the 1st

October 1857. As leader of the 'Forlorn Hope' which on the 21st September 1857 successfully attacked the Cashmere Gate, Delhi, he was awarded the first Victoria Cross given in India.*

The 'attack' involved leading a party of Sappers in broad daylight under murderous volleys of fire to place bags of gunpowder on the Gate and light the fuse. Few of his party returned alive, and four V.C.s were awarded.**

Major Thomas Adams was 'a simple English Major of Foot' whose little-known campaigns in 1763 have been compared to Alexander the Great's. A description of one of his exploits is given by Fortesque, the military historian, in these graphic terms:

> Starting at the height of the hot season, with a handful of British veterans and little more than a handful of sepoys ... Adams marched against the most powerful force in India, trained and partly commanded by European officers. He ... left the enemy no peace till he had forced him back, step by step, 400 miles and finally driven him from his country ... beat him in three pitched battles ... and captured two fortified cities. Had Napoleon ... added such a campaign in India to his exploits in Europe, the whole world would still ring with it ... A marvellous feat of arms, a feat which has hardly a peer in our military history.

Adams died at Calcutta in 1765, worn out from his exertions, before he could hear the news that he had been promoted Brigadier-General in recognition of his services.

Colonel Pennycuick and his son, aged seventeen, were both killed fighting side-by-side in the Sikh wars of 1849. The Colonel had been 43 years in the Army, 27 of these on foreign service seeing action in Java, the Celebes, Burma, Afghanistan, Aden and finally on the Jhelum. His son gained his commission at Sandhurst when only 16 and was appointed to his father's Regiment, the 24th Foot. This Regiment marched on the 13th of January against the Sikh Army, and the *Gazette* relates:

---

*The facts quoted on the epitaph are inexact. His was not the first V.C. in India, although it was one of the earliest, the award only having been instituted in 1856; and the second date should read '14th September'.

**The two Sapper Officers, Lieutenants Home and Sakeld – the latter killed while lighting the fuse – are commemorated on a monument at Fontmell Magna, Dorset. The other two recipients were a British Army Sergeant and a Bugler, a rare honour indeed for 'Other Ranks'. It was not until 1911 that Indian troops could qualify for this award.

It was exposed to the full sweep of the Sikh batteries and to the deadly play of their destructive musketry. More than one-half the Regiment went down in ten minutes ... The elder Pennycuick had fallen, and two soldiers attempted to carry him off while still breathing; but the Sikhs pressed them so closely ... they dropped their honourable burden and drew back. The gallant boy, the son of the noble dead, only 17 years old, now first aware of his misfortune, sprang forward, sword in hand, bestrode his father's body for a moment, and then across it a corpse! Such, Sir, is the simple tale of the deaths of that brave old man and his boy; and if it is not sufficient to obtain for them the honest fame for which they fought so well and died so well – if it does not swell the hearts and moisten the eyes of their countrymen, I know not why generous impulses are component parts of human nature.

A promising young scion of a county family, William Reveley Mitford, was one of the many overcome by the climate. These poignant words are inscribed on his early grave:

Descended from the ancient family of the Mitfords of Mitford Castle, Northumberland and late of Hon. Company's military service on this establishment. Graced with the virtues of early excellence and superior worth and with the abilities that promised in maturer age to render him a bright ornament of his profession; possessed of a noble and handsome exterior, adorned with every manly accomplishment; cherished, beloved and honoured by all who knew him, he fell a victim to pestilential climate, dying at Hazareebaugh on 26th April, 1824, aged 21.

Mercenaries and Freelancers

When political conditions in India became anarchical, following the break-up of the Moghul Empire, private armies were formed by each local Raja, and European soldier-adventurers were not backward in offering their services to the highest bidder. The French-English wars in the second half of the eighteenth century had demonstrated the superiority of European arms and tactics, and the Rajas sought to retain a number of European officers to train and command their native troops, employing French, Dutch, Portuguese, Swiss and English indiscriminately.

The nationality of the mercenary was of little importance when the European nations were confined to their trading enclaves, but once open warfare broke out, with the inevitable widening of the dispute, it became crucial. While the English were emerging as the paramount power, any Raja wishing to remain independent would tend to select a national other than English to command his forces. The days of the English mercenary were therefore numbered, although Sutherland, Brownrigg, Felix Smith, O'Brien and Thomas – colourful characters all – had a good run for their money before leaving their bones in India. The extraordinary life they led is typified in that of George Thomas who died in 1802 and is buried at Berhampore, in the same cemetery as the first wife of Warren Hastings.

George Thomas's Indian nickname was 'Jahaz Sahib' – either from the nearest equivalent rendering of 'Ge-orge Sahib' or, as some think, from the Hindustani word for a ship, indicating a sailor. He kept his origins shrouded in secrecy. He was born in County Tipperary in 1756. He was known to have run away to sea and deserted his ship at Madras to take up a career as a swashbuckling mercenary among the South Indian Rajas, but the knowledge he displayed in his later career as a horseman, as a trainer of cavalry, as a gunner and forger of artillery pieces, and as a fluent linguist in Persian and Hindi both written and spoken, imply an educated background. He first made an impact on the Indian scene when, still in his twenties, he moved to northern India to transfer his service to the Mahrattas and then to Begum Sumroo (see p. 131), who sealed his contract of service by giving him one of the girls in her harem for a wife. His career was one of licensed brigandage, interspersed with periods of consolidation until the pressure to continue paying his troops necessitated another foray against a neighbouring stronghold to extract more booty. At the height of his fame, in 1797, he was known as 'King Thomas', a sort of white Raja and, in his own words, 'dictator in all the countries belonging to the Sikhs south of the Sutlej'. Like all great mercenaries, he was fighting for his own gain and glory and, one suspects, as an Irishman, because he enjoyed fighting; but he retained certain basic loyalties both to the Begum and to the British Crown. He came to the Begum's rescue after her own troops had mutinied (see p. xx), facing odds of over four to one, and forced the rebellious officers to sign an eclectic declaration of obedience commencing: 'In the name of God ... and of the holy apostle of God, Mohammed, and' – after an argument over the inclusion of Christ – 'His Majesty King Jesus Christ.' At the end of his career, broken in spirit, he tried to return to his country, only to die on the way before reaching Calcutta. His troops on hearing of his death refused to serve any other officer, and swore to become sanyasis (mendicants).

The East India Company, with its own 'Company' troops supplemented by 'King's' troops, was only too ready to make use of the services of such military adventurers when the occasion demanded it, particularly when they could bring with them a force of professional cavalry who possessed, mediaeval fashion, their own horse and weapons and owed allegiance only to their personal commander. James Skinner was one of these legendary adventurers. He died in 1841 and was buried in Hansi (north of Delhi) in a 'jagir' of land which he had been granted by the grateful Company. A month later his body was disinterred and brought to Delhi,

> escorted by the whole of the corps and a great concourse of people ... where it was met by all the civilians and officers of the station with a great multitude from the city ... Military honours were paid to the funeral by official command; and 63 minute guns were fired, denoting the years of the deceased. A funeral sermon was preached over the body ... and the veteran soldier was committed to his final resting-place, beneath the altar of the church he had built.

The church was St. James', which he had built partly to fulfil the vow he had made when left for dead on the battlefield, to become a good Christian and forsake his twelve concubines; partly as a gesture to redress the balance after building a mosque for his Muslim wife and a temple for his Hindu mother – so that by one means or another he would go to Paradise; and partly, perhaps, because as the son of a Scottish soldier and an aristocratic Rajput prisoner-of-war, with a 'very black' skin (according to Emily Eden), he wanted a place which he could feel was his own. His youth had been spent very humbly – apprenticed to the printing trade in Calcutta, running away to eke out a living in the bazaar, first as a coolie and then as a carpenter's mate, until his godfather, Colonel Burn, sent him up-country with an introduction to the great French adventurer De Boigne, leading to service with the Mahratta Chief, Scindia; towards the end of his life he moved in high circles, but no doubt he had memories of slights and insults. His family and descendants have been proudly buried in their own churchyard ever since, not willing to put the prejudice of those times – only Europeans were interred in a European cemetery – to the test. His brother Robert, his second-in-command, is also surrounded by legend. He decapitated his wife and her entire household and then shot himself to expunge the disgrace of her infidelity; and of the ensuing auction of his property, Emily Eden writes: 'His soldiers bought every article of his property at ten times its value, that they might possess relics of a man who had shown, they said, such a quick sense of honour.'

The Skinners were a remarkable family and James, known throughout India as 'Sikander' or Alexander, showed what an individual could achieve with dash, integrity and courage in spite of all racial handicaps. It was one of the disappointments of his life that he was only made a Companion of the Order of the Bath and did not receive a knighthood in recognition of his services, but at that period of imperial history such awards were not conferred on Company servants, whatever their descent, only on those holding commissions and appointments directly from the Crown; even to be eligible to receive the C.B. he had to be specially gazetted a Lieutenant-Colonel in the British Army. His epitaph, in his own church, records:

> Here rest the remains of the late Colonel James Skinner C.B. who departed this life at Hansi, 4th December 1841. The body was disinterred, removed from Hansi and buried under this on 19th January 1842.

Another military adventurer to form an irregular cavalry unit was Alan Gardner, who raised Gardner's Horse. Originally an officer of the Highlanders who had left the King's service for a more adventurous and rewarding career with the Mahratta princes, he was dismissed, like Skinner, for refusing to fight against the British, and was subsequently asked by the Company to raise a corps of free-lancers in 1809, which continued to bear his name after they came on to the establishment of the Company's army ten years later. Colonel Gardner, who gave up command in 1828, died in July 1836. His father was a nephew of Lord Alan Gardner, Admiral of the Blue and Major-General of the Marine Forces, who was created a Baron in 1805. Alan, the great-nephew, married a 13-year-old Princess of Cambay, and their son married into the royal house of the Moghul Emperors of Delhi. The Barony became extinct in 1833, but the descendants of the founder of Gardner's Horse form a small impoverished community of 'Gardners' in the family estates near Agra where the eldest representative, another Alan Gardner, is still known as 'Lat Sahib' or Lord. Thus occasionally do East and West meet, under the shield of an English Baron with quarterings of the Begs of Cambay, the Nawabs of Oudh and the House of Timur. Alan's tomb is in the family mausoleum at Chhaoni, which he shares with his father, brother and their high-born Muslim wives.

These 'irregular' units, raised to meet the crisis of the Mahratta wars in the first decade of the nineteenth century, were augmented by similar units during the traumatic days of the Indian Mutiny when the continuance of British rule hung in the balance. Loyal landowners provided a few horsemen each on the feudal principle, to be welded into a cavalry corps by the commander and bearing his name – hence Hodson's Horse, Wale's Horse (later Probyn's Horse), Watson's Horse and so on. An interesting paradox about these forces is that while they were commanded by only a handful of British officers, usually only three to a Regiment, with much greater dependence on Indian officers, they remained one hundred per cent loyal during the Mutiny. Their loyalty was based on personal allegiance. The 'cause' they were fighting for, the 'system' of government which ruled, was unimportant. It was a personal matter of obeying their accepted leader. They were true soldiers.

Residents and Political Agents

Distance from centres of government seems to have brought out colourfulness of character. The mercenaries and freelancers operating outside the boundaries of the East India Company's territory exemplify the rule to a marked degree. Similarly the Residents – political agents of the Governor-General to the various native states – showed extraordinary qualities of originality in their lives, isolated as they were from their own society and depending on their own resourcefulness, with no army to reinforce their authority.

The consequence of this isolation was sometimes exposure to political murder at the instigation of the ruler, when the immediate advantages of such action appeared to outweigh the longer-term probability of retribution at the hands of the Company. Cherry, the Resident at the court of Lucknow, was massacred with all his staff at Benares in 1799; Macnaghten, the political officer in Kabul, was stabbed to death by the son of the ruler of Afghanistan in 1841; Fraser, the Resident at the Moghul Emperor's court at Delhi, was assassinated in 1835 in slightly different circumstances. The instigator of Fraser's murder, the Nawab of Ferozepore, was hanged as a common malefactor, an act unprecedented in British-Indian case law at that time, showing the emergence of British standards of justice and a refusal to consider any exceptions on grounds of religion and title. Fraser himself was described by Jacquemont, the great French botanist, as 'half asiatic in his habits – but an excellent man with great originality of thought, and a metaphysician to boot'.

He had escaped death once before when struck by an arrow in the throat during the siege of Kalanga at which General Gillespie was killed. The monument to his memory – almost totally destroyed during the Mutiny – was erected by his close friend James Skinner, with these words:

> Sacred to the memory of William Fraser Esq. late Commissioner and Agent to the Lt. Governor at Delhi and a local Major of Skinner's Horse, cruelly murdered by an assassin 22nd March 1835. The remains interred beneath this monument were once animated by as brave and sincere a soul as was ever vouchsafed to man by his creator, a brother in friendship has caused it to be erected, that when his own frame is dust, it may remain as a memorial for those who can participate in lamenting the sudden and melancholy loss of one dear to him as life.

Apart from such risks of violent death there were the usual maladies to take their toll, together with the remoteness from proper medical treatment – not always a disadvantage in those days. The Residency at Hyderabad, for example, contains the graves of four Residents, plus the wife of a Resident. It does not include the famous Resident James Kirkpatrick who died on a journey to Bengal and is buried in the South Parks Cemetery in Calcutta. There the inscription on his tomb records:

> To the memory of Lt. Colonel James Achilles Kirkpatrick of the Honourable East India Company's military establishment of Fort St. George who after filling the distinguished station of Resident at the Court of Hyderabad upwards of nine years and successfully conducting during that period various important negotiations, died at Calcutta 15 October 1805, aged 41.
> This monument is erected by his afflicted father and brother.

Seldom can an epitaph have concealed more effectively the real man underneath. James Achilles Kirkpatrick was a remarkable person. Educated at Eton, he sailed for Madras in 1779 as a Company Cadet of 15, and in his early thirties succeeded his brother as Resident at the court of the Nizam, the most important political appointment in the country at that time. He had a taste for splendour, building a magnificent palace with Corinthian columns and 32 marble stairs and decorating it with chandeliers and gilt mirrors purchased from the Prince Regent: he ordered for it a reflecting telescope some 14 feet long costing £500, and exotic plants and animals to stock his gardens – Portuguese orange trees, an Abyssinian goat, an elk. He fell in love with a Mohammedan Princess, Khair-un-Nissa, whom he married in 1800 according to Muslim law. This marriage was viewed with alarm by both the Company and the Government in England, as it was thought that he had become a Muslim. The Governor-General ordered an inquiry, but allowed the matter to die down in view of Kirkpatrick's extraordinary success in negotiating vital treaties with the Nizam to replace the State French troops with a British contingent. The fruits of their marriage were two children, a boy and a girl, their births being commemorated by the sinking of wells, each inscribed with the date – 1802 and 1804 – and a short dedication containing the father's full native title, 'Major James Achilles Kirkpatrick, Bahadur Hushmut Jung'. 'Hushmut Jung', as he was always known, means 'the glorious in battle'. The children were sent to school in England at an early age, and never returned to India, as both their parents died young, but they continued to correspond with their maternal grandmother, Sharif-un-Nissa, who wrote in Persian on paper sprinkled with gold dust and enclosed in a *kharita*, a sealed gold-brocade bag. The girl, Catherine Aurora, married Captain James Winslow Phillips of the 7th Hussars and died at Torquay in 1889 at the age of 87 – she is the 'Kitty Kirkpatrick' of Carlyle's *Reminiscences* (see p. 95).

Other Residents of other courts had an equal claim to fame: Major Ford who died at Poona in 1829; Colonel John Collins – known as 'King Collins' for his imperious ways – who died at Lucknow in 1807 after only one year as Resident; Sir David Ochterlony, who before his military triumphs was the Resident at Delhi and the first Resident of Rajputana. Ochterlony possessed that rare personal magic that went to the making of legends. He shocked Bishop Heber (see p. 34) by receiving him sitting on a divan dressed in 'a choga and pagri' while fanned by servants waving peacock feathers. The Indians were so impressed by Ochterlony's powerful personality that the new Residency he built at Rajputana, with a dedication in English, Urdu and Hindi, was one of the only two buildings in the town not destroyed during the Mutiny, for reasons of superstition; the other being the Masonic Lodge, known colloquially as 'Jadu Ghar', the House of Magic. The local tribesmen held his memory in awe until modern times and brought garlands each year to hang on the wall of the Durbar Hall where he used to hold public state.

Another Resident around whom legend has grown was Josiah Webbe – known throughout India as 'Sree Webbe', Saint Webbe –

who was appointed to the Court of Mysore. He was later transferred to Gwalior but died on the journey to take up his new appointment. A tomb was erected at the spot on the banks of the river Nerbudda and a fakir was left a small salary to guard it; he turned it into a shrine, with a lamp permanently burning on the tomb, and accepted travellers' donations. The inscription read: 'Erected to the memory of Josiah Webbe Esq. by Purnaiya Dewan as a tribute of veneration and respect for splendid talents, unsullied purity and eminent public virtue.' Webbe, though only 36 when he died, made a deep impression on his contemporaries: both the Duke of Wellington and Sir John Malcolm counted him as one of their closest friends. The Duke kept an engraving from his portrait in a prominent place at his home and said of him: 'He was one of the ablest men I ever knew and, what is more, one of the most honest.' Malcolm, passing his tomb 13 years after his death, arranged for a small house to be built and a well sunk to help maintain the garden which had now grown up round it, and noted in his diary:

> I cannot express the feelings with which I contemplated this spot. The remains not merely of one of my dearest friends, but of the most virtuous and ablest man I had ever known ... Poor Webbe: I hope that he wishes us well as we remember him.

An impressive monument was also raised to his memory in St. Mary's Church, Madras, where under a Flaxman statue depicting an officer, a civilian, a Mohammedan and a Hindu mourning over his portrait medallion are these unusual words to a truly remarkable man:

> His mind by nature, firm, lofty, energetic was formed by classic study to a tone of independence and patriotism not unworthy the best days of Greece and Rome. Disdaining the little arts of private influence and vulgar popularity, and erect in conscious integrity, he rested his claims to public honours on public merit. An extensive knowledge of the Eastern languages forwarded his rise to stations of high trust where his ambition was fixed to exalt the honour and interests of his country. But in the midst of a career thus useful and distinguished, preferring the public weal to personal safety, he fell a martyr to an ungenial climate in the prime of life, beloved with fervour by his friends, particularly lamented by the Governors of India, admired and regretted by all ...

Then there was Sir Thomas Metcalfe, Resident at Delhi from 1837
to 1853, who was buried in St. James' churchyard with a simple
epitaph on a tomb which has recently been badly damaged. His
elder brother, Sir Charles, had also been Resident at both Delhi and
Hyderabad before becoming Governor-General in 1835, at the end
of his career; it was he who predicted the Indian Mutiny and made
the percipient remark that 'when India is lost, it will be lost in the
House of Commons'. Again and again these family connections
persist – the Metcalfe brothers; the Kirkpatricks; the Rumbolds,
one Governor of Madras, the other Resident at Hyderabad. Another
common factor, no doubt accounting for their feeling of
identification with the country, was that so many lived in the Indian
style and married Indian women of rank. Because of these
matrimonial links, contact with the Indian aristocracy was much
easier, and conversation was conducted on equal terms in their
language; a Muslim physician might discuss the system of Greek
medicine with the Residency Scottish surgeon; a Hindu financier
might give advice on trading prospects; while astrology, poetry,
painting and music were subjects of common interest. The isolation
of the Resident from European society provided the basis for this
happy state of affairs; but later, as the influence of the Company
spread throughout India, bringing in its wake more administrators,
soldiers and traders, there developed a growing feeling of the
importance of everything British – pride in Western science and
industrialisation, confidence in the universal application of English
education, conviction of the exclusive truth of Christianity – until
the inherent interest in Indian culture withered away in the face of
Victorian arrogance.

Members of Council

The same family names keep cropping up in positions of
importance, whether as Governors, Residents, Generals or
Members of the Presidency Councils. During the first two decades of
the 1800s – 'the Augustan age of John Company' – a large number
of the senior appointments both civil and military were held by
members of the aristocracy of England, Scotland and Ireland. A
Bengal Civil List of this period boasts no less than one Peer, 19 sons
of Peers and 12 Baronets. There were, in addition, many
representatives of influential land-owning families, particularly from
Scotland and Ireland. G.F. Cherry, the Resident of Lucknow who
was murdered in 1799, came from such a family, tracing its lineage
back to William Graham of Abercorn and Dalkeith in the twelfth

century and related to the Dukes of Montrose. Another Cherry – John Hector Cherry, third Member of the Council of Bombay – appears as one of the pall-bearers at the funeral of James Rivett-Carnac. The name Rivett-Carnac resulted from a family alliance between General John Carnac, second-in-command to Clive at the Battle of Plassey before becoming Commander-in-Chief himself for a time, and Elizabeth Rivett, a celebrated court beauty, the daughter of Thomas Rivett Esquire, Member of Parliament for Derby. Her portrait by Sir Joshua Reynolds – considered one of his finest works, now in the Wallace Collection – ensured her immortality. She died in India in her twenties – the General then being in his sixties – and he survived her another twenty years, dying at Mangalore in 1880. The General left all his considerable property to his wife's brother James Rivett who assumed the double name Rivett-Carnac by royal licence. James himself was dead within two years. The full-page, black-bordered announcement of his death and funeral which appeared in the Bombay Gazette of 21 July 1802 is quoted in full below as an example of the paraphernalia surrounding the death of an important member of the government.

On Friday evening last died, JAMES RIVETT-CARNAC, Esquire, second Member of Council of this Settlement.

During a painful illness which defied all medical interposition, he anticipated the approaching event with peculiar equanimity – perfectly resigned, and undisturbedly serene, he closed his well spent life, amidst the sincere and affectionate regrets of relatives and friends, who all equally sympathize the irreparable loss which society has sustained – To them, it will be no inconsiderable consolation to find that his public and domestic virtues are truly appreciated, and that the estimation in which they were held, was evinced by the numerous assemblage who joined affliction's train, and followed him to the sepulchre – Among other mournful tributes of respect which have been excited upon this melancholy occasion, the following has been transmitted by a friend, who has studied to delineate the pre-eminent worth of that character, which now claims so distinguished a place in the register of mortality.

> Gratitude, affection, and esteem
> Now loudly call a tribute forth
> To a beloved, dear, departed friend:
> Tho' sudden snatch'd in prime of years,

His life unblemished, may teach
Some kindred mind to emulate his virtues –
He was distinguished, in his early youth,
For regularity of manners, and refinement of understanding,
Cultivating every science that could adorn
The genuine perfection of his mind.
After true and faithful services in many important situations,
He was called to a seat in council,
At a period when his abilities shone
With the most distinguished lustre;
And to his death continued a zealous
And active member of that board,
In which department, his opinions and conduct
Arose from the purest motives, and which he maintained
With the most laudable inflexibility. –
He was endowed by nature with uncommon discernment
And a large share of circumspection, –
Which preserved his HONOUR and INTEGRITY unspotted.
Adorn'd with every requisite to form a model of human
        perfection,
He was emulous to throw a lustre on the important situation
He held, by a display of the worthiest sentiments.
As a patron, as a father, as a friend,
He was belov'd with veneration;
And his character in general compos'd a pattern
For the rising generation, and a lesson to his progeny,
Which he was always sedulous they should follow –
These endowments with recent instances of his benignity,
Need no comment to immortalize his worth
For he must be UNIVERSALLY LAMENTED
As he was UNIVERSALLY ESTEEMED.

Saturday morning last was ushered in by the melancholy
annunciation of the death of JAMES RIVETT-CARNAC
Esquire – a member of council of this presidency, at day break the
colours of the citadel were hoisted at half mast, and those of the
ships in the harbour were displayed in similar manner – At 3
o'clock the body was privately removed from his residence at the
Breach into the house in Town, appropriated to the second in
council, and at a little past 4 a party of 500 Europeans from the
artillery corps, and his Majesty's 80th, 86th, and 88th regiments
assembled, the whole under the command of major general
Bellasis of the Honourable Company's artillery – The artillery

corps forming towards the Apollo Gate from left to right, and his Majesty's regiments alternately continuing the line in the same order – At five, his Majesty's naval and military, and the Honorable Company's military, civil and marine servants, the gentlemen of the recorder's court, the mercantile gentlemen of the settlement, and the gentlemen commanding country ships having also assembled, the procession, commenced as follows.

· The Reverend ARNOLD BURROWES, the Senior Chaplain, and
    Doctor WILLIAM MOIR, the family Surgeon.
    The Reverend NICHOLAS WADE, the Junior Chaplain.

THE PALL

SUPPORTED BY

Sir WILLIAM SYER, Kt. the Recorder.
Major General ROBERT NICHOLSON, commanding officer of
    the forces.
ROBT. ANDERSON, Esq. superintendent of the marine.
ALEX. ADAMSON, Esq.
JOHN HECTOR CHERRY, Esq. 3d Member of Council.
Captain JOHN SPRATT RAINIER, the senior officer of H.M.
    ships in the harbour.
ROBERT HENSHAW, Esq.
DAVID DEAS INGLIS, Esq.
JAMES FISHER Esq. and Ensign JAMES RIVETT-CARNAC,
    CHIEF MOURNERS.

Followed by the gentlemen who had assembled for the occasion.

The procession moved, whilst the band of His Majesty's 86th regiment, and the garrison band were playing the dead march, and other appropriate solemn music, with accompanyments, towards the government house, and thence to the Apollo street, making a circuit by the adjutant general's office and the lock head gate, passed close to the main-guard, from which moving direct to the CHURCH the line halted at a convenient distance, and formed a street; through which the procession proceeded to the CHURCH – Upon entering it, the funeral service was performed by the reverend chaplains, and the body deposited next to the spot which had many years ago received that of his Sister, the wife of the late brigadier general JOHN CARNAC.

Three vollies from the troops, succeeded by half minute guns from the battery, and the Honorable Company's ship Cornwallis, to the number of 43, being the age of the deceased announced the conclusion of this sad and solemn ceremony.

The speed of the burial arrangements – less than 24 hours after he died; the ranks of society reflected in the pall-bearers; the eulogy delineating 'the pre-eminent worth of that character'; the music, the volley from the troops, the half-minute guns for each year of his life (26 of which had been spent in India); it is all there. James's son became successively Resident of Baroda, Director and Chairman of the East India Company – receiving a Baronetcy – M.P. for Sandwich and Governor of Bombay. Another Governor of Bombay in the 1870s, Sir Richard Temple, was a nephew; a great-nephew, Major J.H. Rivett-Carnac, was Military Secretary to the Commander-in-Chief, Poona in the 1880s. As Kipling put it in the opening paragraph of his story 'The Tomb of his Ancestors':

> Some people will tell you that if there were but a single loaf of bread in all India it would be divided equally between the Plowdens, the Trevors, the Beadons, and the Rivett-Carnacs. That is only one way of saying that certain families serve India generation after generation as dolphins follow in line across the open sea.

The fabric of Bengal society was woven through and through with even more aristocratic families than Bombay and Madras. Lady Anne Vane Monson, the wife of Colonel Monson, Member of the Supreme Council of Calcutta, was the great grand-daughter of King Charles II. Colonel Monson and General Sir John Clavering, another Member of the Council, had also moved in Court circles. They had sailed out with Philip Francis – friend of Burke – to take up the three vacant seats on the new Council in 1774, determined to exercise their majority in thwarting the schemes of the old stagers Hastings and Barwell. The climate of India came to Hastings' rescue after he had endured two and half humiliating years of being outvoted on the Council. Colonel Monson died in September 1776, restoring power to Hastings with the help of his casting vote, and General Clavering followed one year later, giving Hastings a clear majority. Clavering's epitaph was very descriptive of his position but said little of the man:

To the memory of Sir John Clavering, Knight of the Most Honorable Order of the Bath, Lt. General in his Britannic Majesty's service and Colonel of the 52nd Regiment of Foot, second in the Supreme Council of Fort William in Bengal and Commander-in-Chief of all the Company's forces in India. Died August 30th, 1777 in the 55th year of his age and was interred here.

Francis persisted in his campaign a little longer, hoping to drive Hastings from office and take over the position of Governor-General himself, but he departed after being wounded in a duel with him, enabling Hastings to write: 'My antagonists sickened, died and fled.'

The South Parks Cemetery which received the mortal remains of Monson and Clavering had also received the body of the regal Lady Anne – queen of the whist tables in Calcutta – a few months earlier. Her death was the occasion for an unusual demonstration of Women's Lib, when her coffin was carried from the gates of the cemetery to the place of burial by 'six gentlewomen', a remarkable gesture in those days. Yet another person connected with this quarrel of the Bengal Councillors and buried in the same cemetery is Colonel Pease, who acted as Hastings' second in his duel with Francis.

A similar dispute between the Madras Governor, Lord Pigot, and his Council broke out at almost exactly the same time, but on this occasion the climate was on the side of the Councillors, the Governor dying of sun-stroke while under forcible detention. These quarrels in the Presidency Councils were symptoms of the communication problems involved in the attempt to control the East India Company from Leadenhall Street, London. Correspondence with the Directors on controversial questions which flared up among the members of the Council took at least a year to answer, contact between the three main Presidencies was almost non-existent, and influential friends had often been replaced through death and sickness by new faces – not a system conducive to efficiency and Company profits.

Admirals and Naval Officers

According to precedence the Commander-in-Chief of H.M.'s naval forces ranked one below *the* Commander-in-Chief, and several places below the Judges, Bishops and Members of the Presidency Councils. Nevertheless, the navy played a vital part in the history of the British occupation of India. Clive received the credit for the victory of Plassey; yet the victory would not have been possible had it not been for a naval force under Admiral Watson, which transported the relieving force from Madras to Calcutta – voyage hailed as 'a triumph of seamanship'. The Admiral died of a virulent fever during the monsoon, two months after his successes. His tomb in St. John's churchyard briefly records the culmination of thirty years' service – the combined operation against the nest of pirates at Geriah, who had been plaguing the West Coast for a century; the relief of Calcutta following the 'Black Hole' disaster; and the capture of the French settlement of Chandernagore, the loss of which was a body blow to the French Company:

> Here lies interred the body of Charles Watson, Esq., Vice Admiral of the White, Commander-in-Chief of H.M. naval forces in the East Indies. Who departed this life on the 16th day of August, 1757 in the 44th year of his age.
>
> Geriah taken February 13th, 1756
> Calcutta freed January 11th, 1757
> Chandernagore taken March 23rd, 1757
> Exegit monumentum aere perennius – S.O.Fd.

Before he died, Watson despatched news of these victories to England in a small sloop of 60 tons, which battled its way against adverse winds across the Indian Ocean and around the Cape, on a voyage of six months. In those days such hardship was taken for granted.

Admiral Watson's grave was dug near the fresh mound of a midshipman from his own flagship, whose epitaph only hinted at a story of incredible bravery: 'Here lies the body of William Speke, aged 18, son of Henry Speke Esq., captain of H.M.S. Kent. He lost his leg and life in that ship at the capture of Fort Orleans [the French name for Chandernagore] the 24th of March, Anno 1757.' The Kent received 138 cannon shots through the hull, and 111 of her crew were killed or wounded, including the Captain. William would not allow the surgeon to touch his leg until he had first attended to his father, who was lightly wounded, and then to an ordinary seaman, who was severely wounded, lying next to him. When his turn came and his leg was amputated, he did not utter a cry, although fully conscious, and kept inquiring about the condition of his father and his ship. It is typical that there is no memorial of the gallant crew, only of the officers.

Naval supremacy over the Dutch and French and the abolition of the West Coast pirates enabled the English East India Company to be consolidated. The coasts around India contain many graves of naval officers who had either been killed in action or died of some malignant fever, and whose bodies had been brought ashore for burial. The earliest recorded death of an Admiral in India is of Sir Abraham Shipman who died in the 1690s at Anjidiva, a small island fifty miles south of Goa. A century and a half later, in 1839, Admiral Maitland, best known as the Captain who received Napoleon on board his ship, was buried in Bombay. Another famous West Coast sailor was Commodore James, who was commissioned in 1755 to root out piracy along the Mahratta coast and received a baronetcy in recognition of his services. The climate claimed James's first wife, and she was buried at Surat. Contemporary accounts of their humble origins and later rise to fame shed an interesting light on society. James was the son of a miller in Pembrokeshire and, in the vernacular, became a 'cursed' boy when he stole a gamecock from the squire's hall and had to fly the country. Soon after his arrival in India he married and, in the words of the Bombay chronicler:

> The obscurity of his origin did not stand in the way of his achieving distinction, any more than it did in the case of Sir Cloudesley Shovel, and many other famous English Admirals. It may be remembered that his wife kept a public house in the now classic region of Wapping, known as the 'Red Cow'.

James's social climb continued with his second marriage, his daughter marrying Thomas Boothby Parkins, 1st Baron Rancliffe, and his two grand-daughters a Marquis and a Prince.

One of the most brilliant naval actions ever fought, according to some authorities, is commemorated on the tombstone of Captain Edward Cooke in the South Parks Cemetery, Calcutta:

> Sacred to the memory of Edward Cooke Esq. Captain of H.M. ship 'La Sybelle' who received a mortal wound in a gallant action with the French frigate 'La Forte' which he captured in Balasore Roads March 1st, 1799 and brought to this port where he died 23rd May 1799 aged 26 years.

La Forte was the *Bismarck* of the day, the biggest and most heavily armed frigate afloat, one-third larger than Cooke's ship, and its capture created a stir at the time. There is a commemorative tablet to Cooke in Westminster Abbey as well.

The navy also played a spectacular part in the Indian Mutiny, as can be seen from the tombstone of a British Prime Minister's son who had won the V.C. and been created a Commander of the Bath for his service with the Naval Brigade at Sebastopol during the Crimean War:

> To the memory of *William Peel*. His name will ever be dear to the British inhabitants of India, to whose succour he came in the hour of need and for whom he risked and gave his life. He was one of England's most devoted sons, and with the talent of a brave and skilful sailor, he combined the virtues of a humble and sincere Christian. This stone is erected over his remains by his military friends in India and several of the inhabitants of Calcutta. Captain Sir William Peel, R.N., K.C.B., was born in Stanhope-St on 2nd November 1824 & died at Cawnpore on 27th April 1858.

This was a salute from the military to a naval hero, and it is noteworthy that a 'Mutiny V.C.', Major Robert Blair of the 2nd Dragoon Guards,* lies buried in the same cemetery. It must be unique for two V.C.s of different campaigns to share a common graveyard. Peel died of smallpox while in charge of the Naval Brigade from H.M.S. *Shannon*, which he had taken up the river Ganges, with 10-inch guns, to the relief of Lucknow. It was reported that he 'behaved very much as if he had been laying the Shannon alongside an enemy's frigate', bringing his guns within a few yards of the mutineers' defences. A simple tomb at Lucknow records the fate of another member of his party: 'Here lies Mr. Henry P. Garvey, Mate H.M.S. "Shannon", killed before Lucknow March XI MDCCCLVIII.'

To protect its commercial settlements, ports and shipping, the East India Company had formed an Indian Navy as well as an Indian Army. It even built a number of men-of-war at Bombay. However, a career in the navy was considered less attractive than other appointments. 'At all events avoid the Indian Navy, for heaven's sake', wrote Ensign Cary in Bengal to his younger brother in the 1850s. A contemporary handbook explains that while the Indian Navy may not be so desirable as the other services:

> It has its advantages, which become more apparent as its

---

*His brother, Captain James Blair of 2nd Bombay Light Cavalry, also won a V.C. during the Mutiny, pursuing the rebels with only the hilt of his sword left.

members advance up the ladder of preferment. The officers of this service are employed in the steamers which ply between the Red Sea and the island of Bombay; in the Company's schooners and small frigates employed in the Persian Gulf, China and the straits of Malacca, and in the surveys of the seas and coasts in the East ... There are valuable shore appointments distributed among the senior officers.

A reference to a career in the Indian Navy is found on a tombstone at Serampore, not far from Calcutta:

> Sacred to the memory of Captain P. Mearing, formerly of the East India Company's maritime service and subsequently Commander of the ship 'Euphrates' trading to the Persian Gulf, many years a resident of Serampore. Born 26th April 1772, at — in the county of Middlesex, died 4th November 1847, aged 75 (6 months) and 8 days.
>
> A man of the strictest integrity and retiring piety who, whilst living, did good by stealth and blushed to hear its fame; and at his death, left his fortune to numerous charities and friends.

The phrase 'did good by stealth' tells much of the character of this old salt, whose endowments included substantial gifts to native hospitals, the Sailors' Home, the Seamen's Hospital, European orphanages, schools and libraries.

Finally two very nautical epitaphs: to Captain Ambrose Kepling, one of the oldest Commanders out of the port of Calcutta, who died in 1801 at the age of 60:

> In deep distress with sorrows round
> Assist me, or my barks aground;
> From rocks and shoals and dangers of the deep
> God has preserved my soul I hope as yet.

And to Thomas Andrews, the Portmaster of Diamond Harbour who died in 1809 and is buried along with his three infant children:

> With Boreas' blasts and stormy winds
> I was tossed to and fro;
> By God's decree from danger free
> I'm harbour'd here below
> Where at an anchor I do ride
> With numbers of the fleet
> Until again I do set sail
> My Admiral Christ to meet.

Civilians

The best 'epitaph' on the so-called 'civilians', the servants of the East India Company and later the officers of the Indian Civil Service, was written on the occasion the Company took formal leave of them on their transfer to the Crown in 1858:

> The Company has the great privilege of transferring to the service of Her Majesty such a body of civil and military officers as the world has never seen before. A Government cannot be base, cannot be feeble, cannot be wanting in wisdom that has reared two such services as the civil and military services of the Company. Let Her Majesty appreciate the gift – let her take the vast country and the teeming millions of India under her direct control; but let her not forget the great corporation from which she received them, nor the lessons to be learned from its success.

At that time there were just over 800 civilians, all British, to administer a vast country – almost a continent – with an area of $1\frac{1}{2}$ million square miles and a population which at the end of the British Raj approached 400 million. It was a trading company, founded on private enterprise, which had developed into a state within a state to give free rein to Christian commercial expansion – a company which, as John Stuart Mill reminded its detractors, had kept and consolidated the Indian Empire while a succession of Parliamentary administrations had lost another empire on the other side of the Atlantic! It minted its own coins and etched its nickname of 'John Company' so deeply into the everyday life of Indians, that when Queen Victoria's head first appeared on the currency, she was commonly referred to as 'John Kampany Memsahib' – Mrs John Company.

The Writers who came out at first as humble clerks in the small trading stations – the Company had resolved 'not to employ any gentleman in any place of charge' – soon rose in importance and influence as the stations became forts, then the centres of districts, and finally centres of a vast Presidency; their functions changing from commerce to revenue collection and administration of justice. A 'writership' became 'the greatest prize in the East India Lottery', attracting the highest ranks of society, for by the start of the nineteenth century the richest posts, such as the Resident of Benares, were worth £40,000 a year – fantastic wealth. A handbook of British India written in the early 1840s describes the career prospects of a Writer:

It is the first step in the ladder of preferment to the highest civil offices in India. It is, therefore, the most valuable gift at the disposal of a Director, and is reserved for the highest claims of friendship or reciprocal service.

The handbook quotes a starting salary of £300 p.a. from the moment a Cadet sets foot in India; but first he had the 'privilege of studying a language before he enter[ed] upon the duties for which he [was] destined'. This language instruction was given at the East India College at Haileybury, the entry requirements of which throw an interesting light on the social and educational priorities of the day:

> Candidates will be interrogated in an open committee as to their character, connexions and qualifications ...
> Each candidate shall be examined in the Four Gospels of the Greek Testament and shall not be deemed duly qualified for admission to Haileybury College, unless he be found to possess a competent knowledge thereof; nor unless he be able to render into English some portion of the works of the following Greek authors – Homer, Herodotus, Xenophon, Thucydides, Sophocles and Euripides; nor unless he can render into English some portion of the works of one of the following Latin authors – Livy, Terence, Cicero, Tacitus, Vergil and Horace; and this part of the examination will include questions in ancient history, geography and philosophy.

Candidates were also to be examined in arithmetic, geometry and religion, although there was a discretionary loophole that 'superior attainments in one ... shall be considered to compensate for comparative deficiency in other qualifications'. From this appointment system under the patronage of the Directors of the Company, it was a short step to the introduction of an open competition in 1853 – some seventeen years before such a system was introduced for the Home Civil Service – giving birth to a new breed of civil servants, the 'competition-wallahs', and leading to the exclusion of many sons of families long connected with India who may have had a feeling for the East in their blood but no academic ability.

The average life of a Writer in the early days was very short, and the mortality rate continued high, since their work often involved tours to remote and fever-infested jungles. There is a typical epitaph to a promising young civilian at Gaya who died in his early twenties in 1833:

To the memory of Duncan Crauford McLeod Esq., C.S. whose career of public service commenced and terminated in this district where for eighteen months preceding his dissolution he held the office of Acting Magistrate.

Deeply impressed with the responsible nature of his duties, he fulfilled them with zeal, energy and impartiality, anxiously solicitous for the improvement of the natives, he studied and acquired an intimate knowledge of their language habits and feelings; and his intercourse with them was marked by kindness and consideration, which they returned with confidence and affection.

His firm and uncomprising integrity, his singleness of heart, his active benevolence, his tenderness and consideration for the feelings and necessities of others, while they deservedly endear his memory to a large circle of friends, both European and native, add greatly to the bitterness of sorrow which follows the certainty that in this world they can never more be manifested.

The even shorter career of a civilian 'griffin', or newcomer, who did not survive his first monsoon is commemorated on another tombstone:

Charles Clark, a member of the civil establishment of Bombay who arrived in India on 24 May 1828 and departed this life on Sunday 7 September 1828 in the 21st year of his age. He died as he had lived a true Christian.

There were others who lived a little longer and in those short years made such an impression that their memory lingered on in the minds of the local inhabitants, perhaps more legendary than real, as well as being preserved on their tombstones. Such a one was 'Chilli-Milli', as young Cleveland was called by 'his' tribesmen. When he died at sea a few days out from Calcutta (on the same Indiaman on which Warren Hastings' wife was also travelling home), his body was brought back to Calcutta and buried in the South Parks Cemetery with this long epitaph:

Here lie the remains of August Cleveland Esq. Late Collector of the Revenue, Judge of Dewanny Adawlut [i.e. Civil Court] of the Districts of Bhaugulpore, Monghyr, Rajmahal &c &c. He departed this life 12th January 1784, at sea on board the 'Atlas' Indiaman, Captain Cooper, proceeding to the Cape for the recovery of his health, aged 29 years. His remains, preserved in spirits, were brought up to town in the pilot-sloop which attended the 'Atlas' and interred here on the 30th of the same month. The public and private virtues of this excellent young man were singularly eminent. In his public capacity, he accomplished by a system of conciliation what could never be effected by military coercion. He civilised a savage race of the mountaineers who for ages had existed in a state of barbarism and eluded every exertion that had been practised against them to suppress their depradations, and reduce them to obedience. To this wise and beneficent conduct the English East India Company were indebted for the subjecting to their government the numerous inhabitants of that wild and extensive country, the Jungleterry.

Line upon line followed extolling his private virtues. Another monument was erected to him by the natives of Bhagalpur, a massive Hindu-style shrine, with wording in Persian, while on a traditional English-style monument nearby are inscribed these words, reputedly suggested by Warren Hastings:

Who without bloodshed or terrors of authority, employing only the means of conciliation, confidence and benevolence, attempted and accomplished the entire subjection of the lawless and savage inhabitants of the jungle territory of Rajmahal, who had long infested the neighbouring lands by their predatory incursions, inspired them with a taste for the arts of civilised life and attached them to the British Government by a conquest over their minds, the most permanent as the most rational mode of dominion.

These are fine words from the pre-Colonial era – and Hindus, recognising his quality of greatness, came to his tomb to perform *pooja* every year.

'A second Cleveland', at least as claimed on a monument at Cheerapunji dated 1831, was David Scott: the administrator who settled the Provinces of Upper and Lower Assam after the first Burmese war, carried out a survey, opened schools and encouraged missionaries after pacifying the tribesmen. He died in his early forties in the sanatorium he had been responsible for building; and his son, following in his footsteps, died in Rajmahal before reaching the age of 20.

Another bright star in the civilian firmament in the days of the Company was Andrew Stirling. As a cadet he carried off almost every language prize that there was to win, became the 'Persian' Secretary to the Government, and Deputy Secretary in the Secret and Political Department under the Governor-General, and wrote a history of Orissa which is still the recognised authority on the subject. All this before he was 40. And when he died at Calcutta after an illness of ten days, 'his remains were placed in a leaden coffin and followed to the grave by a large concourse of mourning friends European and Native; amongst the latter were observed almost the whole of the distinguished Native Princes, Nabobs, Rajahs and others.'

In Orissa William Nethersole's name is still known throughout the length and breadth of the Sambalpur District, where he carried out one of the most thorough cadastral surveys and land settlements ever undertaken before being thrown from his horse and killed in 1888 at the early age of 33.

Leonard Munn, a geologist who died at Lingsugure as recently as 1935, possessed the same indefinable qualities of strength and gentleness allied to that element of quaintness which goes to the making of legends. His achievement of sinking over 1,000 wells, and bringing water within easier reach of thousands of villagers in the arid farming tracts of Raichore, was considered as supernaturally inspired; and in the minds of the locals his name became identified with their demi-god Manappa.

The civilians filled all the main positions – commercial, judicial, political and military ('Damn your writing, young man, mind your fighting,' as a General advised a future Governor-General in 1810) – but the key post in the service was that of District Officer, the man at the head of a district, an area often bigger than one of the largest English counties, with a population of several millions. He ran the district as magistrate and tax-gatherer, being responsible both for the maintenance of law and order and for the collection of the land revenue and other taxes, taken over by the Company after the breakdown of the Moghul administrative system. This tax-collecting side is seen on the tomb of an old civilian, who obviously endeared himself to the people in spite of the unpopular nature of his job:

Sacred to the memory of Francis Gillanders Esq., many years collector of taxes on pilgrims at Gyah where he departed this life on 27th August 1821, aged 60 years. A faithful and zealous discharge of public duty secured him the unqualified approbation of government; an intimate knowledge of Indian character and customs added to the gentlest manner and kindest heart; with the greatest attention to the wants and comforts of the pilgrims visiting the sacred temples of Gyah gained him their interest, veneration and regard, whilst many amiable qualities, a blameless life and the practice of every virtue within his reach, placed him high in the esteem and affection of his friends by whom this monument is erected to record his worth.

Gillanders confirmed his identity with the Hindu pilgrims by donating a bell to their temple of Vishnupad at Gaya (Gyah) in 1798. This close association of Christian administrators with the Hindu and Moslem customs, at a time when there was no thought of Evangelism, produced the nearest synthesis of East and West that ever came about. Soon the directors of the Company in London were expressing their horror that Christians should be administering 'heathen' rites.

Lady Nugent, the wife of the Commander-in-Chief, mentions meeting in 1812 two civilians with 'immense whiskers' who were 'as much Hindu as Christians, if not more'. James Grant, who died at Gorakhpur in 1815 in his thirties, had, while Collector of Benares seven years earlier, given a bell to the Brahmin priests of the temple of Durga. They had come to the river-bank and prayed for his safety, when he, his wife and children were in a boat caught in whirlpools opposite the Durga temple. It was from these small deeds that the greatest results flowed, and in a land where truth is expressed in paradox, this was nowhere better illustrated than in the life of the ordinary District Officer.

Many of their names may still be read in a disguised form on the map of India today – Closepeth (Brian Close of Madras); Rossghat (Ross); Lyallpur (Alfred Lyall); Abbottabad (Abbott); McCleodganj (McCleod); Kydganj (Alexander Kyd). Sometimes an epitaph confirms the derivation, as on this tomb in the Suran District, where a lamp used to burn continuously over the remains of the Collector Sahib:

In this grave lies Henry Revil, Collector of Customs under the Hon. East India Company from whom the town of Revilgunge derives its name. He first established a Customs Chowkie at the neighbouring bazaar of Semariah in 1788 and during a residence close to the spot he succeeded in gaining the esteem and affection of the surrounding people who raised this tomb over his remains and whose descendants still cherish his memory with religious veneration.

Doctors

The first medical officers in the East India Company were Surgeons on the East Indiamen sailing to the east. The appointment of these Surgeons was in the hands of a 'Surgeon-General' in London, who supplied the medicine chests and trained a succession of apprentices at his own expense. The training was rudimentary – so much so that it was said that 'a man need only sleep under a medicine chest for a single night to become perfectly qualified for the office' – and the Surgeon-General retained a large part of their pay as a perquisite. At an inquiry in the seventeenth century into allegations of various abuses, the Surgeon-General admitted that he had had twenty-seven such apprentices under this retainer system, 'although twenty had since died', but strongly denied keeping as much as two-thirds of their pay, asserting that he took only two months' pay out of their yearly salary as his 'fee'.

Those early Surgeons had to perform a variety of duties. They had to shoulder a gun and even act as ship's barber; for, according to Regulations, 'they shall also cut the hayre of the carpenters, saylors, caulkers, labourers and any other workmen in the Company's said yards and ships once every 40 days in a seemly manner'.

On arrival in India, the Surgeons found that their skills were appreciated much more by the natives than by their own countryman, and they won important trading concessions for the Company as a reward for their cures of local Rajas. Gabriel Boughton travelled out to India in 1645 as the Surgeon on the Indiaman *Hopewell* and was summoned from the trading port of Surat to the Moghul Emperor's court at Agra over 500 miles away to attend to a female member of the royal household. The facts are confused with legends – Was she the daughter of Shahjahan badly burned, or a lady of the harem with a pain in her side? – but whatever the details, Boughton as a reward for his successful treatment obtained a *farman* from the Emperor, giving the Company the right of trading in Bengal free from duty, and paved the way for the first settlement in Bengal. Boughton married an Indian lady and decided to stay out East, but he soon succumbed to the climate and died in Agra, where he lies in an unknown grave.

Another Surgeon, who had a similar experience, has the history of his achievement recorded on his tombstone, a granite slab 6 foot by 3, which was moved from the original grave to the interior wall of Job Charnock's mausoleum at St. John's Churchyard, Calcutta. There in English and flowery Persian prose is written the following epitaph of a surgeon who came out to India in 1711 on the Frigate *Sherborne*, deserted the ship at Madras and made his way a thousand miles north to Delhi as the medical officer of a special embassy despatched there by the Company in 1715 to negotiate a trading treaty. He died two weeks after his successful return:

> Under this stone lyes interred the body of William Hamilton, Surgeon who departed this life the 4th of December 1717. His memory ought to be dear to this nation for the credit he gained the English in curing Ferrukser, the present King of Indostan of a malignant distemper by which he made his own name famous at the court of that great Monarch and without doubt will perpetuate his memory as well in Great Britain as all other nations in Europe.

The Emperor's 'malignant distemper' is less delicately referred to in the diary of the embassy as 'swellings in the groin'. The swellings must have been painful, for the relief from the successful operation was so great that the Emperor showered the Company servants with presents and honours. Hamilton is reported to have suggested as a fee the grant of special trading privileges for his countrymen, and obtained on the Company's behalf a free-trade *farman* and the right of collecting the rent from about 40 villages around the settlement at Calcutta. As a personal reward he received an elephant, a horse, 5,000 rupees, two diamond rings, a jewelled aigrette, a set of gold buttons and models of all his surgical instruments with handles of pure gold – rather better than collecting his 2d-a-sailor fee for hair-cutting. Other Surgeons were quick to get on this band-waggon of being medical adviser to Native princes. Robert Adams went to look after Hyder Ali in Mysore in the 1770s, and Dr. Lloyd in the 1780s; and the pattern soon became general throughout India. European doctors were credited with almost magical powers by their rich Indian patients – surely it was no mere luck that Dr. Fullerton was the only survivor of the massacre of Englishmen at Patna in the 1760s (see p. 141) and that Dr. Brydon was the only man allowed to ride out of Afghanistan with the news of the disastrous annihilation of an army in the 1840s. But while Indians were impressed with some of the results of European medicine, a reverse thought-process was developing in the minds of European doctors in India. 'The Indies have drugs in far greater plenty and perfection than here', wrote one doctor on his return to England; and the view was beginning to be expressed by Company servants that some of the Indian remedies for eastern maladies were more effective:

> Your surgeons diet of Burned Wine to men sick of the flux is by the physicians of this country held rather poisonous than curable, which some of us in our experience have found true.

And commenting on the efficacy of the Company's Medical Chest, he added:

> Being far-fetched and long kept, applied by an unskilful hand and without consideration of the temperature of a man's body by the alteration of climate, they peradventure produce small or contrary effects, and therefore we for our part do hold that in things indifferent, it is safest for an Englishman to Indianize and so conforming himself in some manner to the diet of the country, the ordinary physic of the country will be the best cure when any sickness shall overtake him.

That was in the seventeenth century; and at the beginning of the nineteenth, when a more formal and professional 'Indian Medical Service' had been established, active encouragement was given to young doctors to find out more about Indian plants and drugs, 'the knowledge of which might prove desirable to the European practitioner'. A different attitude prevailed half-way through the nineteenth century, when all forms of Indian medicine were regarded as heathen concoctions and the old Moghul Emperor – the dynasty approaching its end – was privately laughed at by the Governor-General for taking an elixir composed of pearls, coral and rubies ground into a paste. Yet only twelve years earlier, successful experiments were being undertaken by a Surgeon called Edaile in Calcutta to operate on patients under a yoga-induced hypnosis – a real meeting of Eastern and Western technology – and a Mesmeric Hospital was established there in 1846, only to be displaced by the discovery of chloroform a year later.

The standards of the Medical Service in India steadily improved throughout the nineteenth century. At the beginning of the century, boys in their teens were providing the medical treatment of a regiment. By 1822 the rules laid down an age limit of 'not under twenty years', and in 1836 this had been raised to 22. The qualifications for entry also became stricter, requiring a certificate from the Royal College of Surgeons, a certificate from 'the cupper of a public hospital in London of having acquired and being capable of practising, with proper dexterity, the art of cupping', an examination pass in physic, and six months' attendance at an approved general hospital. There was no open competition until just before the '57 Mutiny. Admission to the service depended on nomination by one of the Directors, and ranking was related to the seniority of the sponsoring Directors themselves. This tended to make the Medical Service a preserve for English gentlemen and specifically excluded Indians, the Company insisting that their officers should be of unmixed European extraction although a few exceptions were made in favour of well-connected Eurasians. Yet, in spite of these limitations, there grew up a body of professional men with wide-ranging knowledge, experience and competence. They were both civil and military officers, being on the reserve list for the army and liable to recall at any time, and holding the commission of Lieutenant as combatant officers as well as 'Assistant Surgeon' – the Surgeon ranking as a Captain. The official pay in the 1840s was between £200 and £300 a year for an Assistant Surgeon, but the real income came from private practice. 'Practice, independently of official employment,' comments the Handbook, with a modern ring about it, 'is the grand source of competency ... and this can only be assured by the exercise of undoubted professional skill.'

Much of this social background to the Indian Medical Service, the 'I.M.S.' as it was universally called, can be gleaned from the tombstones of the period: Consider the stone of Gilbert Pasley in St. Mary's Cemetery, Madras:

> This stone will not want power to melt or virtue to amend the heart. It makes the grave the common friend of mankind. It records the memory of the skilful physician Gilbert Pasley and Susan Hannah, the only daughter of Gilbert and Hannah Pasley. Obiit 23 Sept 1781, aetatis 48 – His daughter 17 February 1782, aged 5 months and 4 days. [N.B. He died just after her birth.]

This 'skilful physician' originally enlisted in the Artillery as a 'Lieutenant Fireworks' and came out to India as a Surgeon's Mate in Adlercron's Regiment, the first King's Regiment to serve in India – '*primus in Indis*'; he transferred to the Company's service and became Surgeon of Fort St. George, and finally Surgeon-General of the Presidency, exchanging – as the obituary notice in Hickey's *Gazette* colourfully put it – 'the Sword, Spungeworm and Ramrod for the Lancett, Gold Headed Cane and Snuff-box'. He was a member of an old Scottish family, the fourth son of James Pasley of Craig in Dumfriesshire; but that did not prevent him from acting as agent for military clothing in addition to his medical duties and private practice. His sister married George Malcolm, and one of their sons came out to Madras to stay with the Pasleys when a cadet of 13 – the future Sir John Malcolm, Governor of Bombay in the 1820s.

Mortality, due to the occupational hazards from contagious and infectious diseases, was very high; and if one takes a town in the United Provinces at random – Cawnpore – and examines the death toll of the Surgeons and Assistant Surgeons appointed to that unhealthy place during the 1820s and 1830s, one finds on average almost one death a year – Robert Buchan in 1825 and Robert Merce in 1826, both with less than a year's service in India; Witney Taylor and Clarke Abel, also in 1826; George Reddie in 1827; Patrick Matthew in 1830; David Ramsay in 1831; John Bacon in 1833 and so on. Who were these young men who came out to the East so willingly and who died so quickly? Many, as in any profession, were ordinary, unexceptional men, and no doubt there were a few rogues and a few eccentrics; but there was an unusually high number who achieved distinction in areas outside their own specialised medical field.

In Cawnpore, for example, the Dr. Abel who died in 1826 was a zoologist and naturalist, who spent five years in the interior of China collecting information on animal life. Unfortunately there is no trace of his epitaph and most of his life's work was lost in a ship-wreck. Dr. Benjamin Heyne, who died at Vepery in 1819 after twenty years as Surgeon in the Madras Presidency, was a botanist of note; and Dr. William Griffith, another Madras Surgeon, was a famous botanist whose memorial in the Medical College in Calcutta reads:

> To the memory of William Griffith, Esq. F.L.S. Madras Medical Service. Born at Ham in the County of Surrey, March 1816. As Professor of Botany in this College, he was distinguished by the zeal and activity with which he imparted the knowledge he had himself acquired by personal investigation in the different provinces of British India, and in the neighbouring kingdoms from the banks of the Helmunt and Oxus to the straits of Malacca, where in the capacity of civil Assistant Surgeon, he died 9th February 1845 in the 34th year of his age and the 13th year of his public service in India. His early loss is deeply deplored by the Head of the Government of India and by the leading natural historians of his time. He bequeathed large collections of plants and manuscripts to the Honourable the Court of Directors of the East India Company.

As leading exponents of Economic Science there were a number of Indian Medicos. James Anderson was one – '*Jacobus Anderson, Scoto-Brittanicus, M.D.*', as starts the long Latin epitaph over his grave in Madras, where he was buried in 1809. The tomb, which once boasted a sculptured marble bust and magnifying glass, still records his name around the overhanging dome in four languages – Tamil, Telugu, Hindustani and English – as a token of his wide contacts.

Anderson was largely responsible for the introduction of cochineal, silk, sugar cane, coffee, American cotton and English apples into India. Another was Dr. David Turnbull, the discoverer of Lac dye at Mirzapore, where he died in 1822; and another Dr. Jameson, the first Conservator of Forests in the Punjab, who died at Dalhousie in 1873. (The Indian Forest Service, which dealt with more than a quarter of a million square miles, was one of the finest material legacies of the British Raj.) A doctor was also the first Director General of Telegraphs, in 1852. Doctors were among the few who had received any form of scientific education and understood the mysteries of electricity and magnetism. Another scientific doctor was Robert Tytler, a brilliant eccentric of the Bengal Medical Establishment, who had obtained his M.D. at Edinburgh in 1807 at the age of 19. While Surgeon of the Governor-General's Bodyguards, he found time to devote to zoology, mineralogy, electro-magnetism and Buddhism. He wrote books on each of these subjects, and his works include a dissertation under the pen-name Talib to prove that Adam addressed Eve in Arabic. He held a theory that the centre of the world was in Gwalior, and he was still looking for the magnetic pole there when he died in his palanquin in 1838. His epitaph, now illegible, at one time recorded that he died 'unexpectedly by the bursting of a blood-vessel at the village of Chanda on his way to Gwalior, whither he was proceeding to investigate the magnetic properties of the surrounding country. Lamented by all ...'

There were young explorers, like James Gerard, the medical officer of a Gurkha battalion, who accompanied Alexander Burnes on his sensational journey to Bokhara and was the first European to penetrate the hill tracts above Kotegarh in the Himalayas; he was only 21 when he died, and he is buried at Subathoo, near Simla. And there was the eldest son of the great Niger explorer, Mungo Park, bearing the same name. He was commissioned into the Madras Medical Service in May 1822 and died of cholera in January 1823, aged 23.

The main contribution of doctors to non-medical learning lay in the fields of philology and ethnology. Many of the linguists and orientalists – lecturers and professors at the Hindu College and other early centres for the study of Sanskrit and Indian languages – were medical men: Leyden, Wilson, Sprenger, Gilchrist, Hunter, Dinwiddie. Their studies brought them closer to the orient and helped them understand it; but the ordinary practitioner could bridge this gap too, as did John Glas, for thirty-two years the Surgeon in Bhagalpur District, who died in 1822, aged 72:

Few Europeans were more respected by the natives than Dr. Glas; he was looked up to by them as their common father; to the full knowledge of this profession he added a gentleness and mildness of manners that made him much beloved by a numerous circle of friends and acquaintances,

and as did the young Assistant-Surgeon Joseph Bramley, Principal of the Medical College of Calcutta, whose grateful pupils erected a monument to record

their sense of the zeal and ability with which he watched over their private interests and those of their country and the courtesy and kindness with which he won their affection, which improved their minds. Aged 34.

Why has worth so short a date – while villains ripen grey with time?

Orientalists

At the end of the eighteenth century and the beginning of the nineteenth century, there were many who worked towards a synthesis of East and West through a process of studying the language and literature of India. These orientalists were Europeans, steeped in the Roman-Greek classical revival of the eighteenth century; they were not nationalists in the later nineteenth-century sense, but cosmopolitan. They came out to India with no ambition to change Indian custom, laws and religion, but with a mental attitude of acceptance of what they found and a desire to find out more.

The best example is perhaps Sir William Jones, whose towering monument, an obelisk 60 feet high, in South Parks Cemetery, Calcutta, indicates that he was no ordinary man. 'Harmonious Jones', as he was affectionately known, was a close friend of Dr. Johnson. He was a scholar, lawyer, linguist, naturalist and author. A Judge of the Supreme Court and author of a book on Mohammedan law, he earned the title of 'the Justinian of India'. He was a friend of Warren Hastings, and arranged for the East India Company to pay his chief *pandit* about £400 to translate Manu's Code of Hindu law into English. In 1785 he founded the Asiatic Society of Bengal for the study of the history, science and literature of Asia. His discovery of a Hindu classical age, as he unravelled the mysteries of Sanskrit and realised that it shared a common base with our European Aryan heritage, was sensational. No longer need anyone feel that Indians were culturally inferior: their past was as glorious as Europe's own classical traditions. Jones worked with a handful of dedicated young men to bring this knowledge before the public by an ambitious programme of translating Indian manuscripts. He himself translated the Indian dramatist Kalidasa and compiled a Persian dictionary. He was said to have mastered thirteen languages and to have a working knowledge of twenty-eight Indian dialects. 'He understands almost every language in the world but his own,' commented an admiring French courtier in the hearing of King Louis. '*Mon Dieu*', the King is reputed to have exclaimed, 'then of what country is he?' 'He is, please your Majesty, a Welshman!' After ten years' spectacular work in India, he died of an inflammation of the liver in 1794 at the age of 47, and the epitaph on his tomb, written by himself, reflects a little of his philosophy:

> Here was deposited the mortal part of a man, who feared God, but not death, and maintained independence, but sought not riches; who thought none below him but the base and unjust, none above him but the wise and virtuous; who loved his parents, kindred, friends and country with an ardour which was the chief source of all his pleasures and all his pains: and who having devoted his life to their service, and to the improvement of his mind, resigned it calmly, giving glory to his Creator, wishing peace on earth and wishing good will to all creatures, on the twenty-seventh day of April in the year of Our Blessed Redeemer one thousand seven hundred and ninety four.

There is a monument to him in the Chapel of University College, Oxford, and his fame extended far and wide, influencing many of his younger contemporaries.

A young man who fell under the influence of William Jones was Jonathan Duncan, later to be famous in his own right as Governor of Bombay. This young Scot, who came out to Bengal as a Company cadet at the age of 15, soon became proficient in Persian and Hindi, and he translated Impey's Legal Code into Bengali. In 1791, when Collector of Benares, he proposed the foundation of a Hindu College there – the precursor of the Sanskrit College of today – 'for', in his words, 'the preservation and cultivation of the Laws, Literature and Religion of that Nation at this Centre of their Faith'. His intention was that this should not only be a focal point for research and learning with a collection of rare Sanskrit manuscripts in its library, but also serve a practical purpose as 'a Nursery of future Doctors and Expounders of the Law to assist European Judges in ... regular and uniform advice'. Duncan was that rare combination, a thinker and a doer. He was shocked by the barbaric customs of infanticide and suttee; but, instead of trying to change them by decree, he reasoned with the responsible and leading members of the Hindu community and convinced them that these customs were later excrescences and no part of pure ancient Hinduism. His monument in Bombay, to the man who had been its Governor for sixteen years, records in the scroll: 'infanticide abolished in Benares & Kattiawar.'

The growing understanding of Hinduism led to a belief in some quarters that Christian missionary activity was unnecessary, but by the 1790s such views were being challenged by the British Evangelicals, under the leadership of William Wilberforce. Wilberforce moved a motion in the House of Commons in 1793 to empower the East India Company to send out teachers and missionaries approved by the Archbishop of Canterbury. The immediate reaction of the Court of Directors was to treat the idea of converting Indians to Christianity as absurd. Moreover, as good business men, they considered the scheme both expensive and politically inexpedient. However, the pressures from the Evangelicals steadily increased, and in the Charter Act of 1813 a clause was inserted to permit the licensing of missionaries to introduce into India 'useful knowledge and religious and moral improvements'. This marked the beginning of the end of the opportunity for the two cultures to meet on equal ground; the orientalists were fighting a losing battle. From now on there was a gradual growth in the attitude of moral superiority over the alien culture, with English becoming the dominant language and the means of attaining any recognised education. If slavery in America was morally wrong in an absolute sense, then surely – the Evangelicals argued – the Indian practices of suttee, thuggee, infanticide and the mental slavery of the caste system were equally wrong and should be stamped out by any enlightened government.

One of the last of the great orientalists was Francis Whyte Ellis of the Madras Civil Service who, according to the Tamil inscription on his monument, 'entered into his rest to the deep sorrow of the Goddess of Earth on 9th March 1819 A.D. (1741 of the Salivahana Era)'. The inscription goes on to describe his achievements in the field of oriental scholarship, and there is a recognition of the growing importance of English:

He was deeply learned in the English language, that language which spreads like a creeper penetrating into every nook and corner of the world ...

In his profound learning he shone like a sun wherever he went dispelling the darkness of ignorance. He was well versed not only in three kinds of Tamil but also in Sanskrit. His Tamil was as sweet as fresh ambrosia ... Translated the code of Manu ... caused 27 wells and tanks to be dug ...

The English inscription on the other side of the monument mentions that his 'valuable life was suddenly terminated by a fatal accident in the 41st year of his age'. For twenty years he had been collecting a mass of material for a book on Sanskrit and the literature of Southern India. He was determined to publish nothing until he had exhausted every source of information. Then, his work almost complete, he died after accidentally swallowing some poison during one of his tours. Later, when his property was sold by auction, all his papers were lost or destroyed. However –

The College of Fort St. George which owes its existence to him is a lasting memorial of his reputation as an oriental scholar and this stone has been erected as a tribute of the affectionate regard of his European and native friends.

Another pioneer of modern education in India, who founded the Hindu College in Calcutta in 1816 from the profits of his watch-making and silver-smith's shop, was David Hare, the 'Father of Native Education', the 'Apostle of Native Progress'. Hare was a close friend of Raja Rammohun Roy, the leader of the Bengal

Hindu Reformation movement, and was so closely identified with the Hindus that when he died of cholera in 1842, at the age of 67, he was denied a Christian burial in the European cemetery. Instead, he was interred in the College which he founded and a tomb was erected by subscriptions from the 5,000 Bengalis who attended his funeral. They wanted a death-mask of their benefactor but this proved impossible. He is still remembered by a street named after him and a local public holiday held each year in his honour. These extracts from the inscriptions on the tomb, and on the tablet erected by teachers and students of a branch school, reflect the thirst for knowledge and gratitude to the provider of it:

This tomb (erected by his native friends and pupils) encloses the mortal remains of David Hare. He was a native of Scotland.

He adopted for his own the country of his sojourn and cheerfully devoted the remainder of his life ... to one pervading and darling object ... *viz* the education and moral improvement of the natives of Bengal, thousands of whom regarded him in life with filial love ... in death as their best and most disinterested friend who was to them even as a father.

Ah warm philanthropist! Ah faithful friend
Thy love devoted to one generous end
To bless the Hindoo mind with British lore
And truth's and nature's faded lights restore ...

The men who shared this attitude to Eastern culture came from all walks of life – judges, doctors, generals, civilians and traders. Even some missionaries found their original enthusiasm changed by years of close contact with the East, until they in effect became Indianised Evangelists. A Major-General has a simple epitaph on his tomb in South Parks Cemetery, Calcutta – that he 'departed this life 31st March 1828 aged 70 years' – but what a strange tomb: a model of a Hindu temple, with a carved stone gateway, the recesses on each side of which were occupied by ancient sculptured figures – now destroyed – of the goddess of the Ganges and the goddess of the earth. This is the tomb of 'Hindoo' Stuart – Charles Stuart, born in Ireland, who came out to India in his teens. He soon fell under the influence of oriental culture and used to walk every morning from his house to bathe in the river according to Hindu custom. He built a Hindu temple at Saugor, and when he visited Europe in 1804, he took a collection of his Hindu household gods with him. Yet he was buried in a Christian cemetery; epitomising the fact that any meeting of East and West depended on an absence of rigid dogmatic rules on either side.

Traders

Trade was the motive of most Englishmen who went to India, and even before the days of the East India Company intrepid men, lured on by the stories told by Portuguese sailors, set out for India to seek their fortune. Few records exist of these early traders, and the first Englishman known to have died in India is John Mildenhall. He set off with a small party of merchants at the end of Queen Elizabeth's reign by the overland route, taking five years to reach his destination, the Court of Akbar, the Moghul Emperor, at Agra. By representing himself as the envoy of the Queen – who, though he did not know it, was now dead – he obtained great encouragement; and after he had returned to England he made a second overland journey to India, dying before he arrived, allegedly of a poison draught he had prepared for three of his English associates. His body was carried the remaining 200 miles to Agra for burial in the Roman Catholic Cemetery – locally known as 'John Sahib's Cemetery' – where a Portuguese inscription was put on his tombstone, followed later by this English version of his exploits:

Here lies John Mildenhall Englishman who left London in 1599 and travelled to India through Persia reached Agra in 1603 and spoke with the Emperor Akbar. On a second visit in 1614 he fell ill at Lahore died at Ajmere and was buried here through the good offices of Thomas Kerridge Merchant.

RIP

He left his property to two natural children in Persia, which perhaps explains his preference for the overland route. John Mildenhall was a Roman Catholic; but later traders in the seventeenth century were Protestants, for the East India Company Charter permitted the employment only of members of the established Church. Protestants who died in India were regarded as heretics by the long-resident Jesuit community in Agra, and their bodies were buried outside the cemetery in the garden of the Dutch factory. They included Justinian Offley, who died in 1627 of a lingering sickness; John Drake, killed in 1631 by an arrow fired at the indigo carts which he was taking to Surat for shipment to England; and George Purchas, who died in 1651 at the age of 24, after only two years in India.

It is significant that these early tombstones were of traders, not soldiers. Soon the cemeteries were to receive their quota of Company servants – Writers, Factors, Junior and Senior Merchants – who traded under a royal monopoly and hounded unlicensed traders, the 'interlopers', out of the country. One of these 'interlopers' was Thomas Pitt, the grandfather of William, Earl of Chatham, who made such a success of his first voyage to South India that the Company decided to engage him rather than risk a rival. Pitt returned to become Governor of Madras for thirteen years and retired in 1710 with an enormous fortune. This included the Pitt Diamond, which netted him a profit of over £100,000 before becoming one of the French Crown Jewels. It was not until 1813 that the India trade was opened to other merchants and the Company's monopoly ended. Finally, in 1833, the similar monopoly to China was abolished and all the Company's 'commercial business and make sale of all their merchandise, Stores, and Effects at Home and Abroad' closed for ever. Parliament had come to the conclusion that the Company, with its involvement in fighting wars, administering the territory secured, and collecting the revenues, should not be connected with trade. It had been a gradual process, from checks on Company servants engaging in private trade – the Cornwallis reforms of 1804 – to the elimination of all Company trade. As the Company surrendered its interests in trade, 'free-merchants' were licensed to take over the running of plantations, banks, agency houses and other businesses. 'It is strange, very strange,' as Macaulay said at the time in Parliament –

> that a joint stock company of traders; a society, the shares of which are daily passed from hand to hand; a society, the component parts of which are perpetually changing, a society which, judging *a priori* from its constitution, we should have said was as little fitted for imperial functions as the Merchant Taylor's Company or the New River Company, should be entrusted with the sovereignty of a large population, the disposal of a larger clear revenue, the command of a larger army than are under the direct management of the Executive Government of the United Kingdom. That a handful of adventurers from an island in the Atlantic should have subjugated a vast country divided from the place of their birth by half the globe ... a territory inhabited by men differing from us in race, colour, language, manners, morals, religion: these are prodigies to which the world has seen nothing similar. We interrogate the past in vain. The Company is an anomaly: but it

is part of a system where everything is anomaly. It is the strangest of all governments but it is designed for the strangest of all empires.

The 'merchants' of the Company concentrated on government, leaving the commercial field open to enterprising individuals, mainly Scots, to build up and run family businesses and plantations – indigo, jute, tea, sugar, tobacco, mining and engineering industries – turn them into agency houses and the large corporate companies of the late nineteenth and twentieth century – with names so revealing of their connections north of the border: Macneill & Co., McCleod & Co., both agency houses for collieries and tea estates; Jardine, Skinner & Co., Begg, Dunlop & Co., jute and general agents; Hamilton & Co., Orr & Co., silversmiths of Calcutta and Madras respectively; Bruce, Fawcett & Co., Forbes & Co., general agents of Bombay; Turner, Cadogan & Co., Mackinnon, Mackenzie & Co., Thomas Duff & Co., Birkmyre Bros., Duncan Bros. – the Scottish names roll on and on.

John Farquhar's career illustrates a typical free-merchant of this early period. Born in 1751 of humble Scottish parentage, he joined the Company's service as a Writer and then resigned to become a licensed free-merchant and sole contractor of the government's gunpowder factory at Pulta – a profitable line of business. He had deliberately equipped himself for this job by studying the chemistry of saltpetre, and he husbanded his financial resources by doing without the numerous servants who were normally considered indispensable to a European household, giving his only bearer two annas a day (less than twopence) to provide him with food. When the Company's monopoly was removed in 1813, he set up Basset, Farquhar & Co., and also had an interest in Whitbread's Brewery in London at a time when the export of 'India Pale Ale' was increasing rapidly. This shrewd Scot not only made a fortune but preserved his health. He retired to Fonthill Abbey, which he purchased in 1822 for £330,000 – a fabulous amount for those days – dying four years later at the age of 75. He had, during his Indian days, been a great admirer of Hindu philosophy and in his will he left £1 million to a Scottish university to endow a School of Atheism, a tantalising offer which had to be rejected as contrary to the religious charters of that institution.

The 'Prince of British Merchants', as John Palmer was known, had an even more spectacular commercial career. Born in the West Indies in 1767, he was captured by the French and eventually joined his family in Calcutta, where at that time his father, Major William

Palmer, was acting as Confidential Private Secretary to the
Governor-General, Warren Hastings. John started work as a clerk in
the office of licensed merchants and on the death of one of the
partners took his place; by a series of amalgamations he emerged as
the principal of a Banking House known as 'Palmer & Co'. He had
many powerful friends and connections who included Tucker, a
Director and future Chairman of the East India Company and Pitt,
the Prime Minister. His half-brother William was the power behind
the Hyderabad throne, aided and abetted by the Marquess of
Hastings, the Governor-General; and his step-mother, Princess Faiz
Baksh, was related to the ruling Moghul family in Lucknow and
Delhi. Yet, in spite of money, power and influence, the Palmer
House failed in the spectacular 'crash' of so many banking houses in
the 1830s, and it is estimated that his losses amounted to £17
million. The remainder of his life was devoted to helping some of the
worst victims of this financial disaster, the widows and poor; and
when he died of quinsy at the age of 68 in 1836, he was carried to the
grave by a 'more numerous concourse of friends and others who
respected his memory than perhaps ever attended any funeral in
Calcutta'. The legend on the statutory bust that was erected in the
Town Hall in his honour contained these words:

> To superior talent he united a mind well-cultivated and richly
> stored with a heart susceptible of every generous and benevolent
> impulse, ready at all times to sympathise in the sorrows and
> sufferings of his fellow creatures ... He lived in the respect and
> affection of a numerous circle of friends, European and native ...
> who have caused this monument to be erected to his memory.

Even an exceptional person like John Palmer could not break
down the social barriers that were so strictly observed in India
between the 'officials' – both civil and military – and the rest. As late
as 1857, the *Times* correspondent Russell was writing:

> Wealth can do nothing for man or woman in securing them
> honour or precedence in their march to dinner ... A successful
> speculator, or a 'merchant prince' may force his way into good
> society in England ... but in India he must remain for ever
> outside the sacred barrier, which keeps the non-official world
> from the high society of the services.

The one area where the non-official reigned supreme was the
plantation, remote from the interference of Company Magistrates,

Collectors or other representatives of the Government. The planters, a number of whom had come from the West Indies, ran their estates much as they pleased. They were a law unto themselves and represented a strong voice of British opinion – mostly Scottish. They dominated the English Press in India and often indulged in bitter attacks on Company policy for placing the interests of the 'natives' before those of their own countrymen. But they lived lonely lives, working hard to develop their plantations – first indigo, then from the 1840s jute, sugarcane, tobacco, cotton and tea. The inscription on the grave of Bruce at Tezpur in Assam tells of the start of the tea industry:

> In memory of Charles Alexander Bruce born 11.1.1793 died 23.4.1871; aged 78 years; 3 months; 13 days … The first explorer of tea tracts in the province and discoverer of the indigenous tea plant in Assam who was appointed Superintendent of tea culture under the Government of India until the tea industry was adopted by private enterprise …

The plantation industries were always at risk from the invention of synthetic substitutes – such as killed indigo – or from a glut on the market. It was no easy life, and many planters who lived near unhealthy jungle tracts found early graves in an unconsecrated corner of the Manager's garden. The present kitchen garden of the Dooriah Concern contains the graves of a number of the pioneer indigo planters, such as George Christy, who died 18th August 1812.

Indigo was first cultivated here in the Tirhut district in 1780. One of the earliest managing proprietors was Arthur Jones. He was followed by John Finch and William Howell. In the 1840s the factory passed into the hands of the Tirhut Indigo Association of London, which experimented with sugar cane. About twenty years later the Association sold the concern, which was again growing indigo, to Messrs. Studd & Lachlan Macdonald. The estate covered an area of over 200 square miles, and as it was not lawful until 1833 for a European to be a direct owner of land, a system of leaseholding developed, with the peasant-farmers contracting to sow a certain area of their holdings in indigo and the factory contracting to pay a fixed price per acre. An indigo concern generally consisted of a number of these factories under the supervision of one manager, usually with a European assistant at each 'outwork'. There was not much scope for social life, medical care or any of the little luxuries that even the mofussil towns could boast. Instead, these rugged characters created their own interests, which usually centred on a huge airy bungalow with wide encircling verandahs, extensive lawns and prolific flower and vegetable gardens growing every local and imported variety that could be encouraged to survive the hot season with the aid of systematic irrigation and manuring. And it was in these gardens, which they supervised with so much care, that many planters knew that they would leave their bones, unless they could defy the fevers which were so prevalent. A young Assistant in his fifteenth year shares the garden graveyard of the Rajpore concern with an unknown colleague – the brief record of his short life surviving on this inscription cut upon a simple slate slab:

Sacred to the memory of George Benjamin Havell who departed this life on the 19th day of September 1810 aged 14 years.

Family Connections

A tour round the cemeteries of India, from Bombay to Calcutta to Madras, reveals a surprisingly large number of inmates who, although not famous themselves, were closely related or connected with famous people in England: some with the Court, the natural sons and daughters of the Royal Family; some with the nobility and the ruling families of church and state; some with the best-known literary figures of the time – Milton, Dickens, Scott and Burns; and some with celebrated artists and stage personalities. Others were the forefathers of men later to become household names, who by building up a fortune in the East provided a foundation of power and leisure for their sons to pursue their political and literary careers in England; this was the background of politicians such as Pitt and North, and writers such as Addison and Thackeray.

The earliest connection with the royal family was provided by an unexpected character called Tom Coryate (see also p. 181). He was educated at Westminster and Oxford, spoke nine languages (including Persian) and knew Johnson, Donne, Drayton and Shakespeare. He made a 2,000 mile walk through Europe which he described in his *Crudities*, and then travelled overland to India on foot as a pilgrim in oriental attire, earning this epitaph written by Terry, the chaplain at Surat in 1617:

Here lies the wanderer of his age
  Who living did rejoice
To make his life a pilgrimage
  Not out of need but choice.

He had a gift for acquiring patrons, and was appointed by King James I as a companion to his son, Prince Henry, becoming a kind of Court jester; on one occasion he described James as 'the refulgent carbuncle of Christendom'. He is remembered for having introduced the fork from Italy to England, an exploit that earned him the nickname 'Furcifer'.

More direct connections with the Court were provided by Lady Anne Monson, the great-granddaughter of Charles II through his mistress Barbara Villiers, who died in Calcutta in 1775. She has already been referred to in the section on Members of Council at the time of Warren Hastings. And there was the humble Mrs. Dalton who died at Madras in 1813 at the age of 32, married to a surgeon in the Madras Medical Service who was the grandson of King George III and a love of his youth, Hannah Lighfoot, 'the Fair Quaker'. George III's second son, the Duke of Clarence, later King William IV, sent three of his natural sons by Dora Jordan, the reigning queen of comedy, out to India in the King's army, where two of them died: Frederick FitzClarence attained the rank of Lieutenant-General and Commander-in-Chief Bombay before his death in 1854 at the age of 54 near Poona, and his remains were shipped back to England; Lieutenant Henry FitzClarence at the age of 23 'sunk under the fourth day of a fever at Allahabad on the evening of 2nd instant [September, 1817] whilst on his progress to the Upper Provinces in the suite of the Governor-General', according to the *Calcutta Gazette*. The epitaph and monument erected over his tomb have unfortunately disappeared.

The family influence of the Pitts was built on the fortune which grandfather Thomas Pitt accumulated when Governor of Madras at the start of the eighteenth century, as described in the section on Traders (see p. 86). Another earlier Governor of Madras (1687-92) who amassed a huge fortune was Elihu Yale (see also p. 136), the founder of Yale University; two of his daughters married into English aristocratic families, enriching them with his Indian wealth. The eldest daughter married Dudley North, the grandfather of Lord North the great Prime Minister, and the second daughter married the younger son of the 1st Duke of Devonshire. The epitaph on Elihu's tomb in London where he was buried in 1721 records his varied life:

Born in America, in Europe bred
In Africa travelled, in Asia wed,
Where long he lived and thrived – in London dead.
Much good, some ill, he did, so hope's all even
And that his soul through mercie's gone to heaven.

Gladstone's father built his fortune on Eastern trade and sent the first vessel from Liverpool to Calcutta after trade in the East was thrown open. Among other Prime Ministers with relatives buried in India was Sir Robert Peel, whose 'V.C.' son died of smallpox at Cawnpore in 1858, as described under Naval Officers (p. 66); and Lady Peel's grandmother, Rebecca Darke, died at Trichinopoly in 1797. Lord Liverpool's mother was the daughter of 'Begum' Johnson whose mausoleum still stands in St. John's churchyard, Calcutta, with an epitaph proudly declaring the connection (see p. 116). And Cromwell, the Lord Protector, must not be forgotten; several of his descendants died in India – Frankland, his great-grandson, Governor of Bengal, in 1728; another great-grandson, Sir Francis Russell, died in Calcutta in 1743; and a great-great-grandson, Nicholas Morse, Governor of Fort St. George, died in 1772.

Literary connections were numerous, and it would be hard to name an author of the eighteenth and nineteenth centuries who did not owe a little in some way to India. Addison acknowledged his debt; two of his brothers, one a Governor of Madras, died at Fort St. George, and it was the inheritance of the Governor's fortune that enabled him to bring off his marriage with the Dowager Countess of Warwick – the 'Chloe' of Holland House – with whom he had so long been in love. Sterne had a notorious love affair with Mrs. Eliza Draper (see p. 114), born in Angengo, near Cape Cormorin: 'Not Swift so loved his Stella, Scarron his Maintenon, or Waller his Sacharissa as I will love thee and sing thee, my wife-elect', as he said, in anticipation of the possibility of her becoming widowed; and he made Eliza the heroine of his *Sentimental Journey*. It was remarkable that this young woman, born and educated at a small Indian factory settlement, and reputedly very plain, should have been able to attract so much attention from men who were preeminent in the world of letters. Abbé Raynal gives this eulogy on her:

> Territory of Angengo, you are nothing, but you have given birth to Eliza. One day these commercial establishments founded by Europeans on the coasts of Asia will exist no more. The grass will cover them, or the avenged Indians will have built over their ruins; but if my writings have any duration, the name of Angengo will remain in the memory of men. Those who read my works ... will say, – It is there that Eliza Draper was born; and if there is a Briton among them, he will hasten to add with pride, – and she was born of English parents.

It is a curious fact that the historian Orme – the 'Indian Thucydides' – was also born at this small outpost some fourteen years before Eliza, though he had the advantage of being educated at Harrow. Eliza died at the age of 35, and the inscription on the shield of her graceful monument in Bristol Cathedral, with two classical virgins bending over it, simply states her name and dates, and adds: 'In whom genius and benevolence were united.' This contrasts with Sterne's London epitaph, a few years earlier: 'Alas! Poor Yorick ... Ah! *molliter ossa quiescant.*' Sterne had been introduced to Eliza by 'Mr and Mrs James', who figure largely in his memoirs, and it was to James that he consigned his only daughter – the same Commodore James, naval hero of Severndroog in 1755, who stamped out piracy on the Bombay coast, became Chairman of the East India Company, Member of Parliament, Governor of Greenwich Hospital, and was commemorated by a monument on Shooter's Hill, London, which stands 140 feet higher than the elevation of St. Paul's, and is now converted into tea-rooms (p. 98).

The Indian connections persist; Thackeray was himself very influenced by India. He was born in India and both his father and grandfather were Bengal 'Collectors' who died in Calcutta; his great-uncle was a famous elephant-hunter; one uncle of 19 was buried at Cuddapah, while another uncle was killed near Surat. A romantic story is told about Thackeray's mother: she first fell in love with an Indian Army Lieutenant, Carmichael-Smith, who was related to Fanny Burney. Her family disapproved and pretended he had died. She married the elder Thackeray and gave birth to William Makepeace. Then, quite unexpectedly, she met her old love again. When she was widowed, she married him.

Thackeray dedicated *The Virginians* to 'Sir Henry Davison, Chief Justice of Madras ... by an affectionate friend, London, 7th September 1859'. Sir Henry received this book only a few months before he died at Ootacamund, aged 55. It was while in residence at Ootacamund that Macaulay, who hated India and was always homesick for England, came nearest to something he appreciated; he described his cottage

buried in laburnums, or something very like them, and geraniums which grow in the open air ... the vegetation of Windsor Forest or Blenheim spread over the mountains of Cumberland.

And it was at 'Ooty' that Richard Burton, after visiting St. Stephen's Church in 1847, commented on its cemetery as being 'so extensive and so well stocked' that it made him 'shudder to look at it'. Nearby in St. Martin's Church, Bangalore, is a tablet to the son and heir of Sir Walter Scott, a Colonel in the Hussars, who died at the Cape on his way out to India in 1847, making the Baronetcy extinct. Scott's brother-in-law, Charles Carpenter, was Commercial Resident in Salem, and Scott must have listened to many stories about India, for his characters Middlemas and Begum Moti Mahal in *The Surgeon's Daughter* are Reinhart and Begum Sumroo thinly disguised, just as Thackeray's character Major Gahagan is a composite of those two famous Anglo-Indian 'freelancers' Skinner and Gardner. The Presidency of Madras also holds ties with John Milton – his grandson, Caleb Clarke, being parish clerk of St. Mary's; and Thomas De Quincey had a daughter living there.

Apart from the connections with the Thackerays, Calcutta was rich in other literary associations. Charles Dickens's son, Lieutenant Walter Landor Dickens, is buried at the Bhowanipore cemetery; and the occasional Anglo-Indian slang in Dicken's novels betrays his interest, as with the term 'gum-gum', a little drum, in *Sketches by Boz*:

'Did you ever hear a tom-tom, Sir?'
'A what?'
'A tom-tom.' 'Never.'
'Nor a gum-gum?'
'Never.'
'What *is* a gum-gum?' eagerly enquired several young ladies.

Walter Savage Landor, the godfather of Dickens' son, wrote the beautiful ode to Rose Aylmer – the love of his youth – who lies under a delicately shaped twisting stone monument in the South Parks Cemetery (see p. 104). Landor also wrote verse to Theodosia Garrow, the kinswoman of Anthony Trollope, who had three 'nabob' relatives in cemeteries in Madras Presidency. The South Parks Cemetery also contains the bones of Fanny Burney's half-brother, not far from the steepling obelisk of Sir William Jones; and both Fanny and Sir William were close friends of Dr. Johnson. Walter Bagehot, the economist and man of letters, obtained entrance to the world of politics through his father-in-law James Wilson, who is also buried in South Parks. The epitaph on the tomb of Lucia Palkh, in the same cemetery, is quoted by Rudyard Kipling in *City of Dreadful Night* (see p. 102); and Charlotte Hickey, the wife of the famous diarist William Hickey, also lies there.

Bombay has its share of connections with men of letters even though some of them are a little indirect, as with Thomas Chisholm Anstey. To him belongs the credit for preserving the only record of

Carlyle's *Lectures on European Literature*, delivered in 1838 without notes and unreported at the time. Anstey's private verbatim notes, in the form of a volume of 214 pages, was bequeathed to the Bombay Branch of the Royal Asiatic Society when he died there in 1888. Carlyle was fascinated by Catherine, the daughter of the Resident of Hyderabad and a Mohammedan Princess – the Kitty Kirkpatrick of his *Reminiscences* and the Blumine of his *Sartor Resartus* (see p. 56). The novelist Charles Reade had a brother George in the Bombay Civil Service, who died at Calicut in 1816 at the age of 18. Robert Burns had a daughter-in-law and grandson buried in Neemuch within a few weeks of each other; and his closest friend, Chaplain Gray, who had been a master at Dumfries High School during Burns's schooldays and saw to the schooling of his sons, was buried north of Bombay where he had come to teach the Rao of Kachh (Cutch), with this brief inscription on his tomb:

> Sacred to the memory of James Gray of Scotland, Chaplain of Bhuj, tutor to H.H. Rao Desaljee, who died 25th March, 1830 aged 60 years.

On the other side of his tomb is an inscription to his wife, who died at Bhuj in 1829.

Others were literary figures in India in their own right, who maintained contact with the world of letters in Europe. William Delafield Arnold, who wrote several books and tracts under the pen-name 'Punjabee', was the brother of Matthew Arnold the poet. Matthew wrote 'Southern Night' in memory of his brother, and this stanza from it commemorates William's death in Gibraltar on the journey home from India and his wife's death at almost the same time at Dharmsala:

> Ah me! Gibraltar's strand is far
> But farther yet across the brine
> Thy dear wife's ashes buried are
> Remote from thine.
> For there, where morning's sacred fount
> Its golden rain on earth confers
> The snowy Himalayan mount
> O'ershadows hers.

Two English authoresses sleep in the cemetery at Poona: Emma Roberts, who wrote a number of well-known travel books, and Mrs. Fletcher, a friend of William Wordsworth. Mrs. Fletcher married

one of the chaplains in the East India Company and fourteen
months later fell a victim to cholera, while travelling with her
husband back to Bombay from Sholapur, their first station. A few
weeks before, she had written of India as a land –

> where Death is such a swift and cunning hunter, that before you
> know you are *ill*, you may be ready to become his prey – where
> death, the grave and forgetfullness may be the work of two days.

A close friend on hearing of her death wrote:

> Will you tell Mr. Wordsworth this anecdote of poor Mrs.
> Fletcher's? I am sure it will interest him. During the time that
> famine in the Dekkan was raging, she heard that a poor Hindu
> woman had been found lying dead in one of the temples at the
> foot of an idol, with a female child still living in her arms. She and
> her husband immediately repaired to the spot, took the poor
> orphan away with them and conveyed it to their own home ... to
> be brought up as a Christian.

Apart from these literary connections of family and friendship,
India provided the inspiration for many characters and plots of the
great novelists and story tellers. Rudyard Kipling was one of the
greatest of those who captured the 'feel' of India, the sounds and
scenes and smells, from first-hand experience, having been born and
brought up there. Rider Haggard was another; his mother's family,
the Dovetons, had continuous Indian contact for over a hundred
years, with uncles and great-uncles in the Bengal Army, the Madras
and Bombay Civil Service, each no doubt with their accumulated
store of quaint and original happenings on this magnetically elusive
Continent; until in the process of time the ordinary Englishman in
his little urban island was made familiar with some of India's
folklore. Perhaps the man in the street was influenced more by the
Music Hall versions – the Poona Colonel, the 'mad dogs and
Englishmen' of Noel Coward – than by the histories, memoirs and
travelogues produced by men like Elphinstone, Mackintosh,
Malcolm, Duff, Kaye and, of course, Winston Churchill – men who
did much of their work with the thermometer in the hundreds while
many of their contemporaries slept through the hot afternoons
under the punkah. But these writers, whatever the influence of their
works, succeeded in enriching the English vocabulary with dozens of
new Indian and Anglo-Indian words which have now passed into
everyday usage – blighty; bungalow; verandah; cot; cummerbund;

loot; jungle; juggernaut, khaki; gym and gymkhana; phut; punch-bowl (from 'panch' meaning five, the number of ingredients); pukka; puttee; pariah, shampoo, thugs and mugs; the many culinary terms – curry, chutney, kedgeree, mulligatawny, pilau, cochineal; and materials – calico, gingham, jute. Perhaps these will be some of the more lasting memorials of the British connection with India.

Artists, no less than writers, were influenced by India. Recording strange and picturesque scenes, ornate and unusual architecture, colourful people taking part in exotic religious festivals, tigers and elephants, beautiful flowers and butterflies, they hoped to bring these to the eyes of their countrymen and make a fortune for themselves in the process. Zoffany, Ozias Humphry, Thomas Daniell and his nephew William Daniell – leading painters of their day – were all out in India at the same time and returned to exhibit their folios of drawings and paintings. Others were not so fortunate. Tilly Kettle died at Aleppo in 1790, going overland to Bengal for a second visit. George Farrington, brother of a well known R.A., and himself classed by his compeers with Carracci, arrived in India in 1783 and died a few years later at the age of 34 as the result of fever contracted 'by exposure to the night air while sketching native ceremonial rites'; Samuel Daniell, brother of William, succumbed to a fever in Ceylon; John Smart, the miniaturist, spent five years in India, and his son, who also exhibited miniatures at the Academy, died at Madras in 1809; George Chinnery, after twenty years active work in Calcutta, died near Canton in 1848. A number of artists found it more profitable to be attached to the Court of one of the Native princes, where they received rich fees in money and jewellery for their work – more lucrative than painting a succession of conventional miniature portraits for European patrons at the standard rate of about £25 each. Robert Home was painter to the Nawab of Oudh and died in his old age at Cawnpore in 1834; his son was killed at Sobraon in 1841; his brother Edward was the first president of the Royal College of surgeons and his brother-in-law was Hunter, the great anatomist. Home's position at the Court was taken over by George Beechey, who became almost completely 'Indianised' and settled down with his Indian wife and family in Lucknow to paint and send occasional pictures to England for exhibition. He died in 1855 and his ghost is alleged to haunt his bungalow still.

James Wales became the official artist at the Peshwa's Court at Poona, inducing the Peshwa to establish a school of drawing in his palace, and he lived there as superintendent of the school until his premature death five years later, in 1795. The Court at Poona was a stimulating centre in more senses than one, and recorded an instance of 'streaking' which set the bazaar tongues wagging, when two high-born ladies were induced to walk unclothed through the great new hall of mirrors to claim a valuable piece of jewellery each from the Peshwa. They were nicknamed 'Crouching Kate' and 'Susan Straight' from their respective modest and brazen approaches to this ordeal; what a pity Wales did not paint the scene for posterity!

Many famous personalities of the theatre had close family links with India. Two of the most brilliant actresses of the eighteenth century sent sons to serve the Company. Sarah Siddons had a son who became Postmaster-General in Bengal before dying in Calcutta, and three grandsons in John Company's army. Dora Jordan, who lived at Bath with the Duke of Clarence, sent three of the five sons she bore him to India (see p. 91). A son-in-law of Mrs. Jordan, who married her eldest daughter (the progeny of her liaison with Daly, the manager of the Dublin theatre), also went to India and found a premature grave in the North Parks Street cemetery, Calcutta in 1824.

3 Women and Children

The original charters of the East India Company prohibited women, and the first factory settlements were run on college lines, with morning prayers in chapel and dinner in hall. This monastic pattern of life was not unusual at the time, and the same conditions would have been found at the Merchant Adventurers' factory in Middleburg or the Levant Company's trading post at Aleppo. The rule proved impossible to enforce when there was a ready supply of attractive local Goanese women, the progeny of Portuguese predecessors, and the Directors of the East India Company became concerned about the morals of their servants and, more important, the religious consequences of taking wives from the Roman Catholic Goanese community established round the Presidency towns of Madras and Bombay. They sought to reverse this trend by arranging for occasional boat-loads of young Protestant girls to come out and by laying down a formal order that no Christian inhabitant of their settlements should presume to marry without the Governor's consent – adding in justification:

> Many of the young gentlemen in the Company's service, being of good families in England, who would be very much scandalised at such marriages as were likely to be contracted without the consent of the President.

The Directors were only following the practice already established by the Portuguese of drafting out a supply of women to their possessions in the East and attempting to control European marriages. The French at Pondicherry did much the same, and the Dutch went further and set up a Court to adjudicate on the suitability of marriages. Chaplains who consecrated unauthorised unions were liable to dismissal; Clive dismissed one in 1765, and as late as 1817, a Chaplain's allowance was suspended for this offence.

The first records of women coming out under this system are found in the 1670s in both Bombay and Madras. In 1671, twenty women were sent out to Bombay at the Company's expense for one year. They were described as 'of sober and civil lives'; but scandals followed, and they were warned that they would be put on bread-and-water and shipped back to England unless they applied themselves to 'more sober and Christian conversation'. At Madras, the need for wives appeared to be smaller; only three unmarried women were sent out in 1678 – 'having neither relations nor recommendations to any person in this place'. These women were divided into 'gentlewomen' and 'other women' according to the accepted social stratification of those times. They were not given dowries, but they were provided with one set of wearing apparel and were maintained by the Company for up to one year while they sought husbands. It is hardly surprising that women sent out in these circumstances should have adopted a somewhat mercenary attitude to the whole matrimonial procedure, and this is openly reflected in their letters and diaries. As one experienced wife wrote cynically to her friend Maria in England in the early nineteenth century:

> What a state of things is that, where the happiness of a wife depends upon the death of that man who should be the chief if not only source of her fidelity. However, sad is the fact in India: wives are looking out with gratitude for the next mortality that may carry off their husbands, in order that they may return to England to live upon their Jointures; they live a married life in absolute misery, that they may enjoy a widowhood of affluence and independence. This is no exaggeration I assure you.

The 'jointures' were the prize sought by the English damsels who braved the long and arduous voyage and the dangers of the Indian climate; the East India Company provided an allowance of £300 a year on marriage to a civilian, and this continued for life even if the wife was widowed. English girls were not the only ones; the Dutch girls of Capetown cornered part of the marriage market. Many officers of the East India Company spent their leave in South Africa owing to the absurdity of the furlough regulations, which laid down that all leave at, or eastward of, Cape Colony counted as service with full Indian pay and retention of Indian appointment, while westward both appointment and allowances were lost. Naturally, in the words of Rawlins –

> many flocked to the Cape, and spent a pleasant furlough there, as the Dutch people are famed for their hospitality and sport and their daughters are exceedingly agreeable and good-looking ... few young men could resist the charms of the fair maids of Capetown; consequently many a Cape girl married an Indian officer, or civilian better still, as the latter was always worth, dead or alive £300 a year! and these alliances afforded them much pleasure, as their parents were ambitious and rejoiced to see their girls lifted in the social scale and thus happily united.

The arrival of any unmarried women in Calcutta became a social event, and it was unusual if engagements did not ensue within a matter of days. Church on Sundays was the recognised marriage bazaar; after the arrival of a 'Europe ship' bringing new beauties to the city, the gallants congregated on the church steps awaiting the young ladies' arrival, to greet them as they stepped down from their palanquins. The ritual was described by a young maiden who came out to Calcutta with her father as protector in 1783:

> I have been at church, my dear girl, in my new palanquin where *all* ladies are approached by sanction of ancient custom, by all gentlemen indiscriminately, known or unknown, with offers of their hands to conduct them to their seat. Accordingly those gentlemen who wish to change their condition (which between ourselves are chiefly old fellows, for the young fellows either choose country-born ladies for wealth, or having left their hearts behind them, enrich themselves in order to be united to their favourite Dulcineas in their native land), on hearing of a ship's arrival, make a point of repairing to this holy dome and eagerly tender their services to the fair strangers, who, if this stolen view happens to captivate, often, without undergoing the ceremony of a formal introduction, receive matrimonial overtures, becoming brides in the utmost splendour, have their rank simultaneously established and are visited and paid every honour to which the consequence of their husband entitles them. But not so your

friend; for, having accompanied my father to India, no overtures
of that nature will be attempted previous to an acquaintance with
him ...

Rudyard Kipling refers to the rush into matrimony in *The City of
Dreadful Night*, as he muses on Lucia Palkh, who found an early
grave in Calcutta:

> What pot-bellied East Indiaman brought the 'virtuous maid' up
> the river, and did Lucia 'make her bargain' as the cant of those
> times went, on the first, second or third day after her arrival? Or
> did she, with the others of the batch, give a spinsters' ball as a last
> trial – following the custom of the country?

Lucia's death at the age of 23 is commemorated in 'the stiltedness of
the old-time verse' on her tomb:

> What needs the emblem, what the plaintive strain,
> What all the arts that sculpture e'er expressed,
> To tell the treasure that these walls contain?
> Let those declare it most who knew her best.
>
> The tender pity she would oft display
> Shall be with interest at her shrine returned,
> Connubial love, connubial tears repay,
> And Lucia loved shall still be Lucia mourned.
>
> Though closed the lips, though stopped the tuneful breath –
> The silent, clay-cold, monitress shall teach –
> In all the alarming eloquence of death
> With double pathos to the heart shall preach.
>
> Shall teach the virtuous maid, the faithful wife,
> If young and fair, that young and fair was she,
> Then close the useful lesson of her life,
> And tell them what she is, they soon must be.

The size of Lucia's tomb proved that her husband was a rich man;
in Kipling's words, he gave her –

> all that her heart could wish. A green-painted boat to take the air
> in on the river of the evenings, Coffree slave-boys who could play
> on the French horn, and even a very elegant, neat coach with a
> genteel rutlan roof ornamented with flowers, very highly finished,

ten best polished plate glasses, ornamented with a few elegant medallions enriched with mother-o'-pearl, that she might make her drive on the course as befitted a factor's wife ... She was a toast far up the river. And she walked in the evening on the bastions of Fort William and ... exchanged congratulations with her friends on the 20th October, when those who were alive gathered together to felicitate themselves on having come through another hot season. ... But Lucia fell sick, and the doctor – he who went home after seven years with five lakhs and a half [i.e. 550,000 rupees], and a corner of this vast graveyard to his account – said that it was a pukka or putrid fever, and the system required strengthening. So they fed Lucia on hot curries, and mulled wine worked up with spirits and fortified with spices for nearly a week; at the end of which time she closed her eyes on the weary, weary river and the fort for ever, and a gallant, with a turn for *belles lettres*, wept openly as men did then and had no shame of it, and composed the verses above set ... But the factor was so grieved that he ... could only spend his money – and he counted his wealth in lakhs – on a sumptuous grave. A little later on he took comfort, and when the next batch came out ...

Young women were a great source of entertainment in the male-dominated society of those times, and one of the largest and most ostentatious tombs in Calcutta, in the shape of a huge pyramid 24 feet high, is to the memory of Elizabeth Barwell, the young wife of a senior member of the Supreme Council, who died in 1779. In her maiden days she had set Calcutta society alight with her escapades, and many young men were constantly pursuing her. She had a solution to this embarrassment of bachelors. She accepted invitations from each and every one to the same fancy-dress ball, and instructed each to match her dress by wearing an exotic and ridiculous pea-green costume and not to tell anyone else. On the night of the ball a dozen young suitors appeared in their pea-green attire hoping for the sole company of Elizabeth, and each was astonished to meet eleven competitors for her hand. However, once the absurdity of the situation had sunk in, they formed a solid group, escorting her round the hall in her palanquin singing roisterous songs.

A sadder young woman, who left her poet-lover, Walter Savage Landor, pining in England and resisted immediate matrimony in gay Calcutta, was Rose Aylmer, who is buried close to Lucia and Elizabeth under a tapering twisting column (p. 99). Until the plaque was recently shattered by vandals, her tomb carried Landor's words below some lines from Young's *Night Thoughts*:

> To the memory of the honourable
> Rose Whitworth Aylmer
> Who departed this life March 2 AD 1800
> Aged 20 years

> What was her fate? Long, long before her hour
> Death called her tender soul, by break of bliss,
> From the first blossoms, to the buds of joy;
> Those few our noxious fate unblasted leaves
> In the inclement clime of human life.

> Ah, what avails the sceptred race!
> Ah, what the form divine!
> What every virtue, every grace!
> Rose Aylmer, all were thine.

> Rose Aylmer, whom these wakeful eyes
> May weep, but never see,
> A night of memories and of sighs
> I consecrate to thee.

According to William Hickey, Rose Aylmer died from eating too many pineapples, and many of these young girls died through not taking proper care of their diet and dress in the humid climate. Lord Valentia writes of the custom at the end of the eighteenth century of dancing through the night from 9 p.m. to 5 a.m., which was said to cause consumption by the excessive physical strain followed by exposure to the cold, damp night air:

> I have seen them dancing on 'feverish nights' when the pearly drops have trickled down their necks in showery profusion, notwithstanding the aid of Punkays, etc. This is amusement!

As a consequence the young things 'were in the habit not infrequently of dancing themselves into the grave'. Some of the newly arrived ladies quickly adjusted to the needs of the country and –

> when the Minuets are ended they go home with their partners to undress and after a little refreshment return again in the purest innocence of muslin and the simplicity of a nightgown.

Right through the nineteenth century there occurred this sudden and shattering mortality among the young and beautiful, more noticed perhaps because of the scarcity of unmarried girls in India. In 1886 when the Governor of Madras was visiting Poona he had been enchanted by a gay and vivacious young girl, Helen Portman, and a few months later he received a letter to say she had been 'laid in a damp earth grave ... in the little white and silver coffin'. It seemed that all recreations were tinged with death. One favourite pastime was known as 'taking the bark' – for which purpose Kipling's Lucia had been given the 'green-painted boat' – but Mrs. Rebecca Parnell, younger daughter of J. Slaughter, indigo planter, has this sad and precise epitaph on her tomb in Monghyr: 'She met her death by the upsetting of her boat at Soorujsgurrah on the evening of 23rd February, 1837, aged sixteen, one month and twenty days.' Another common relaxation was the evening drive, the *hawa khana* or 'eating the air' as it was called, and Russell, The *Times* correspondent in Calcutta in 1857, associated even this with death, as it was also the hour for funerals:

Is this a limbo in which all races, black and white, are doing penance on the outside of strange quadrupeds and in the interior of impossible vehicles? The ride in Rotten Row, the dreary promenade by the banks of the unsavoury Serpentine, the Bois de Boulogne ... are haunts of frivolous, reckless, indecorous, loud-laughing Momus and all his nymphs ... compared with this deadly *promenade a cheval et a pied*, where you expect every moment to hear the Dead March in Saul, or to see the waving black ostrich plumes sprout out of a carriage top.

By the middle of the nineteenth century, the annual exodus of young marriageables from England, which had begun on a small scale, had grown into a social phenomenon known as the 'fishing fleet', with girls sent out at the insistence of their family often against their own will, in the hope of making a good match with one of the wealthy middle-aged merchants. In England a girl might be 'without dowry, rich relations or beauty, and consequently without hope of marriage'. But as soon as she sets foot in India she is overwhelmed with offers of marriage 'from old and young, military and civil, nobles and commoners':

Her aunt tells her, day and night, that she should not lower herself by dancing with anyone below a very senior civilian or a military officer holding a staff appointment and in a position to give her the three things considered in India to be the first essentials of conjugal felicity: a massive silver teapot, a palanquin and a set of bearers to use by day, and a carriage in which to drive in the evening.

She is thus impelled by an outrageous ambition to refuse in the course of a few months some really eligible wooers of whom she would not have dreamt in England, while she dances till she is out of breath and her hair gets dishevelled in order to draw into her curls some old nabob with spindle legs, in whose mummy there is not a spark of heat, whose soul for the past twenty years has been concentrated on rupees.

Thomas Hood, in 'I'm going to Bombay', satirises the ambitious husband-hunter:

> By Pa and Ma I'm daily told
> To marry now's my time,
> For though I've very far from old,
> I'm rather in my prime.
> They say while we have any sun,
> We ought to make our hay –
> And India has so hot a one,
> I'm going to Bombay!
>
> My cousin writes from Hyderapot
> My only chance to snatch,
> And says the climate is so hot,
> It's sure to light a match.
> She's married to a son of Mars,
> With very handsome pay,
> And swears I ought to thank my stars
> I'm going to Bombay!
>
> Farewell, farewell my parents dear,
> My friends, farewell to them!
> And oh, what casts a sadder tear
> Goodbye to Mr. M.!
> If I should find an Indian vault,
> Or fall a tiger's prey,
> Or steep in salt, its all *his* fault,
> I'm going to Bombay!
>
> (verses 4, 5 and 8)

Locally, too, steps were taken to meet the ever-increasing demand for wives, and the Orphan Girls School in Calcutta – divided into two parts to preserve the social distinctions of the day, one for the children of officers and gentlemen and the other for the children of soldiers – began to hold monthly bachelor balls to which men came from up-country stations, several days journey away, to select and carry off a bride 14, 13 or even 12 years of age. 'A grisly bombardier of 40 unites himself to a girl of 12,' comments Mrs. Postans in her memoirs; and a Bombay newspaper announced at the close of the eighteenth century a union in which the disparity of ages shocks us now, though it was quite usual at that time:

> At Tranqebar, H. Meyer, Esq., aged sixty-four, to Miss Casina Couperas, a very accomplished young lady of sixteen, after a courtship of five years.

Some of these child-brides hardly got to the altar before they were carried off, and many died in the first year or two of their marriage, from a fever or childbirth, as the epitaphs prove. One of the most poignant of these epitaphs – now disappeared – was on a tomb at Azamgarh in the United Provinces, 'Sacred to the Memory of Mrs Sarah Ammaun and her stillborn son who departed this life on 29th June 1820':

> Just fifteen years she was a maid
> And scarce eleven months a wife
> Four days and nights in labour laid
> Brought forth and then gave up her life
>
> Ah! loveliest of beauties
> Whither art thou flown?
> Thy soul which knew no guile
> Is sure to heaven gone
> Leaving this friend and thy kindred
> Thy sad exit to mourn.

An even younger wife, yet already widowed, is buried at Jaunpore, U.P.:

> Sacred to the memory of Elizabeth Smith, widow of late Fife-Major John Smith, 16th Regiment Native Infantry, who departed this life on 22nd February, 1829, aged 14 years, 9 months and 21 days.

There is a cluster of graves of young wives in the South Parks Cemetery at Calcutta where, taken at random, one reads of the death of Mrs. Mary Haywood in 1804 at the age of 17; of Mrs. Elizabeth Hunt in the same year at 18; of Mrs. Elizabeth Wells in 1805 at 16; of Mrs. Margaret Gibson in 1810 at 17; of Mrs. Anna Townsend in 1822 at 16, and so on. Some of them had large families, such as Mrs. Anna Maria Thompson who died in 1817 aged 20, leaving behind four children after six years of marriage; and Mrs. Ann Riley of the same age who also left four children after a teenage marriage. A number of girls appeared to die from grief at the loss of their child or husband; such as Anne Becher who, in the words of her epitaph, 'after suffering with patience a long illness occasioned by grief for the death of an only daughter', died aged 18 and was buried in St. John's churchyard, Calcutta. Another wife came out from England to join her husband, who had left England some years before, a few weeks after their marriage, and who had not yet seen their offspring; she landed in Bengal in 1805 only to hear that her husband had died of a fever that very same day. She pined away and died six weeks later, and the child died soon afterwards. During her decline she used to go every day to the landing-place and weep over her child, and so the place came to be called 'Melancholy Point'.

The records of child deaths often reveal not so much the acute personal tragedy the parents suffered, but their calm acceptance of death and perseverance with which they continued to try to raise a family. Five children of Sir Frederick and Lady Hamilton are buried under a row of lofty obelisks at Bhagalpur. Six children of a more humble couple, Joseph and Elizabeth, at Benares are simply listed on one tombstone:

John died 11th March, 1834, aged 7 months
Jesse died 18th August, 1835, aged 8 months
Henrietta died 3rd June, 1838, aged 6 months
Oliver died 14th August, 1839, aged 13 months
Arnold died 22nd November, 1841, aged 5 months
Joseph died 29th May, 1842, aged 5 months

Three children of Lord Roberts, the famous Commander-in-Chief born in Cawnpore, are commemorated on a stone slab in Simla:

Nora Frederica born Mean Mir 10.3.1860; died Simla 18.3.1861
Evelyn Santille born Clifton 18.7.1868; died at sea 8.2.1869
Frederick Henry born Simla 29.7.1869; died 20.8.1869

One can imagine the tombstone being lifted up and the fresh inscription added for each successive loss. Sometimes the grave was finally closed when an adult member of the family died, as with grandmother Herklots, who died at Chinsurah in 1846 aged 72, claiming to have 105 living descendants. She was buried in the same grave as five of her children and four of her grandchildren, whose ages are given as follows – 6 days; 9 days; 1 year and 8 months; 2 years and 2 months; 5 years, 9 months and 23 days; 5 days; 1 month 11 days; 6 months 22 days; and 10 months.

At times an entire family was annihilated within the space of a few days, as with the three children and their father at Dharmsala:

Lt. Francis Tigue Reilly died 13th July 1875, aged 45, 2 months, 3 days.
Edmund Patrick aged 5 years, 9 months and 19 days ⎫ died
William aged 3 years, 5 months and 9 days ⎬ 6 to 10th
Mary Agnes Alice aged 1 year, 5 months and 23 days ⎭ July 1875

The epitaph found on a number of infant tombs at Dharmsala's cemetery of St. John's in the Wilderness, situated among the Himalayan pines, echoes this feeling of acceptance of God's will: 'He shall gather the lambs with His arms and carry them to His house.' Other inscriptions are equally moving in their pathetic sentimentality:

The lovely babe beneath this tomb was cut off in the bud
But she in Paradise will bloom and ever live with God.

On a tomb at Ghazipur, where Lord Cornwallis had died a few years earlier, one child's life was counted in hours:

To the memory of Louisa, daughter of Elizabeth Rowthorn (of His Majesty's 17th Foot) who departed this life 21st May 1818, aged 7 months, 7 days and 1 hour.

Good attendance was applied
Physicians proved in vain
For God thought fit to call her hence
And ease her of her pain.

'In the morning it was green and growing up, in the evening it was cut down and withered like a flower.'

Regimental women like Elizabeth Rowthorn had a rough life. Only a limited number were permitted to travel with the Regiment from England, and there was a lower age-limit of 25; there was so much competition that there used to be a ballot for selection among those eligible. They lived in a screened-off portion of a large barrack room where they had little privacy; they conceived, gave birth, and brought up their children, fought with other wives and rowed with their own husbands within ear-shot of dozens of soldiers. It was from the ranks of these practical and tough women that the station midwife was usually found: witness the tombstone in the Saran District to –

> Isabella Magowan, the wife of Private Magowan, died returning from attending to the Collector's wife, 1829.

She had travelled over twenty miles to reach the bedside of the expectant mother and paid the penalty of exposure to the climate.

The problems and difficulties in rearing a child in India are illustrated in this extract from Mercer's diary in the 1850s, which shows why those who could afford it sent their children to England as soon as they were of school age or even earlier, leaving their upbringing to grandma or other relatives:

> About the middle of November, our dear boy Franky (aged 7½) was attacked with Ophthalmia which lasted for about 12 days. He was just recovering from this when he was seized with a bad sore throat. For some wise purpose we were not permitted to see any danger in this. The usual remedies were applied but the Doctor who attended our family was equally misled. On the 30th November we observed a great difficulty in his breathing and I wrote at once to the Doctor asking if he advised me to try a mustard blister. Suspecting that my report was dictated by a little over anxiety, he neglected to come and judge for himself what was the state of the throat. The next morning, the 31st, he came and to his infinite horror and surprise found that the disease had taken another form. Laryngitis or inflammation of the throat had set in. Our dear child was in imminent danger. Every remedy was then resorted to but alas! it was too late – in 36 hours we were bereft of our child – perhaps the most promising of our flock ... He had even in these early years evinced a love of Christian truth, an early piety, and an acute discernment between right and wrong which, had our eyes not been blinded, might then have struck us as an indication of a ripeness for eternity ... A long dark

night of sorrow followed this sudden bereavement. The bitterness entered into our souls like a sharp iron. Often had we grieved for those that were not, amongst our children and others most dear to us, but as the buoyancy of youth passes away, the heart seems more alive to sorrow; more deeply impressed with the exceeding awfulness of death. This blow we did not recover from for years. His body lies in the cemetery at Ferozepore under a Sarcophagus of the shape shown in this sketch [see p. 122] with a cypress tree at each corner. The inscription is as follows:

Sacred
To the memory of
Francis Gordon Mercer
The beloved son of
Capt. and Mrs T.W. Mercer
Who died after a few hours illness
On 1st December 1857

(XVIII Matt 10 Ver)
'I say unto you that in Heaven their angels do always behold the face of my Father which is in Heaven.'

Captain Mercer also had a son by his first wife, Maria Caroline Herklots, whom he married in 1844. By a strange coincidence the main events of her life all occurred on the 7th of November. 'She was born 7th November, 1826; she was married 7th November 1844 and she died 7th November 1845 – the additional circumstance of my having first trod the shores of India on 7th November 1842,' wrote the Captain in his diary. His second wife had been married to a gentleman in the Company's service in Singapore, and had borne her first husband two children, before he died there in the third year of her marriage. She bore Mercer ten children, nine sons and one daughter. The daughter and three sons died in infancy, Francis in early childhood and another son in his late teens – six out of ten; such was the toll of India. Yet birth succeeded death, remarriages took place, and large families were still somehow raised. Mercer, now a Colonel, retired to England, where his wife soon died; but he married a third time and had a daughter sixty years after the birth of his first child. They were certainly tough, morally and physically, in those days.

A succession of marriages was not unusual in the circumstances of such high mortality, but a few extreme cases are noted on the tombstones. For example at Simla, the headquarters of the Government during the hot weather and monsoon, there lie the seven wives of Mr. Hogan, Head Clerk of the office of the Commander-in-Chief's Military Secretary. He lived just below the cemetery and there is a local tradition that his wives were buried within sight of 'Glen Hogan', as his residence was called. Then there was the Judge who earned the nick-name among later generations as 'the Blue-Beard of the Civil Service'. This was Judge Waters of Chittor in South India, who after a long and distinguished service retired to Brighton where he died in 1882 at the age of 90. He was well and truly 'salted', as the expression went for those who, after surviving the first few years of high risk from fevers, seemed immune from all diseases of the orient. Not so his wives. A large octagonal mausoleum at Chittor contains the graves of his first two wives, who died in 1823 and 1828 respectively. Their coffins are suspended by chains from the roof and the vault door is secured by three heavy iron locks to discourage grave-robbers, as there is a local legend that much valuable jewellery was buried with the ladies. Whether it was the Judge's intention to 'hang' all his wives in the same mausoleum is not related, but his third wife died in 1831, his fourth in 1833, his fifth in 1857 – by which time he was aged 65 – and he married a sixth time in 1871. Early mortality was not confined exclusively to women, although the undertakers and traders in funeral attire found them the more profitable side of their business, selling mourning dresses and mourning scarves and even displaying rhyming advertisements in their shop-windows:

Ladies caps to adorn the head
Shrouds to wrap them in when dead.

Many women survived, only to be widowed with a large family of young children to bring up, like Mrs. Keighley. She was married at 18 to an officer who had a brilliant career ahead of him and an established reputation as an outstanding linguist and oriental scholar, but soon, in the words of Rawlins –

he was suddenly called away and left a young widow with seven children disconsolate at his loss. For a time poor Mrs. Keighley was well-nigh crushed and fallen, but being a woman of great energy and character and having seven young children entirely dependent upon her, she determined to brave her sorrow for their sakes, and to succeed; she came to England, established a charming home for Indian* children and by her kind and

*Europeans from India.

maternal treatment soon obtained a reputation which filled her house and enabled her to live in the greatest comfort.

Mrs. Ommaney, the wife of the Judicial Commissioner at Lucknow, was left with her six children 'to sorrow, not without hope, for the one thus suddenly cut off' – as she put it on the gravestone – when he died as the result of Mutiny wounds. Another brave widow was Mrs. Hermitage, who had already lost five children when her husband, a Branch Pilot at Calcutta, died suddenly, and then lost two more in their early childhood – the eight tombstones in the South Parks cemetery record the bare facts:

Henry Mathias Hermitage, died 24.9.1826, aged 2 years, 9 months, 26 days

James William Hermitage, died 8.8.1827, aged 5 months, 4 days

Charles Edward Hermitage, died 11.3.1828, aged 1 month, 25 days

John Francis Hermitage, died 20.10.1832. aged 14 years. 9 months

Henry William Hermitage, died 4.6. 1833, aged 2 years, 9 months, 22 days

John Mathias Hermitage, died 28.10. 1833, aged 42 years, 9 months, 20 days

Emmeline Felicia Hermitage, died 7.6. 1842, aged 8 years, 9 months, 4 days

Caroline Claudine Hermitage, died 7.8.1846, aged 14 years, 6 months, 17 days

Other young widows added a personal touch of their own to their husbands' epitaphs. Sarah, the wife of D.W. Taylor, the 'Assistant Apothecary Hon. Company's Service' who died at Chunar, U.P. in 1834, 'aged 29 years and 22 days', wrote:

That blameless virtue which adorned thy bloom
Lamenting Sarah, now weeps o'er thy tomb.

And, not to be outdone, another Apothecary's widow at Chunar a few years later writes this inscription to her husband H. Spinks, who died aged 30 in 1839:

Thy wife, dear Henry, o'er thy mouldering earth
Erects this tribute to departed worth.

Widowhood, however, was not always as tragic in the long term as it might seem, for the demand for wives was so great that a widow was frequently proposed to on the steps of the church after burying her husband. Mrs. Postans writes in her memoirs of 1838 of a gunner who died of fever and left an attractive widow:

> An hour after her husband's death three of his comrades proposed to her, and before a week expired, her weeds were laid aside. The woman's second husband also died and she again married with similar promptness. A third time death severed, and Hymen retied the mystic knot; and last of all, but again a widow, the woman died also.

These speedy remarriages were far from uncommon, encouraged by the system of taking army widows 'off-pay' soon after their husbands' death, and there were cases of a wife engaging herself to a suitor during her husband's life who 'trusts to the chance provided by attack and the climate for the fulfilment of the contract'. As Sterne wrote to Eliza in 1767 (see p. 92):

> Talking of widows – pray Eliza, if ever you are such, do not think of giving yourself to some wealthy nabob, because I design to marry you myself. My wife cannot live long.

Remarrying provided a means of social climbing, as observed by Emily Eden when introduced to the ladies belonging to the Gwalior contingent in 1838 and meeting an officer's wife; the Captain remembered her as

> a little girl running about barracks a soldier's daughter, but she was pretty, and, by dint of killing off a husband, or two, she is now at nineteen the wife of a captain here.

One of the most celebrated much-married women was 'Begum' Johnson, whose splendid mausoleum in St. John's churchyard, Calcutta, records her succession of husbands:

> Beneath are deposited the remains of Mrs. Frances Johnson. She was the second daughter of Edward Crook Esq. Governor of Fort St. David on the coast of Coromandel and was born the 10th of April 1725. In 1738 she intermarried with Parry Purple Templar Esq., nephew of Mr. Braddyll, then Governor of Calcutta by whom she had two children who died infants. Her second

BEGUM JOHNSON'S TOMB

husband was James Altham of Calcutta Esq., who died of small-pox a few days after the marriage. She next intermarried with William Watts Esq. the senior member of the Supreme Council of Bengal by whom she had issue four children

Amelia, who married the Rt. Honourable Charles Jenkinson – afterwards Earl of Liverpool by whom she had issue one child, Robert Banks now Earl of Liverpool &c &c
Edward, now of Hanstoke Park in the county of Bucks Esq.,
Sophia, late the wife and now the widow of George Poyntz Ricketts, late Governor of Barbadoes
and William who died an infant.

After the death of Mr. Watts she in 1744 intermarried with the Rev. William Johnson, then principal Chaplain of the Presidency of Fort William by whom she had no issue. She died 3rd of February 1812 aged 87, the oldest British Resident in Bengal, universally beloved, respected and revered.

The girl, who had first married at the age of 12, earned herself a State funeral, with the Governor-General in his state coach drawn by six horses, and a detachment of the Bodyguard to escort her mortal remains to the churchyard. All the bells in Calcutta tolled for the passing of this great character, who had lived life to the full and had taken part in country dances until a few weeks before her death.

The shortage of European women in the East and the great risks and discomforts of living so far from 'home' accentuated the different approaches of men and women towards matrimony. Men's motives were seldom mercenary; women's often were, for what else could induce them to face the hazards of India, unless it was missionary zeal or true love? As Ovington wrote of Englishwomen in India:

A modest woman may very well expect, without any very great stock of honour or wealth, a husband of repute and riches there, after she has run all this danger and trouble for him.

The qualities men looked for in their partners can be judged from the epitaphs they wrote on their wives' graves; for instance the daughter of Capt. P. Crawford, buried in Shergati Cemetery in the Gaya District, who –

became the wife of G.J. Morris Esq., once Judge of this District, to whose happiness she was permitted by God to contribute for

nearly thirteen years. He resigned her to the Lord ... on 26th
December 1831, in her 31st year.

The assumptions of the subordinate role of the wife, her duty to her
husband, her basic function of rearing a family, are evident on many
such tombstones throughout India up to the middle of the
nineteenth century. They abound in such phrases as 'affectionate
wife', 'tender mother', 'amicable and accomplished woman',
'exemplary discharge of her several duties', 'exemplary in her
conduct as a wife' (1839), and we see this attitude being passed on
with Mrs. Frushard, daughter of Mary Jones of Hackney, 'whose
loyal and virtuous conduct she faithfully copied during her whole
life'. Occasionally a more positive and assertive female character is
revealed:

Hands that the rod of Empire might have swayed
Or wak'd to extacy the living lyre,

as was inscribed on the tomb of Mrs. Woodhouse at Cuddalore in
1777. The family motto was '*Frappe forte*'; perhaps she needed this
strength of personality to control her husband, who 'spent a
considerable fortune in every species of fashionable dissipation'; yet
in the rest of the epitaph he describes her revealingly in terms of the
ideal of womanhood of that period:

Her form was elegant, her deportment noble. Possessed of every
virtue, every grace that could adorn her sex, she was religious
without superstition, prudent without meanness, generous
without prodigality, the sweet companion and the steady friend.

Men's horizons of interest tended to be much wider than
women's. Their work brought them into contact with all levels of
Indian society, while the Memsahibs, partly through the influence of
the caste and purdah systems which confined their Hindu and
Muslim 'sisters', were thrown in on their own society, and were
often unaware of Indians as real people, other than their servants. A
letter from Madras in 1837 describes this attitude, which was still
found in some Memsahibs as late as 1947:

I asked one lady what she had seen of the country and the natives
since she had been in India. 'Oh, nothing!' said she. 'Thank
goodness, I know nothing at all about them, nor I don't wish to:
really I think the less one sees and knows of them the better!'

There were the exceptions: Lady Canning was permitted a rare meeting with the ladies of the harem of the Nawab of Oudh at Lucknow and, in the words of Rawlins –

> expressed the great pleasure she derived from her visit to the royal dames, and described some of them as being most elegant in appearance and prepossessing in their manners.

The Nawab's establishment of ladies was said to be as numerous as his horses, about 70 to 80, and the early European visitors to India set out to imitate this style of living, although on a somewhat smaller scale. Even at the start of the nineteenth century it was the accepted custom to keep a *'cara amica* of the country' or, in local parlance, a beebee, who usually lived in a separate house – the *beebeeghar* – adjacent to the main bungalow, with her own female servants, and seldom ventured beyond her own quarters. Sometimes in towns an entire property was devoted to the maintenance of a beebee, as suggested in the following advertisement, which appeared in the *Calcutta Gazette* of the 16th June 1809:

> To be sold by private sale, a garden house and grounds situated at Taltolah Bazar, which to any gentleman about to leave India, who may be solicitous to provide for an Hindostanee Female Friend, will be found a most desirable purchase.

Most of the early beebees were buried in unrecorded graves, or cremated, according to the customs of their religion. Sometimes a humble Moslem-style tomb is found in a European garden, and there are occasional references on tombstones in the Christian cemeteries: 'Lucy, his woman ...' (see p. 46). A grave in the Scotch and Dissenters' Cemetery in Calcutta is inscribed to Charlotte 'who departed this life April 10th 1838 aged 3 years, 3 months and 13 days, the most lovely and beloved child of Charles Reed and Bebee Jan'. Six years later, 'Bebee Jan' was also buried in the same grave, the Scots being less particular in this respect than the Established Anglican church, which a quarter of a century earlier had denied a Christian burial to Arabella, the half-caste mistress of General John Pater. He overcame the interdict by burying his beloved in a field close by and erecting over her grave a church which he donated to the East India Company, later consecrated as St. Mary's, Masulipatam.

Young officers, both civil and military, generally had no thought of marriage until well into their thirties, partly because they lived

almost permanently in debt and could not afford a wife, and partly because it was officially discouraged as interfering with the efficiency of the Service, which required frequent moves from one uncomfortable station to another; suitable married accommodation was usually nonexistent. A military officer was expected to have attained the rank of Major before seeking permission from his Commanding Officer to marry, or to have had at least fifteen years' service if a Captain or Lieutenant. These late marriages, apart from encouraging the keeping of beebees, led to the growing custom of sending unmarried sisters out to India to look after their brothers. This became quite widespread in the middle and late nineteenth century when the demand for wives was being met and it was becoming more difficult for a girl to find a suitable husband. Keeping house for a brother provided a base for a longer-term approach to matrimony. A tombstone of 1834 in Calcutta commemorates 'Mary Bird, daughter of R. Bird of Taplan, Bucks and sister of R.M. Bird Esq., C.S. who have quitted her home and country to comfort an afflicted brother ...' After staying with her brother at Gorakhpur, she then went to look after another brother at Calcutta whose wife had died of cholera. She herself also died of cholera, on her birthday; when she mentioned this anniversary to a friend at her bedside, his cheerful reply 'was suited to the spirit of the suffering Christian that it would probably be her eternal birthday'!

The growth of the 'fishing fleet' of English girls led to relentless pressure for a reduction in the age men were allowed to marry and for the abandonment of beebees. English women saw beebees as a threat to their position, and by combining this fear with a growing feeling of racial superiority and a moral justification based on Evangelical piety, they inculcated into successive generations a sense of revulsion towards any 'black' connection, whether with an aristocratic Ranee or a sweeper's wife. A Hudibrastic poem of 1816, *The Adventures of Qui Hi*, on a young Englishman and his beebee Gaulaub, satirises their disapproval:

Poor Gaulaub now was in *that* way
That those 'who love their lords' should be;
And in a week to Qui Hi's joy
Produced our youth a chopping boy.
... Our hero now without pretence
Thought himself of some consequence;
A child he'd got, and what was curious,
He knew the infant was not spurious
For tho' Qui Hi was never tied

By licence to his Indian bride,
Yet he was confident that she
Had acted with fidelity.
How many husbands to their shame,
Would hesitate to say the same;
But now he finds he must submit
To European damsels wit;
Wherever Qui Hi did appear,
The spinsters titter, chat and jeer.
'O dear, Miss Pinchback, have you heard,
La! what a scandal – on my word;'
... 'The fellow! but we'll send him out
Of our society, no doubt;'
... That Qui Hi's creature, it is said,
The other day was brought to bed.'
'Oh heaven!' exclaimed Miss Indigo,
'And could he then have used me so?
And with a *black one* too connected,
My fortune and myself rejected;
If such a thing's allow'd to pass,
What then is to become of us?
If this is privileg'd 'tis plain,
To Europe we must go again.
A precious precedent's begun,
A mistress first and then a son.'

The collective strength of the Memsahib, as exercised through the
Club and formal social occasions, succeeded in morally outlawing
concubinage, and after the Mutiny the break was almost complete.
The Memsahibs came into their own, bringing Little England into
India and cultivating English flowers in gardens modelled on
English lines. Their menfolk accepted the more comfortable and
familiar regime, forgetting their beebees; and with their
disappearance from the social scene there was a further loss of
contact and understanding of eastern ways.

Until the 1850s, India had been a famous matrimonial market.
Even so, one military officer wrote home in despair when the Mutiny
was still in progress in February, 1858:

If I do come home some day, how will the ladies be inclined to
marry Indian Officers and risk their lives in the East, or has the
year 1857 made the danger too great in their eyes for us to have
any chance?

(Lieutenant Stanhope Cary, the writer of this letter, never married; he died of consumption in a remote Indian station in Rajputana four years later.) By the 1870s, the marriage boom was over, diarists now, instead of noting that a certain Miss — had married within a few weeks of landing and received a settlement of x thousand rupees, or that a certain girl had received three proposals at her first ball, were writing a different story. As Rawlins described it:

> But now they droop and languish, and nobody comes to woo, and charming girls often spend four or five years in India and then return as spinsters to their mother country ...

And minor poets were expressing the change in their fortunes:

> Now sail the chagrined fishing fleet
> Yo ho, my girls, yo ho!
> Back to Putney and Byfleet
> Poor girls, you were too slow!

The truth is that communications between India and England had improved to such an extent, with the opening of the Suez Canal and with fast steamers, that most officers preferred to choose their wives from their familiar native background, on one of the more frequent visits they made 'home'.

Much has been written disparagingly about the Memsahib, but many of them led devoted lives, following their husbands around in the most uncomfortable conditions, enduring heat and fevers, seeing their children snatched from them and often joining them in an early grave. India brought out the best in them as well as exposing some of their weaknesses. As Olive Douglas put it so well, writing about the Memsahib in 1913: 'The women who are pure gold grow more charming, but the pinchbeck wears off very soon.'

4 Other Westerners

During the historically brief period of the British Raj, India became the preserve of the Scotch, Irish, Welsh and English representing the paramount British power as traders, administrators and soldiers. But many other races also took part in the incursion of Europe into Asia. The Portuguese had preceded the British by a century, the Dutch arrived on the scene at the same time, while the French contested paramountcy throughout the eighteenth century.

In the following pages I have selected a cross-section of these other Westerners from the tombstones and memorials they left behind, to give a glimpse of the motives that led them to India and what they achieved. Some were fortune-hunters, like the British; some were fugitives from political and religious persecution, like the Poles and Huguenots; some, like the Danes, were full of missionary zeal. The main nationalities are taken in their order of arrival in India. Hence the Portuguese come first, followed by the Dutch, French and Danes. The other national groups are taken in no particular order.

Portuguese

The Portuguese began the quest for a sea-route to India after the Ottoman Turks had effectively blocked European trade via the mediaeval land routes to the East. They were encouraged by the Pope, who conveniently divided the maritime spheres of influence

between the Spanish in the West and the Portuguese in the East, so
it fell to the lot of Portuguese mariners, led by Vasco da Gama, to
open the Indian Ocean to Western trade, rounding the Cape of
Good Hope and landing in Calicut (south-west India) in 1498 after
a voyage of ten months and twelve days. Vasco da Gama made two
further visits to India, the last in 1524 when he was appointed
Viceroy of all their Eastern possessions; he died within three months
of landing at Cochin. No monument marks his burial place, as his
body was exhumed and conveyed to Portugal in 1558, where it
received a hero's funeral before being interred at Vidigueyra. From
then on Portuguese power in India was consolidated, with
settlements established along the Malabar Coast (the west coast)
until in 1570 Albuquerque, the greatest of all Portuguese Viceroys,
took Goa, which remained the capital of their dominions in India
down to modern times. The Portuguese also opened up other centres
of trade on the east coast – in Chittagong, known by them as Porto
Grande; and at Satgaon near Calcutta, known as Porto Piqueno.
Many events interfered with peaceful trade, and trade itself was
subordinated to religious conversion, which ultimately led to the
undoing of the Portuguese. When Goa was beseiged by local Rajas in
1570, it was successfully defended by '700 European soldiers
supported by 300 friars and priests', some indication of the
importance given to religious conversion: the aim was to compel every
person residing on Portuguese territory to adopt Christianity.

The Portuguese enjoyed a short period of influence at the Moghul
court in the 1580s, when the Emperor Akbar was pursuing his ideals
of religious toleration; in a House of Worship he sat and discussed
with Jesuits, Jains, Parsees and Hindus the basic tenets of their
faith. But Akbar's successors followed a policy of reaction and
persecution, and after the capture of the Portuguese town of Hugli in
1632 several hundred prisoners were taken to Agra and attempts
were made to convert them forcibly to Islam. A number died and
were buried in the cemetery variously called 'the Martyrs'
Cemetery', 'John Sahib's Cemetery' (see p. 85) and 'the Old Agra
Catholic Cemetery', the oldest cemetery in northern India. A few
inscriptions are still legible: 'aqui iazo Padre Mel D'Anhaya, clerigo
morto pelo fee na prisao a 2 d'Agusto, 1633' (here lies Father Mel
d'Anhaya, a priest killed for his faith in prison, on 2 August, 1633),
and 'aqui iazo Padre Mel Garcia, clerigo morto no carcere pela fee
...' (23.3.1634). The early Portuguese made no attempt to copy the
grandiose style of the Moghul tombs for their own dead, preferring a
plain stone slab bearing heraldic arms and devices, with a bare
mention of name and age, sometimes adding length of married life

and status, but avoiding laudatory epithets.

The most famous Portuguese tomb is that of saint Francis Xavier, a courtier in Navarre who, under the influence of Ignatius Loyola, became a Jesuit missionary and spent ten years in India and Japan, dying off the coast of China in 1552. His body was embalmed by Chinese (or, according to some, was miraculously preserved) and brought back to Goa, where it is periodically exposed to public view as a focus of Catholic worship. A different sort of Portuguese tomb at Surat commemorates the life of Donna Lucia, who was one of an annual batch of women shipped to India by the Portuguese government in the 1700s. She was captured at sea by Mussulman pirates and sold as a slave at the Surat slave-market. She married her purchaser, a rich Dutchman, according to the rites of the Dutch Reformed Church, an event which caused a local scandal among the strict Protestant merchants as he allowed his wife 'to continue her Papist practices'.

The demand for wives from Portugal soon increased, and the practice of marrying local women led to a mixed population of Catholic 'Goanese'. The Catholic faith was firmly insisted on, and some Portuguese customs, such as dress, were adhered to, but an odd synthesis between the two races developed; in food and other matters, there was a general conformity to Indian traditions. This cultural adjustment came very naturally to a people from an almost tropical country who had already absorbed several Moorish elements into their way of life.

Another Portuguese woman to marry outside her co-religionists was the daughter of Favier de Silva, the celebrated astrologer. She accompanied her father when he was sent out to India by the King of Portugal to advise the Raja of Jaipur in his astrological studies, and she married a wandering native of northern Ireland, Thomas Legge. Legge was an eccentric, practising alchemy and divination and ending his days as a fakir living naked in a deserted tomb. He died in 1808 near Jaipur, and both his wife and son are believed to have died in India, but their graves are unknown.

An unidentified Portuguese tomb was dug up in 1852, when a sugar factory was being built near Bombay on the site of the ruined church of Nossa Senhora da Vida, containing the bones of a man and a horse, and a rusty rapier. The man was a defender, perhaps, of the port, now one of the greatest cities in the world, which the Portuguese Catharine of Braganza bestowed on her husband Charles II of England as part of her dowry, and he in turn sold off to the Honourable East India Company for ten pounds.

In St. George's Cathedral, Madras, lies Francesco Marques de

Souza Lisboa, son of the Chevalier Joze Marques Lisboa, ex-Envoy Extraordinary and Minister Plenipotentiary of His Majesy the Emperor of Brazil to Her Britannic Majesty Queen Victoria; Francesco died at the youthful age of eighteen as a Midshipman in the Royal Navy in 1852. In Agra are interred several generations of the De Silva family from Goa, all doctors by profession, who emphasised their good Portuguese descent by including 'don' or 'donna' after their name and then, curiously, an inscription in Persian – this as late as 1859. The last of the line has a simple English inscription: 'In memory of Joseph Augustin De Silva, physician, born 6th January 1838, died 9th June 1909. R.I.P.' Joseph was the author of a work on comparative Indian, early Greek and European medicine exploring an interesting link between East and West that has received too little attention.

Dutch

No nation observed the *culte des morts* more than the Dutch. They not only systematically pulled down the Portuguese tombs in the settlements they took over towards the end of the seventeenth century – their sailors being ordered to smash them with sledgehammers, according to a contemporary Dutch writer – but also erected elaborate mausoleums for their own dead, importing stone-masons trained in Holland to execute deeply-etched carvings and finely-wrought lettering to stand the test of time to the *laste opstaanding*. At Pulikat, 25 miles north of Madras, where the Dutch established a trading settlement in 1609, there is a well-preserved lych-gate to the cemetery, flanked by two stone skeletons. Further south, over the grave of the wife of Matthys Pfeiffer, is a carved bas relief of an eighteenth-century piper playing a recorder. Nearby is a stone sculpture of a bygone Mynheer wearing a three-cornered hat. On the west coast, at Surat, is a grave to a celebrated Dutch toper, a relation of the Prince of Orange who became King William III:

At the top was a great cup of stone, and another at each corner. Opposite each cup was the figure of a sugar-loaf. Dutch drinking parties used to frequent this tomb, brewing their punch in the large stone basins; remembering their departed companion they sometimes forget themselves, singing

Would that a Dutchman's draught could be
As deep as the rolling Zuyder Zee.

VAN REEDE'S TOMB

This grave, alas, no longer exists, but there is another almost regal
mausoleum at Surat still standing, to the memory of Baron Van
Reede. Bellasis, a civil servant, writing about the old tombs of Surat
in 1868 with the purpose that the proceeds of the sale of his
pamphlet be applied to preserving them from decay, says that it

> exceeded all the rest in magnificence; and it was built with the
> intention of eclipsing that of Sir George Oxinden. It consists of a
> double cupola of great dimensions with a gallery above and
> below, supported on handsome columns. It was formerly adorned
> with frescoes, escutcheons and passages from Scripture and the
> windows were filled with much beautiful wood carving.

A relative of Reede visiting the tomb in 1886 comments: 'I saw the
very identical commemorative tablets – the wooden tablets – which
of the same epoch I find in my own parish in Holland to my own
ancestors.' And the Dutch inscription, in white letters in a cursive
script on a large black wooden tablet, translates:

> Here rests the corpse of his high nobility the Lord Henry Adrian
> Baron of Reede of Drakenstein, Lord of Meydight, graced with
> the order of Knighthood and usually delegated by the same order
> as deputy of the Noble and Mighty Lords the States of the
> Province of Utrecht; Commissary of the United Netherlands
> Licensed East India Company of India, representing in that
> quality the assemblies of the Noble Lords the Seventeen.
> Departed the 15th December, anno 1691, on board of the ship
> Dregerlant sailing from Cochim to Souratta abreast of the
> English fort Bombay, aged about 56 years.

The accession of a Dutch Prince, William of Orange, to the
English throne (1689) ended the hostility that had existed for years
in the East between these two maritime powers, and the Dutch
concentrated on their East Indies – the Archipelago and Spice
Islands of Java, Sumatra and Celebes – leaving the English to
consolidate their position in India. Dutch influence was still exerted
through a few individual mercenaries and traders such as John
Hessing, who is buried beneath another magnificent tomb at Agra,
almost a miniature Taj:

> ... on a square basement with many windows of pierced
> sandstone and corners reminiscent of Akbar's elevated throne of
> Fatehpur Sikri. It has four arched entrances at cardinal points

and eight arched niche-like verandahs. A dome rises above it and the whole is surmounted with a cross. At each of the corners is a minaret with a small domed canopy at the top and a slender pillar-like minaret on either side.

The inscription on the tomb commemorates

John William Hessing, late Colonel in the service of Maharaji Daulat Rao Sindia, who after sustaining a lingering and very painful illness for many years with true Christian fortitude and resignation, departed this life 21st of July 1803, aged 63 years 11 months and 5 days ... He was a native of Utrecht and came out to Ceylon in the military service of the Dutch East India Company in the year 1752.

There are many unusual Dutch tombs and quaint inscriptions in the cemeteries near the trading posts they established around the coasts of India – Bimlipatam, Cochin, Palakol, Pulikat, Negapatam and Tuticorin in the Madras Presidency; Balasore, Berhampore and Chinsurah in Bengal; Broach and Surat in Bombay. For instance, these two at Surat:

Here lies buried the honourable, chaste lady, Magdalena Haijers, when alive housewife of the honourable Director Paules Croocq; buried 29th November 1642, aged 27.

Here below rests till a blissful resurrection the corpse of the umquhile lady Bastina Theodora D. LeBoucq, consort of the noble, honourable, worshipful lord John Schrender ... born at the Cape of Good Hope 15th May anno 1708, and departed here the 7th May 1743 being 34 years, 11 months, and 22 days of age.

But perhaps the saddest – a solemn reminder that the Indian climate generally had the last say – is the epitaph mentioned by William Hickey, on the tombstone of a Dutchman at Sadras on the Coromandel coast:

Mynheer Gludenstack lies interred here,
Who intended to have gone home next year.

French

Compared with the Portuguese, English and Dutch, the French

appeared late on the Indian scene, their official Company – 'La Compagnie des Indes Orientales' – not being formed until 1664, and then never receiving adequate backing from home. Their main settlement was at Pondicherry, some eighty miles south of Madras, with another at Chandernagore near Calcutta, and others of lesser significance at Mahé on the Malabar coast, Karikal on the Coromandel coast and Yanaon near the mouth of the Godaveri. The relative importance of these French settlements fluctuated with their success at arms on European and Indian battlefields; and in spite of the efforts of Dupleix, De Bussy and a number of talented soldier-adventurers in the service of Indian Rajas hostile to the English cause, their influence – military and commercial – was never consolidated. By the end of the eighteenth century it had virtually disappeared.

De Bussy returned to France loaded with honours, one of the few from France or England to be so recognised after an Indian career. He lived in France for twenty years until, late in his life, he sailed once more to Pondicherry, to take charge 'of all the French forces of land and sea in all their possessions east of the Cape of Good Hope'. He died at Pondicherry in 1785 at the age of 67, while playing cards, and was buried there. His body had been embalmed, as was the custom among certain noble families, and when the French Revolution broke out it was removed secretly from its first resting-place to an obscure grave opposite the cathedral in case it should be desecrated by French soldiers. Babel, another French General, serving under Raja Basalat Jung, earned himself the nickname of 'zephyr' and the following heroic epitaph on his grave at Guntoor in south India:

Cheri de fortune et favori de Mars
La victoire suivit partout ses étendards
D'Hercule il égale les travaux et la gloire
Mais une mort trop cruelle a trompé notre espoir. (1770)

Francois de Raymond commanded the troops of the powerful Nizam of Hyderabad and became a legendary figure after his death in 1798, in spite of political influence passing to the English. Each year on the 5th of January, the anniversary of his death, a special parade took place beside his lonely grave on a hill near Hyderabad: a salute of twenty-one guns was fired, the band of his old regiment played the Marseillaise, and token gifts of a bottle of beer, a box of cheroots and a box of matches were placed in a shrine opposite his grave. This ceremony by Mohammedan troops continued for over a hundred years, until the First World War; when it formally ceased, it was replaced by an informal pilgrimage of Hindus each year. Such is the power of personality in India, transcending even religious boundaries.

Many other French soldier-adventurers lie in graves scattered across India; Ferez and Etienne in the little cemetery at Gudaspur in the Punjab; Dubignon at Ludhiana; Allard at Lahore; Viscount Alexis de Falieu at Ferozepore; Le Vassoult near Sardhana. Colonel Vassoult died a chivalrous death in 1798 as the result of a suicide pact with the Begum Sumroo, made when fleeing from her own mutinous troops. The lovers had evidently agreed that they would kill themselves rather than fall into the hands of the mutineers, and when escape seemed impossible, the Begum, who was travelling in a purdah-carriage with her woman attendants while the Colonel rode behind, made a mock attempt to stab herself and ordered her servants to display her blood-spattered blouse to him through the curtains. Vassoult immediately put his pistol to his head and fell dead to the ground. The Begum was taken back to Sardhana by the mutineers and chained between two guns for seven days, without food except for that smuggled to her by her faithful maidservants. She was rescued by another European adventurer-paramour, Thomas (see p. 51).

One of the most influential Frenchmen in India was Claude Martine, who died at Lucknow in 1800. He ran away from home at the age of 15 and joined the French army in India. After a series of escapades he found himself an Ensign in the Company's service in charge of a body of French cavalry raised from volunteers among the prisoners-of-war. He continued to serve the Company when he was sent to the Court of the Nawab of Oudh, where he was able to give full expression to his diverse talents. He was a skilled diplomatist, a shrewd businessman, an indigo planter, a money-lender, builder and architect, caster of cannons, experimental balloonist, bibliophile – accumulating a library of over 5,000 books in Latin, Italian, French, English, Persian and Sanskrit – and a patron of art (he invited artists such as Zoffany, Beechey, the Daniells and Tilly Kettle to come and stay with him and accumulated a collection of 150 oil paintings). He was also a philanthropist, leaving his fortune of half a million pounds to endow three schools famous to this day (the La Martinière schools at Lucknow, Calcutta and Lyons, his native town), and providing in his will charitable legacies for the Hindu, Muslim and Christian poor, the distribution of which is still made at Lucknow. This remarkable man, whose motto was 'Labore et constantia', retained control of his own fate down to the smallest

details. Knowing that the Nawab envied and wished to appropriate
the palace he had built himself – 'Constantia', an extraordinary
composite of Byzantine, classical and oriental architecture –
Martine stipulated that he should be buried in its basemenet, thus
desecrating the place in the eyes of the Nawab, as no Mohammedan
may live in a tomb. His will continued to specify:

> When I am dead, I request that my body may be salted, put in
> spirits, or embalmed, and afterwards deposited in a leaden coffin
> made of some sheet lead in my godown, which is to be put in
> another of sissoo wood, and then deposited in the cave in the
> small round room north-east in Constantia, with two feet of
> masonry raised above it, which is to bear the following
> inscription:

> > Major-General Claude Martine, born at Lyons, January 1738,
> > arrived in India as a common soldier, and died [at Lucknow,
> > the 13th September 1800] a Major General; and he is buried in
> > this tomb. Pray for his soul.

The French were the innovators of those days. Another balloonist,
Robertson, met his death near Lucknow in 1836 in probably the first
recorded human ascent in Asia. Schmaltze, a chemist, engineer,
mathematician and musician, who was reputed to be the inventor of
the modern flute, died near Calcutta in 1799. Louis Bonnaud was
the first indigo planter: requiring building materials, he improvised
the making of lime by exhuming skeletons from the neighbouring
Moahmmedan cemetery. He died in Bengal in the early 1800s.
'Hadjee Mustapha' was a little-known but important French writer,
one of the first Europeans to enter Mecca incognito; he died at
Calcapore in 1791. Jacquemont, the famous botanist and writer who
was alleged to have seven wives, Hindu and Muslim, died near
Bombay in 1832 at the age of 31. His body was exhumed by the
French Academy in 1881 and reinterred in France in accordance
with their proudly stated policy that 'la nation Francaise n'oublie
pas ses enfants celebres même quand ils sont morts a l'estranger'.
When the coffin was put aboard the French ship *La Clocheterie*, at
Bombay, a wreath of small delicate flowers was laid on it with the
message: 'Voici le fleur que Victor Jaquemont a introduisit dans
Bombay de la Cachemire et qui porte son nom Jacquemontia.'
Then there were members of the old French royal family,
descendants of the renegade Bourbon who founded the family of
Bhopal Bourbons; and aristocrats such as Boileau who died at

Allahabad in 1847, one of several of that name who served the English East India Company, descendants of Nicholas Boileau, created Lord of Castelnau in 1600, whose grandson fled to England at the revocation of the Edict of Nantes. The De L'Etangs, father and son, ran the Company's horse-stud at Pusa and were both buried at Ghazipur, sharing a common tomb, the inscription on which reads:

Chevalier Antoine de L'Etang, Knight of St. Louis
Born 20th August 1757 died 1843.

Lieutenant Eugene de L'Etang, 1st European Regiment
Born 5th May 1803 died 15th November 1829.

The father, as an officer in the French army, had performed an act of wartime courtesy typical of those times during the wars between the French and English in South India, when he warned the English officers of the 'revolutionary' tendencies of his own men and saved them from an ambush. In those cosmopolitan days the officers and gentlemen in opposing armies often felt that they had more in common between themselves than with the soldiers of their own country.

Danes

In 1616, shortly after the English and Dutch had formed their companies to trade in the East, the Danes – not to be outdone – established a Danish East India Company, and they sent a fleet to South India in 1620 to lay the foundations of a hoped-for empire. The Danish ships were chased away from Ceylon, where they first attempted to land, by the Portuguese who then held the island; and the Danish sailors eventually landed some 200 miles south of Madras, at Tranquebar – 'the village of dancing waves' – which they purchased from the Raja of Tanjore and turned into a fortified trading settlement. A century and a half later, in 1755, the Danes established another Factory at Serampore, fifteen miles north of Calcutta, and these two seemingly unimportant trading posts, which remained under direct royal control of the Kings of Denmark until purchased by the English in 1845, exercised an influence on Indian affairs out of all proportion to their size. Tranquebar and Serampore became two of the four cradles of Christianity in India, the other two being Goa and Kerala – and the only Protestant missionary centres, as proselytising was debarred until 1813 in the territory administered by the English East India Company. Here came Bartholomew Ziegenbalg, the father of the Protestant missions in India, sent out under the royal warrant of King Frederick IV of Denmark in 1706. He achieved remarkable success among the Tamil population and remained in close touch with King George I, the Archbishop of Canterbury and Christian societies in England. When the Society in England for the Promotion of Christian Knowledge sent him a commendatory address in Latin, he replied in humble Tamil; and just before his death at Tranquebar at the age of 35, he received the following extraordinary letter from the Archbishop of Canterbury which would have made a fitting epitaph:

> I consider your lot is far higher than all church dignitaries. Let others be prelates, patriachs and popes; let them be adorned with purple and scarlet; let them desire bowing and genuflexions. You have won a greater honour than all these and far more generous recompense shall be given you.

Ziegenbalg was succeeded by Schwartz, a missionary of world fame, once described by Hyder Ali as 'the only Christian in India', whose epitaph at Tanjore, where he died in 1798, was written by the young Raja of Tanjore, and whose sculptured monument at Madras contains this summary of his career:

> Sacred to the memory of the Rev. Christian Frederick Schwartz, whose life was one continued effort to imitate the example of his Blessed Master. Employed as a Protestant missionary from the government of Denmark, and in the same character of the Society in England for the Promotion of Christian Knowledge, he, during a period of fifty years 'went about doing good', manifesting, in respect of himself, the most entire abstraction of temporal views, but embracing every opportunity of promoting both the temporal views, but embracing every opportunity of promoting both the temporal and eternal welfare of others. To him religion appeared not with a gloomy aspect of forbidding mien but with a graceful form and placid dignity.

Seventeen ministers from Halle lie in the graveyards of Tranquebar and pious hands annually repaint the letters on their eighteenth-century tombs. Many appear to have attained a ripe old age, perhaps due to the Danish custom of keeping their drinking water sweet by stirring it with a red-hot crowbar. Kiernander, a Swede by race, trained at Halle and engaged in missionary work in

Tranquebar before becoming the first official missionary of the Church of England in India, died in Calcutta in 1799 at the great age of 88 and was buried in an immense family tomb painted blue, the colour of heaven! Later English missionaries in the early nineteenth century, such as Carey, Marshman and Ward (see p. 38), were buried in the Danish settlement at Serampore, which by its position of sturdy neutrality enabled these Baptists to build a flourishing printing press and Mission for the dissemination of the Gospel. For many years these two Danish trading centres remained the main source of inspiration for Protestant missionary effort in the whole of India, and their cemeteries contain inscriptions in nine languages – Danish, Dutch, English, French, German, Latin, Portuguese, Swedish and Armenian.

Apart from religion, Tranquebar and Serampore, in their later days, secured a European reputation for scientific research. John Gerhard Koenig, the famous botanist, was the Surgeon of Tranquebar for ten years and died of dysentery when travelling along the coast to Calcutta in 1785. Another celebrity was Colonel Mathias Jurgen von Muhldorf, reputed son of King Frederick V, who was exiled to Tranquebar after a political plot had failed. Muhldorf was buried in a nameless tomb in 1836 at the age of 86, leaving an unsolved mystery; he told his friends that the letters written over the archway of his old house, 'D.E.M.E.P. anno 1791', contained the clue to the secret of his life. He also left five daughters 'from whose veins the blood royal of Denmark has flowed into several Madrassi families'.

Americans

The first contact between America and India occurred through 'free-traders' or 'interlopers' in the days before American Independence. Men born in the then Colony of America were lured to the East by tales of fortune, and often finished up respectably as servants of the East India Company. Such a man was Elihu Yale who, born in Boston, became Governor of Madras and later Governor of the British Colony of New York, as well as being the benefactor of the University that bears his name. He was also responsible for many other public and private acts of charity, including the founding of a new Hospital in Madras to replace the old one which was run on very inadequate Church funds augmented by fines on individuals for 'rather infrequent violations of Sunday observance'. Not all his acts would stand up to the same moral scrutiny, as acknowledged on his epitaph (see p. 91). Included on the debit side, no doubt, would be his action in sentencing his English groom to death by hanging for spending the night outside the confines of the settlement, in the 'Black Town' which was out of bounds, an offence which in Yale's opinion justified the supreme penalty. The autocratic power wielded by the early Governors is hard to imagine in these bureaucratic days of rapid communications when no administrative step is taken without confirmation from some superior authority or committee. When Yale's small son David died he named the new fort at Tevenapatam 'Fort St. David' (now Cuddalore) after him to rank with the other forts around the coast named after the ruling sovereigns – as Fort William at Calcutta and Fort St. George at Bombay. The Latin inscription on this boy's epitaph reads:

> Hic jacet David filius honorabilis Elihu Yale praesidentis et gubernatoris Castelli St Georgii et civitatis Madrassiae, natus fuit 15 Maii 1684 et obiit 25 Januarii anno 1687/8.

A few Americans are known to have joined the band of European soldiers of fortune in the eighteenth century. There are references to a Colonel John Parker Boyd who joined the 'campoos' of the Mahratta Chiefs in the late 1790s, although his last resting-place is uncertain; and a Major James Murray, a native of Newport, U.S.A., came over from serving with the Mahrattas to join the Company forces in 1803 and died at Calcutta two years later, where his grave bore this epitaph:

> He dignified the character profession and courage of a soldier by the practice of the mild and social duties of justice, humanity and benevolence.

And there was the famous Alexander Gardiner, born in America in 1794, who became Chief of one of the Afghan tribes, and lies in an unknown grave in the Punjab where he died in 1848.

Several other soldiers of the East India Company were born in America and died in India. General Sir David Ochterlony (see p. 43), whose monument still towers over Calcutta, was born in Boston in 1758. A Commandant of Company Pensioners buried at Ganjam, on the east coast between Madras and Calcutta, clearly retains his loyalty to the Crown:

> Ensign Samuel Pippett, aged LXX and 10 months, born at Mount Holley in New West Jersey in Burlington City, North America. Served King and country for fifty years.

There is a remote grave beside the ruined Fort of Nurpur, commanding the valleys of the western Himalayas; it is that of John Harlan, aged 19, the reputed son of General Josiah Harlan, a Philadelphia Quaker, agent of Ranjit Singh in the Punjab and 'Raja' of Nurpur, who was in India from 1823 to 1841. John was born in Kabul, and whether he was adopted or the progeny of a union with an Afghan princess is open to speculation. There is no mention of the boy in Josiah Harlan's memoirs, perhaps out of deference to his family, as both his parents were ardent members of the Society of Friends. Philadelphia Quakers were no strangers in India. Early in the nineteenth century a group had come out at the invitation of the Bengali intellectual Rammohun Roy to explain the philosophical background of Christianity, without any idea of conversion. Josiah Harlan was not a missionary, but a self-taught doctor. He became an Assistant Surgeon in the service of the East India Company, and then travelled to Afghanistan, earning from the Shah of Kabul the romantic titles of 'King's Nearest Friend' and 'Companion of the Imperial Stirrup' before settling down in the Punjab for seven years under Ranjit Singh. He imaginatively attempted to export camels to the United States Army to be used as beasts of burden in the deserts of Texas and Arizona, and he tried to introduce Afghan grape-vines into Central America and also to California, where he died in 1871.

After the 1840s, American traders began to take an increased interest in the potentialities of trade with the East, once the East India Company's monopoly had been lifted out and the Treaty of Nanking had opened the door to European manufactures. American ice-ships visited Calcutta, Bombay and Madras in the hot weather, carrying as ballast huge blocks of ice from the Wenham lakes. This 'delightful luxury' was stored in domed Ice Houses and retailed at an exorbitant profit. Twelve American cotton planters were invited to south India with their cotton-seed to improve the condition of the locally grown crop, but without much success, and again the tombstones tell the story. At Bellary is an inscription to 'James Morris, cotton planter of Natchez, Adam's County, Mississippi, USA. Died 18th March, 1846.'

One of the main exports from America was missionaries, as soon as the East India Company had opened the door in 1813. The father of the American Missions is generally considered to be Gordon Hall who died of cholera in Nasik in 1826. The first Mission to be established in the Punjab was the American Presbyterian Mission at Ludhiana in 1834. Mission graveyards up and down the country testify to the number of Americans who came to the country and never returned; for instance, at Allahabad: 'Howard, W., "Our father", born at Nantucket, 1835-1905.'

At Allahabad there is an interesting memorial to an American, Mrs. Dodge, who came on a visit to India in 1893 with her wealthy husband and died of smallpox. As a mark of his gratitude for those who had nursed his wife through her fatal illness, and as a practical token to her memory, he provided a large endowment, half to go to the Cathedral building fund and half towards the salaries of two clergymen, one to minister to Europeans and the other to the railway people of Allahabad.

Italians

Italians came to India from the seventeenth century onwards as travellers, explorers, priests, doctors, mercenaries and highly skilled artisans; seldom as traders, for they had no nation state at that time to organise and support a trading company like those of the Portuguese, Dutch, English, Danes and French with their navies.

One of their earliest graves, only identified in the early twentieth century, is one of a famous Venetian jeweller who was engaged by the Moghul Emperor to work on the Taj Mahal. He was named as the architect by one contemporary account but was more probably concerned with the highly ornamental inlays around the interior walls. His epitaph at the Old Catholic Cemetery, Agra, merely states:

Aqui jaz *Jeronimo Veroneo* faleceo em Lahore 2 d'Agosto de 1640.

Another artisan of the Moghul Court was a Venetian lapidary who was summoned to cut a large diamond – perhaps the Koh-i-Noor? – and was reputed to have magical powers, as was the Hindu girl widow he married. His grave, close to that of Veroneo, carries this inscription:

Aqui esta sepultado *Hortenzio Bronzoni* Veneziano faleceo aos 11 de Agosto do anno 1677.

Manucci, the famous seventeenth-century traveller and writer turned doctor and surgeon, was also a Venetian by birth. He spent many years in India and lies in an unmarked grave near Madras dated about 1710. Constantine Beschi, the distinguished Jesuit missionary, was a native of Castiglione. He adopted native costume and customs and became known as 'the white Brahmin', or 'Veeramahamunivar', 'the great fearless man of God' in Tamil, the language and dialects of which he spoke perfectly. He died in 1747 in Trichinopoly and shares a little monument with two other Jesuit Fathers.

A Venetian architect, Tiretto, designed the church at Patna in 1772, and other highly skilled Italian artisans were employed at the courts of various wealthy Rajas. In the late eighteenth and early nineteenth centuries, as the break-up of the Moghul empire encouraged Native princes to form their own private armies, a few Italian officers who had been in the French army made their way easterwards and offered their services to the highest bidder. There was Michael Filose, a Neapolitan muleteer who enlisted in the French army in India before becoming a mercenary. His two sons Fidele and Jean Baptiste were born in India and both followed in his footsteps; Jean Baptiste joined the campoos of the Mahratta Chief Scindia at the early age of 12. Fidele committed suicide in 1801, and his wife and two children died one after the other in Gwalior in 1803; but his brother lived to be over 70 and was buried in the same family mausoleum there in 1846. Another soldier adventurer was Reuben Ventura, a Colonel in Napoleon's army who made his way to India after Waterloo and was taken on by Ranjit Singh, the 'lion of the Punjab', to train and lead his army. On one occasion Ventura was despatched to Peshawar to secure a celebrated horse of 'surpassing beauty and excellence', for Ranjit lived up to the famous saying attributed to him: 'Four things greater than all things are: women and horses, power and war.' Ventura accomplished this delicate mission successfully and was appointed a General, being given the titles of Kazi and Governor of Lahore, with the third seat in the Sikh Durbar, a position of great honour and influence. He married a Jewess called Anna Moses amid scenes of oriental pomp and ceremony, attended by Sikh couriers, and ended his distinguished career in retirement in Italy, his wife returning to the Punjab after his death and dying in Ludhiana.

In a cemetery in Simla, a few miles to the north of Ludhiana, are the mortal remains of a nineteenth-century pop group. Four young Italian musicians – Nicola Navallo, aged 13; Francis Pizzo, aged 14; Joseph de Giradi, aged 14; and Ferdinand Depasqua, aged 17 – were touring India playing in different centres before both Indian and European audiences. On 28th June 1871, as they went up to Simla by bullock cart, a large rock fell from the hillside and crushed them to death. One of the first people on the scene was the Viceroy, Lord Mayo, who himself met a sudden death at the hand of an assassin a few months later (see p. 22).

Germans

The town of Halle sent a succession of Lutheran missionaries to the Danish settlement of Tranquebar, as already noted. Besides these, there was Father Tieffentaller, born in Bolzano, educated in Germany: a priest, mathematician, astrologer, geographer and linguist, who travelled to India in 1743 and spent the next forty-two years methodically compiling a Sanskrit-Persian dictionary. He also published a Gazetteer on India at Berlin before he died at Lucknow in 1785, his body being buried at Agra Old Cemetery.

A number of German army officers entered the service of the Mahratta chiefs, although most of them transferred their allegiance to the East India Company in 1803 when war broke out between the Company and the Mahrattas, as did Captain John von Stubenvoll who eventually died at Calcutta in 1820. Colonel Johan Frederick Meiselbach, a native of Jena, served the Raja of Bundlekhand, married at Cawnpore in 1798 and became widely known as the 'father-in-law of the Old Bengal Army'. He lies in an unknown grave somewhere in Northern India.

The most famous, or infamous, German mercenary of all was Walter Reinhart, about whom no two authorities agree. Even the evidence of epitaphs is highly contradictory. At the foot of the Patna memorial to 200-odd Europeans massacred by him in 1763 are the words 'Walter Reinhart alias Sumroo, a base renegade', while the Persian inscription on his ostentatiously designed tomb at Agra, a handsome octagon surmounted by a dome, translates:

The death of Sumroo Sabah – the leader of virtuous dispositions – roasted the bosom of the universe with the fire of sorrow. From the date of the Messiah's ascension to the heavens, the Zodiac declared the date of his death. From the perfume of the floor of the Garden of Paradise, 1778.

On another side of his tomb is an altogether simpler inscription in Portuguese:

A qui lazo Walter Reinhart morreo aos 4 de Mayo no anno de 1778.

At the time of the massacre he was in the service of the Nawab of Bengal, Kassim Ali. The Nawab, warring with the English, attacked and captured a large number of English residents at Patna and ordered them to be executed. None of Kassim's own native officers came forward to undertake this, but Reinhart, wishing to ingratiate himself with his new employer, agreed to carry out the execution. Details of the murders are given in the *Annual Register*:

Somers [Reinhart] invited about forty officers and other gentlemen who were amongst these unfortunate prisoners, to sup with him on the day he had fixed for the execution, and when his guests were in full security, protected as they imagined by the laws of hospitality, as well as by the right of prisoners, he ordered the Indians under his command to fall upon them and cut their throats. Even these barbarous soldiers revolted at the orders of this savage European. They refused to obey, and desired that arms should be given to the English, and that they would then engage them. Somers, fixed in his villainy, compelled them with the blows and threats to the accomplishment of that odious service. The unfortunate victims, though thus suddenly attacked and wholly unarmed, made a long and brave defence, and with their plates and bottles even killed some of their assaultants, but in the end they were all slaughtered ... Proceeding then, with a file of sepoys, to the prison where a number of prisoners then remained, he directed the massacre, and with his own hands assisted in the inhuman slaughter of 148 defenceless Europeans confined within its walls – an appalling act of atrocity that has stamped his name with infamy for ever.

This man, who carried out one of the worst atrocities in Indian history, before which the Black Hole of Calcutta pales into insignificance, was yet capable of evoking strong feelings of affection and loyalty among the troops he commanded. 'Homage is offered to Shri Ganesh Mr. Walter Reinhard (Samroo Sahib)' declares the dedication on a well he built near Agra in 1744.

Reinhart was born at Salzburg in 1702, the son of a butcher. One of several thousand fugitives to Prussia in 1730, he reached Pondicherry on a French frigate in 1750 and deserted to join the Company's army before starting on his career as a freelance. He was nicknamed 'Sumroo' on account of his dark complexion – supposedly an Indian corruption of the English word 'sombre'. He served twelve different Indian Rajas before finally tendering his services to the Moghul Emperor and settling down at Sardhana with Begum Zeb-un-Nissa, the 'Ornament of her Sex', who became his wife. Here he put down roots, doubled the revenues of the estates, and on the battlefield perfected a strategy of minimum involvement – 'to draw his brigade out into a line, fire a few shots, form squares, and retreat' – by which he preserved his reputation and never lost a gun. His guns were, however, used by his troops to extract money from their commander whenever their arrears of pay reached an intolerable level. A cannon was left out in the sun to get hot, then he was debagged and sat astride it until he agreed to pay them something on account.

After Reinhart died, his Begum asserted her own equally forceful personality. She led her troops into battle like Joan of Arc; she had a succession of European lovers and kept a harem of girls. When two of her slave girls tried to elope with their paramours, setting fire to a house in the process, she sentenced them to be flogged until senseless and buried alive, and put her own bed on top of the grave and slept on it for a night to prevent their rescue. This savage punishment was described by her Roman Catholic biographer in the 1880s as 'not greater than the crime deserved and the occasion demanded'. In later years she gained the approval of the Church, and was baptised 'Joanna Sumroo' by the Carmelite Friar, Father Gregory, who acted as chaplain to the many Roman Catholic freelancers in the area. She also exercised her considerable influence to have her own chaplain, Father Scotti, elevated to the episcopate of Sardhana as 'Father Julius Caesar'. She built a cathedral at Sardhana, and a church at Meerut. She sent large sums of money to the Pope and the Archbishop of Canterbury and received the Papal title of 'Joanna Nobilis'.

Swiss

Swiss mercenaries were common on the European battlefields, and so it was not surprising to find them serving in India wherever there was fighting to be undertaken for a fee. The occasional tomb at Agra and other old settlements testifies to their presence, but at Seringapatam in South India are a large number of graves of 'Swichter Troops' employed by the East India Company who were killed in the campaigns against Tippoo Sahib in 1799. These were men of the regiment raised by Comte de Meuron at Neuchatel in 1781, who served the Dutch Company at the Cape and later at Ceylon, but transferred their allegiance to the English when they took over the island. During the siege of Seringapatam the Regiment fought with Colonel Sir Arthur Wellesley, and earned his unstinted praise for their bravery. Earlier, when fighting beside the French at Cuddalore in 1782, the garrison had included the young Sergeant Bernadotte, to become King of Sweden and Norway. Giants marched across the Indian scene in those days, and the Swiss played a part, as the tombstones at Seringapatam record – for instance, that of a soldier killed on 28th November 1802, whose descendants became planters in Ceylon:

> Francois Piachaud, late a Major in His Majesty's Regiment de Meuron, aged 40 years. Erected to his memory by his disconsolate widow.

Poles

The occasional Polish officer is found among the campoos of the Mahrattas or in service of one of the other native princes. A tombstone at Meerut (Sardhana) records a distinguished officer who joined Reinhart's forces at Sardhana and became another lover of his irresistible Begum:

> Major Gotlieb Koine, native of Poland, born Sunday, 25th December AD MDCCXLV, died Sunday, p.m. 11th September MDCCCXXI, who was in the service of Her Highness Begum Sombre for fifty years, the last thirty-two of which as Collector of Bhudhana. He lived and died with the reputation of an honest

man and a pious Christian.

Another Pole who lived well into his seventies was John Christian, founder of the indigo concern at Madhipura, who died there in 1846. He was one of the many Europeans who found their way to India to escape persecution. He was born in Poland in 1769, and at the division of that country in 1793 he left for England to avoid conscription by Russia, and from there made his way out to India. He started indigo farming at Monghyr and Madhipura in the province of Bihar, and the Mongyr concern remained in his family for five generations.

Greeks

Scholars, merchants and shopkeepers came from Greece, then part of the Ottoman Empire of the Turks, to continue a connection with India that had commenced with Alexander the Great. At Benares is a grave to a Greek orientalist, one of the first to translate Sanskrit manuscripts into the kindred Greek language, who left behind this intriguing Persian epitaph in the Greek Church at Calcutta:

> To the memory of Demetrius Galanos, an Athenian, who died at Benares the 3rd May 1833, aged 72. Manifold griefs! Demetrius Galanos has gone away into Paradise from this world! Beside themselves with grief [people] cried out: Alas! He who rivalled Plato in eloquence has departed.

The building of the Greek Church was inspired by a Greek called Ageery, the first eminent member of his community to settle in Calcutta around 1770. He acted as the Arabic interpreter on the British mission to secure freedom to trade with Suez, and at the outset of the voyage vowed to build a church in Calcutta on their safe and successful return. All went well, and the Patriarch of Constantinople consented to send a Greek priest to Calcutta, but Ageery himself died in 1777 before his plans were much further advanced. His epitaph refers to him as 'Hadjee Alexios Ageery, native of Philippolis': Ageery had made his pilgrimage to Jerusalem and earned the title of 'Hadjee', as a Mohammedan would for visiting the holy city of Mecca. The work of building the church was taken up by Parthena of Corfu, and the foundation stone was laid in 1780, thanks to the encouragement of the Governor-General. Hastings contributed generously –

setting an example of the English to encourage the pious intentions of Greeks ... English gentlemen mainly contributed and the few poor Greek traders to Bengal added their mite to the aggregate.

As European commercial interests expanded over the sub-continent, Greeks prospered, and a successful Greek was likely to be found in almost every business community. In Delhi, a number of years before the city came under the direct administration of the East India Company, the usual enterprising Greek, Michael Keryack, had found a niche for himself. His tombstone is in the Lothian Bridge Cemetery (see p. 147). The lettering was carved by a trooper of the 16th Lancers, who has added his signature at the bottom: 'M. Fennerty 16th L.'

The Greeks who came to India tended to stay there, unlike the majority of the English to whom their Indian career was an episode before retiring 'Home'. Second generation Greeks sometimes, instead of following in father's footsteps, became anglicised through boarding-school education in England, and returned to posts in the civil service, as evidenced on this tombstone in Simla:

> Demetrius Panioty, Assistant Private Secretary to His Excellency the Viceroy, son of Emanuel Panioty a Greek Gentleman of Calcutta. Born at Calcutta 1830. Died at Simla 17th July 1895. A devoted husband, a good father, a true friend and faithful servant of the government. He tried to do his duty.

Armenians

The Armenians, another community of Christians from the Ottoman Empire, established themselves as merchants at the Moghul centres of power before the arrival of the European trading companies, and consolidated their position under the Christian commercial expansion that ensued. The community at Agra dates back to the time of Queen Elizabeth, and many Armenians had very influential positions with the Court of Akbar, while others were merchant princes on their own account – such as this very rich and holy Armenian buried in the old Agra Cemetery. His Persian inscription translates:

> Here lies the Holy Khoja, or Khwaja, Mortenepus, Armenian, who was a professed disciple of Christ, and who was a righteous man; whatever he had he gave in charity to the poor in token of

fidelity to his Master in the year 1611 from the birth of Christ.

Delhi had a similar congregation of Armenian Christians although the epitaphs in their cemetery were destroyed during the invasions from Afghanistan in the second quarter of the eighteenth century. Gradually these Armenians established themselves in different towns, some retaining their Christianity while others around 1820 embraced Islam, perhaps as a silent protest against their social rejection by their European Christian brothers.

In the early days of the East India Company it had been the policy – for reasons of economy – to employ a number of Asians in preference to Europeans, but after the Cornwallis reforms at the start of the nineteenth century, recruitment was restricted to European-born officers. The Amenian community was, however, given official recognition and supported with a church provided the congregation numbered more than fifty. In their own cemetery at Calcutta are the tombs of a number of early members of the community, the Armenian inscriptions frequently in the form of a miniature biography spoken by the deceased with occasional exhortations to the passer-by:

> My body was placed in this sepulchre of rest. I am a pilgrim and the son of Bektan and my name is Malcolm. I am a native of Julfa and in my old age went on a pilgrimage to Holy Jerusalem which was my fervent desire and ultimate object. Died in Calcutta on the 9th Hamirah in the year of Our Lord, 1791. Oh! Thou who mayst pass by this tomb, pray for me.

In Madras Presidency, at Vepery, is a tomb to Petrus Uscan De Coja Pogus with a long impressive epitaph in Latin. 'Coja' means 'a man of distinction' and 'Pogus' means 'Paul' in Armenian. This great Catholic benefactor built the Marmalong bridge, installed steps from the foot to the summit of St. Thomas' Mount and endowed a chapel to Our Lady of Miracles to be built over the grave where he was laid to rest in 1751. His will also provided for his heart to be removed – '100 pagodas to the Surgeon' – and placed in a golden casket before being taken to Julfa in Persia for burial. An oil-painting of him hangs over it in the Cathedral there and on the picture a heart is painted, with this distich:

> My heart longs for home, where should I be unable to go, I desire that when my last day comes, my heart be sent to my native land, so that I Petrus Uscan, may have a grave there.

What other Eastern country has such a collection of Western bones buried thousands of miles from their native home? Only the larger national groups have been mentioned. Many have been omitted: Swedes, who attempted to establish a trading settlement at Surat; Norwegians, who as part of the Danish kingdom took part in the early Tranquebar settlement and in modern times have been active missionaries among the tribes of Assam; Canadians, who now have a number of important Christian Missions in India, and who in earlier times sent a few sons to fight in the Company's army, such as Major H. Maxwell who died at Chunar in 1829, the son of Captain W.H. Maxwell, born in Canada in 1787; South Africans, represented by twenty Boer prisoners-of-war at Ambala, and by lonely Swanepoel at Solan who died in 1902; Brazilians, by a Major in the Brazilian army buried at Chunar; Hungarians, by the compiler of the first *Dictionary and Grammar of the Thibetan Language –* Cosma de Koros – who died at Darjeeling on his way to Lhasa in 1847; Roumanians, by the pilot of a plane which crashed at Benares in 1931 – all have contributed in one way or another to making modern India.

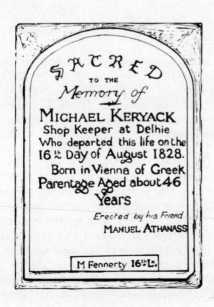

Man needs but little here below
Nor needs that little long.

(over the gateway to Karnal cemetery)

5   Epitaphs and Grave Stories

The epitaphs can often provide a glimpse of the character of the inmate, and a commentary on the society in which he or she lived. The names on the tombs can tell one something about the origins in their own country of the Europeans who came to India: thus the Puritan 'Ordonicus' and 'Tryphena' show that the early British merchants were from London, the Home Counties, Bristol and Devon. Political events at 'home' changed the pattern of emigration: a scattering of Huguenot Chardins, Crommelins, Amsincks, LeFevres and Trapauds arrived at the end of the seventeenth century and in the early eighteenth, with an increasing number of Scots towards the end of the eighteenth century, the Macs and the Stuarts, after the two rebellions and the Highland clearances. The shields and initials engraved on the monuments give interesting information to the genealogist and to those interested in the development of Freemasonry in the East. But quite often the epitaphs are interesting simply as epitaphs, for their wording, their poetry conscious or unconscious, or their attitudes to death. This chapter collects a representative selection of the different types found, some speaking for themselves, others requiring a brief commentary.

Sad and Pathetic

To Dr. J. Harris, Residency Surgeon at Jaipur, 1846, aged 43:

> This tablet a hapless widow rears
> To prove her love and to record her tears
> To him on lasting marble to attest
> How good her husband was, herself how blest.

To Major Eagle, 3rd Regiment Native Infantry, at Delhi, 1811:

> Silent grave, to thee I trust
> This precious pile of worthy dust,
> Keep it safe in the sacred tomb,
> Until a wife shall ask for room.

To James Nixon, Conductor of Ordnance at Delhi, 1826, aged 43
– from County Tyrone:

> Where now alas my dearest James
> Shall Hannah seek for rest?
> Where, but in your Saviour's arms
> Reclining on His breast.
>
> Oh may I seek and tread the road
> You sought and ever trod
> And in the end find that repose
> Which now you have with God.

At Tranquebar:

> Here lie the remains of the terrestrial body in which once lived the
> heavenly-minded soul of Maria Willads, born 9th December
> 1753, died 9th December 1777.
> After 9 months and 11 days of sorrowful matrimony she left her
> husband the Rev. H.J. Willads bereft of earthly happiness and
> her child Christian of 11 days old motherless. We hope to meet in
> heaven.

At Kangra, H.P.:

> To the memory of Catherine, the beloved wife of C.H.D. Spread,
> 72 Reg B.N.I., and much lamented daughter of Lt. Col. and Mrs.
> Wilkinson of the same Corps, who died on the 19th Aug. 1847

aged 20 years, 8 months and 24 days, endeared to all her friends by her many aptitudes and amiable qualities. Her premature death is a source of deepest affliction.

At Amritsar, Punjab:

Ellen Belcham Flinn – one of the most affectionate of human beings

Born 25th July 1857   Married 1876   Died 8th June 1878

Erected by parents to their son, O.A.S. Boodrie, a Ticket-Collector, buried at Amritsar, Punjab in 1879, aged 18:

Go home my loved ones and shed no tears
I must be here till Christ appears
Short was my stay and long my rest
Christ took me where he thought it best.

In Lower Circular Road, Calcutta:

Lucy Maria, wife of Mr. P. Pereira, who was suddenly removed from the bosom of a fond husband, an affectionate mother and brother, and of attached friends, by an attack of Cholera, on the 29th January 1846 at the early age of 19 years, 4 months and 3 days:

Go fair example of unsullied truth
Go smiling innocence and blooming youth
Go female sweetness joined with manly sense
Go winning wit that never gave offence
Go soft humanity that blest the poor
Go saint-eyed patience from affection's door
Go modesty that never wore a frown
Go virtue and receive *thy heavenly crown.*

Humourous and Quaint

At Peshawar, Pakistan:

Here lies
Captain Ernest Bloomfield
Accidentally shot by his orderly
March 2nd 1879.

Well done, good and faithful servant.

At Surat:

> Here lies Francis Breton, who, after he had for five years discharged his duties with the greatest diligence and strictest integrity, went unmarried to the celestial nuptials, on July 21st, 1649.

At Negapatam lies Mary Harris, a fond wife, for whom all went according to plan:

> [her] soul, perfect in all earthly ordained virtue, departed on 4th March 1799 at the early call of its Guardian Author for its next assigned function in the Eternal Kingdom.

One man died, according to the stone mason (United Provinces):

> Craving a large widow and family to mourn his lot.

To Private J. Saffory, Infantry Invalids (Pensioner), 1832, aged 66, Buxar, Bihar:

> My flesh shall slumber in the ground
> Till the last trumpet's joyful sound
> Then burst the tomb with sweet surprise
> And in my Saviour's image rise.

There is a nice example of co-existent religions at Simla. One grave contains a chaplain, Rev. Pitcaithly, who in 1848 aged 44

> ... left a family of six young children with unfaltering confidence to the care of *his* God.

– and in a nearby grave lies a native Mohammedan lady:

> ... dearly loved and devoted wife of Lt. Col. T.D. Colyear, ret'd, a good mother and a firm friend who lived in the service of *her* god.

Colyear was the natural son of the last Earl of Portmore, died 1875.

An extravagantly humble epitaph is this, translated from Armenian, in Calcutta:

> This is the tomb and resting place of the body of a certain unhappy and wretched clergyman, hardened in sins.

I am the unworthy Rev'd Johanness, a great sinner and son of the Rev'd Zachariah, the chaste clergyman of the family of Deelakheantz.

Oh! you my venerable father and brethren who may pass by this sepulchre, I pray thee with a mouthful of dust, to deign me worthy of your prayers, perchance through you I may share the clemency of the great tribunal.

The 13th Hamirah, 1790 A.D.

The Resident to the court of Rasagee Bomslah, who died at Nagpore in 1791, has a sonorous and assertive epitaph:

God is free from want. This is the tomb of G. Forster, the strengthener of the Empire, the preserver of the country, possessed of intrepidity, Sardar of the old British Company, who had come to this country as an agent from Calcutta. Aged 39.

The emotion shows through the doggerel in this, to John Vaughlin, Livery Stable Keeper, 1824, Calcutta:

His early death involves in grief severe
A loving partner and ten children dear.

An appropriate quotation was found for Shakunthala Menezes, killed by falling down a lift shaft in 1972, in New Delhi:

'Let the bones which thou hast crushed rejoice'

(Ps.30 v.10)

The family of Peter Bunter Tapsell, who died aged 35 in 1898 at Dharmsala, showed an anguished acceptance of Providence:

Had He asked us, well we know
We should cry 'Oh! spare this blow'
Yes! with streaming tears should pray
'Lord we love him, let him stay'.

But the Lord doeth nought amiss
And since He hath ordered this
We have nought to do but still
Rest in silence on his will.

Heroic and Humble

Robert Atkinson, Commander of Ordance, R.A., buried at Lothian Bridge, Delhi, in 1815, aged 48, has a plain slab surrounded by large ostentatious tombs:

> This modest stone what few vain marbles can
> May truly say 'here lies an honest man
> Of manners gentle, of affections mild
> In wit a man, simplicity a child
> A safe companion and an easy friend
> Unblamed through life lamented in his end'.

John Carvalho, buried at Fort St. George, Madras, in 1723, has one of the few epitaphs with a pagan sentiment found on Christian tombs in India – a reminiscence of Horace Odes 1.4.13, which also appears on the tomb of John Ross, merchant, in the Charnock Mausoleum, 1751:

> With equal pace impartial fate
> Knocks at the palace and the cottage gate
> Nor should our sum of life extend
> Our growing hopes beyond their destined end.

In the case of Sgt. H. Orchard, buried in 1876 at Muree, Pakistan, aged 26, dying amounted almost to desertion:

> Farewell, dear comrades, one and all, goodbye,
> My stay was short but God knows why
> He called me to himself – He knew but why –
> From the King's Regiment. I hope I was prepared to die.

To the chief of a settlement, Madras, eighteenth century:

> Though without wealth of a Governor, was rich in the real worth
> of a man.

To Julia Anne Dyce, aged 31, Meerut, 1820, of Begum Sumroo's entourage at Sardhana (the second couplet is also found on Mrs. Woodhouse's tomb at Cuddalore – see p. 117; a particularly successful or touching verse was often repeated):

Alas! In this neglected spot is laid
A heart once full with the celestial fire
Hands that the rod of empire might have swayed
Or waked to ecstasy the living lyre.

Admonitory

To George Maflin of Hon. Company's Marine Service, 1834, aged
29, Calcutta:

Good Christians on me cast an eye
As you are now, so once was I
As I am now, so you must be
So then prepare to follow me.

This was a popular sentiment, with many variations – such as this
to Sgt. A. Aitchison, 92 Highlanders (Gordon) 1859, aged 31, at
Jhansi:

Stranger or friend, as you draw nigh
As you are now, so once was I
But as I am, so shall you be
Prepare yourself to follow me.

To Capt. C. Sandford, 1858, re-erected 1877:

Strangers, respect the lonely resting-place of the brave.

To a Salvation Army worker, Palampur, H.P.:

She has done her bit – what about you?

The epitaph of Charles Weston, 1731-1809, in Calcutta, pays a
long tribute to his generosity (he gave 100 gold mohors a month to
the poor); referring obliquely to the fact that he was an Eurasian 'A
striking example that character and refined sentiments are not
confined to complexion or climate' – then adds:

This stone is no flatterer – go and do thou likewise.

At Bankipore:

Here lay deposited the earthly remains of the truly gallant Major

Rankfurlie Knox, who, after having lived many years in the military service of the Hon'ble United East India Company, universally esteemed and beloved, died on the 28th of January 1764, aged 34.

Reader! Whatever the Principles of thy religion may be, form thy life after his example, so shall the pious tears never be wasting to be shed to thine as to his Memory.

Short

On a tomb in Kolasi Factory, Purnea District, Bihar:

Our Alice

To Lt. Maxwell, aged 27, Meerut, 1827:

Alas!! Poor Maxwell!!!

Major Nairn, killed at Aligarh, 1803, achieved fame for attacking a tiger armed only with a spear:

This was a man

To the Rev. Beddy, aged 64, died 1852, Calcutta:

Tandem Felix

To John Campbell, M.D., aged 24, died 1803, carried off by a sudden fever, buried in South Parks, Calcutta:

Eheu! Fugaces!

To Judge Sextus Phillpots, died 1883, Hursole, Bombay:

His sun went down at noon

Col. J. Guthrie, who gave his name to a Regiment later known as 'Three Brahmans', died 1803, Fatehgarh:

Peer of the Moghul Empire

On the tomb of J.A. Fanthome, at Agra, who died in 1907 aged 19, are three bars of music and then:

> Excelsior. Excelsior. Excelsior.
> I go to my Father

One laconic and gloomy stone at Saugor, C.P., about 1840, says briefly, without any details:

> The wages of sin is death

Long and Prosaic

This gave the stone-mason over 170 words to cut:

> To the memory of Alexander Patrick Johnstone, Esq. late on the Bengal Civil Establishment of the East India Company who expired on the 11th November 1803, aged 25 years, 11 months, & 1 day, who, to the strictest integrity and to uncommon maturity of judgement united the mildest manners, extensive benevolence and all the social and tender affections; under the guidance of which principles he invariably maintained the character of a public officer with credit and honour to himself and in the most pious and exemplary manner the various duties of a man, brother, husband, father, and a friend. To commemorate these virtues this monument has been erected by her who is best able to judge of their influence and effects; and who is anxious to record this testimony of the felicity of their conjugal union during a period of nearly four years, of the affection, love, gratitude and reverence which she feels for his memory and of the deep and indelible anguish which the premature loss of him has impressed upon her mind.

To the 18-year-old wife of C. Raikes of the Bengal Civil Service, who died in 1835 and was buried in Landour Cemetery, U.P.:

> Those who in agony, but in humility deplore her loss deem not her death premature, for through the mercies of that Saviour in whom she trusted she was already meet for immortality; her rare personal and mental endowments were but the blossoms of the tree whose fruits were Christian purity and holiness. May those who now mourn her on earth be made partakers with her in the resurrection of the blessed.

An afflicted and disconsolate father described as follows the death of his son, Warren Hastings Larkins, at the age of 4 years 20 days in 1788:

An uncommon promising genius, and engaging and amiable disposition made him the delight of his father and a favourite of the settlement; in this season of innocence the hand of Providence visited him with a mortal disease and removed him from the presence of his earthly parent, to the kingdom of his Heavenly Father and Redeemer. The dictates of reason and religion may teach us to acknowledge the benefits derived to him from the change; but the lenient hand of time only can reconcile the feelings of paternal affection to the disappointments of hope, on what it had fondly rested, and what have been thus untimely destroyed.

Matilda Gwyne, the wife of William Dickson, married at 13 and died in Cawnpore in 1827 aged only 23:

This monument is erected by her afflicted husband in commemoration of her virtues as an affectionate wife, a tender mother and a faithful friend during a union of nearly ten years. If worth were to be esteemed by the unspeakable grief of a disconsolate husband, and the deep and unfeigned grief of all who had the happiness of her acquaintance, hers would rank high indeed; but alas! she has fled from erring human judgment, to that tribunal, which alone can duly appreciate the mild and gentle virtues which adorned her admirable mind.

This translation from the Armenian, in Calcutta, is in quite a different style but just as wordy:

To thee are my words, oh, thou passer-by who may chance to fix your gaze at this spot.
    I, Arratoon Catchick, a follower of the Saviour was born in the great city of Ispahan ... and came to India to trade ...
    Annie was the name of my wife who was adorned with the heavenly graces. She bore me children like angels ... but alas! Inconstant and cruel destiny spares not even the tender years of youth for the unendurable gall of death fell on our dear children ... our beloved pair of turtle-doves.
    My devoted wife through excessive grief succumbed to consumption ... then I who was left alone asked the Lord ... to

give me rest to my soul who sent anon His Angel ... into whose hands I yielded my soul.

Now the end of my painful life took place in the year one thousand and eight hundred plus fifty-two on the 26th day of the month of February on the day of the feast of Simon the Old who was happy to exchange life with death.

The days of my life being 82 years of which deduct 38 days only.

Living in the Present

Elizabeth Bull wrote her own epitaph two years before she died at Allahabad in 1828, aged 27 and 7 months:

Today and Tomorrow

Today, man's dressed in gold and silver bright
Wrapped in a shroud before tomorrow night:
Today, has fed upon delicious food
Tomorrow, dead, unable to do good.
Today, he's nice and scorns to feed on crumbs
Tomorrow, he's himself a dish for worms.
Today, he's honoured and in vast esteem
Tomorrow, not a beggar envies him.
Today, he rises from a velvet bed
Tomorrow, lies on one thats made of lead.
Today, his house though large he thinks too small
Tomorrow, can command no house at all.
Today, has forty servants at his gate,
Tomorrow, scorned, not one of them will wait.
Today, perfumed as sweet as any rose
Tomorrow, stinks in everybody's nose.
Today, is grand, majestic, all delight,
Ghastly and pale before tomorrow night.
True as the scripture says, man's life's a span
The present moment is the life of man.

By Eliz. Bull Jan 31 1826.

This tomb is erected by a tender, kind and indulgent husband, as a mark of his esteem and regret.

Susan, the wife of Sergeant Costello of the Chunar Magazine, died in 1833 aged 16 years, 9 months and 17 days:

Let the vain world engage no more
Behold the gaping tomb
It bids us seize the present hour
Tomorrow death may come.

Social Virtues

Captain George Nugent, Fort Adjutant and Barrack Master Chunar, died in 1839 aged 39, only four years after being made a Captain:

He was a man of most honourable and upright principles, a tender, kind and indulgent husband, a fond and affectionate father, a warm and sincere friend possessing an elegant mind and energy and wit blended with the most affable manner; he was a charming companion and an excellent member of society.

John Henry Stephenson, solicitor of Bombay, died at Bussorah 21st February 1816, aged 37; his epitaph is in St. Thomas' Cathedral, Bombay:

Still let the trophy'd urn and sculptured bust
Of shrouded grandeur, mock the slumbering dust;
His sterling worth no borrowed aid requires
From breathing sculptures or poetic fires.
The social virtues of his generous mind
Live in each friend's memorial breast enshrined,
And those, the law to his protection gave
Still bless'd the hand that reached them but to save
Still bless'd the heart, just, liberal, candid, bold,
Unswayed by interest, prejudice or gold.
Asia admir'd – bewail'd his short career
And o'er his ashes shed the grateful tear.
No prouder monument can marble yield!
No brighter trophy blazon virtue's shield!

At Ludhiana:

Sacred to the memory of Eliza the beloved wife of Major John Holbrow who departed this life with resignation befitting a Christian and in charity with all mankind, 13th July 1838, aged 31 Years & 7 Mths to the unspeakable grief of her fond relatives. In the several relations of wife, mother, daughter and sister, she was adored; and by society at large she was respected and esteemed.

Infants and Centenarians

To Thomas W. Adams, Calcutta, aged 1 year, 11 months and 19
days, 1810:

> Beneath dear sleeping Tommy lies
> To earth his body lent
> More glorious he'll hereafter rise
> Though not more innocent
>
> When the arch-angel's trump shall blow
> And soul to body join
> Millions will wish their life below
> Had been as short as thine.

To Ralph Edward Crawford, Gaya District, Bihar, aged 1 year
and 17 days, 1844:

> I was dumb,
> I opened not my mouth,
> Because Thou didst it.

To John Blyth, infant, Surat, 1773:

> Happy the babe, who privileged by fate
> To shorter labour and to higher weight
> Received but yesterday the gift of breath
> Ordered tomorrow to return to death.

Ann O'Brien, Cawnpore, 18??, aged 18 months and 9 days:

> Oh, the tempest was unkind
> And stern the shower
> And cruel was the wayward wind
> That wrecked so sweet a flower.

To Alice Olympia, child of Major G.T. Green of Engineers, died
1848, aged 1 year and 8 months:

> The star of comfort for a moment given
> Just rose in earth then set to rise in heaven.

This verse was written by Elinor Jenkins who died at the age of twenty in 1918. Many of her family served in India, and she was a cousin of Evan Jenkins, a Governor of Punjab:

> Father, forget not, now that we must go,
>   A little one in alien earth low laid;
> Send some kind angel when thy trumpets blow
>   Lest he should wake alone, and be afraid.

This commemorated the children of Lt. Col. J.G.W. Curtis and his wife, buried at Kasauli – Maria Charlotte, born, 5.2.1834, died at Neemuch 23.10.35; Grace Mary, born 10.9.1843, died at Simla 7.10.43; Robert Ruddock, born 24.8.1846, died at Ludhiana 9.3.47:

> And we must wander witheringly
> In other lands to die
> And where our father's ashes be
> Our own may never lie.

These 'two children', buried at Howrah, were J.J. Heritage, aged 4 years, 9 months, 11 days, and C.M.A. Heritage, aged 8 years, 11 months, 15 days:

> Beneath this stone two children lie
> Who raised many a tear in their father's eye
> Because when young their parents parted
> Which might have made them die broken hearted.
>
> Go home dear parent, shed no tear,
> We must be here, till Christ appear.

One wonders what forgotten tragedy lies in these words (Surat, eighteenth century):

> Annesley, son of Lt. Col. Thomas Brownrigg, aged 2 months and Margaret his mother who fell a victim for him.

At St. John's Trichinopoly, this verse commemorates four children – Robert Trower, who died 2nd June 1821, aged 2 years and 4 months; Henry Trower, died 11th October 1820, aged 5 months 27 days; Robert Trower, died 26th October 1821, aged 22 days (the second Robert to die in a year); and Alexander Trower, of H.M. 2nd Battalion or Royal Regiment:

These four lovely sons so young and fair
Called hence by early doom
Just came to show how sweet a flower
In paradise would bloom.

In contrast, Sgt. J. Williams of an Invalid Battalion, Chunar, died aged 101 and 1 day:

Life is the time to serve the Lord
The time to win the great reward
And while the lamp holds out to burn
The last sinner may return.
There are no acts of pardon gra[ced]
In the cold grave to which he haste
But darkness, death and long despair
Reign in eternal silence there.

The Barrackpore Burial Register records on the 4th of September 1849 the death of 'Sancta Victoria – supposed 100 years – a pauper', but a grave at Chunar outdoes her:

Sacred to the memory of Mrs Catherine Mingle, born 16th March 1760, died 22 November, 1869. 'May she rest in peace.'

'Grave' Stories

Epitaphs often conceal as much as they reveal. The cold dignified slab to Sir Alexander Fleetwood Pinhey, a Resident of Hyderabad, surrounded by exquisite marble railings carved in open Moghul decorative pattern – a gift from Indian admirers – tells nothing of the pandemonium at his funeral caused by swarms of bees. He contracted typhoid and was the fourth Resident to die in office at Hyderabad, being buried in the Residency graveyard a short distance west of the Residency, alongside the other Residents and several of their wives. His funeral service was held under the main Residency porch. When the band started playing appropriate music, the bees which swarmed every year in the roof cornices descended, sending the crowd, and the horses harnessed to the waiting gun-carriage, flying in all directions. No doubt many omens were read into this dramatic event, hardly a propitious start to a long lonely journey. A more touching memorial to Pinhey was erected at Neemuch by the family Ayah, who gave directions in her will that all her jewellery should be sold and a well erected 'in memory of her Sahib'. This was faithfully carried out and the inscription on the well records that it was –

> Built in grateful memory of Sir A.F. Pinhey, C.I.E. C.S.I. by his faithful servant Jenna Ayah, 1924.

The death of another senior civil servant gave rise to a superstitious practice of saluting cats walking out of the front door of Government House at Poona. Sir Robert Grant, who was the Governor of Bombay from 1834 to 1838, had a habit of walking up and down a particular path in the grounds of Government House every evening after the sun had set. He died of apoplexy following a fever while in residence there, and after sunset on the day of his death, a sepoy sentry saw a cat leave Government House by the front door and stalk up and down the same path. Rumour soon travelled round the Hindu guard that the soul of Sir Robert had transmigrated into the cat – an ironical fate for so staunch a Christian, who had written 'O worship the King' and other well-known hymns – and the guard commander gave orders that the cat must be given every honour to which the late Governor was entitled. Complications arose over identifying the particular cat out of the many at Government House so, to avoid any possibility of discourtesy, *every* cat seen leaving the front door after dark was given the full treatment, with the sentry presenting arms. This custom continued for over twenty years.

Animals and birds were closely connected with superstitions in the East. There was a common Indian belief that when a British soldier died his soul transmigrated into a newborn crow, which accounted for the crow's cunning; and Frank Richards relates that after a Battalion had lost a number of men from cholera during the monsoon of 1906, it was noted that as soon as the burial party arrived at the graveside –

> a solitary crow would alight on the cross of a tombstone a few yards from them and stay there watching the proceedings. When the coffin was lowered into the grave the crow would start to caw, maliciously as it seemed, and even the three volleys that were fired over the grave did not frighten it away. Then, as the company left the cemetery, it would fly behind them, still cawing, until the last man had passed through the gates; after which it would fly silently away. If they did not happen to bury a man one day they buried two the next, to make up for it; and the crow – they all swore that it was the same crow – never failed to present itself at the graveside. This so got on the nerves of the Company that they believed that they would continue to lose men so long as the crow appeared. And the queer part of the story is that they were right. At the funeral of the thirteenth man the crow did not put in an appearance, and this was the last man the company lost for the rest of the summer.

The British troops had an equally strong superstitious belief in their regimental mascots. One battalion had a goat – 'the Goat' as it was called – which had followed the battalion around in Malta and Crete, to India and all the various stations in India over the eight years of its regimental service in the early 1900s. When the goat died of old age at Meerut, it was buried in the shade of a large tree where several rebels were hanged during the Mutiny, and a large cross was put over the grave giving full details of its honourable service. One old soldier present at the burial ceremony expressed a wish to be buried under the same tree when his time came. In the ensuing years more interest was taken in maintaining the goat's grave through voluntary fatigue duties than in all the soldiers' graves in the nearby cemetery put together, or so it was alleged. Another regiment grew so attached to their goat that when it died its head was mounted on silver to make a huge snuff-box coaster, to be passed around the Officers' Mess on special occasions as a lucky talisman.

Belief in transmigration of souls is closely connected with spiritualism and astrology, and the European community of

Bombay in the late eighteenth century was much affected by these oriental beliefs, encouraged by their Governor, Thomas Hodges, who consulted a Brahmin 'sorcerer' over every decision he had to take and died in macabre circumstances predicted by the Brahmin's divinations. The Brahmin had established his influence over Hodges by prophesying many years before that he would become Governor, but adding that a black cloud was before him and according to the Hindu calender the 22nd February 1771 was an unlucky night. On that evening the Governor refused to go out and 'take the air' in his customary fashion. 'This is going to be a critical night for me,' he is reported to have said, and the next morning he was found sitting up in his bed with his finger on his lips – dead. It is interesting to compare him with such modern figures as the Prime Ministers of both India and Ceylon, who are commonly rumoured to consult their astrologer-advisers before committing their country to any major course of action. The *Sunday Times* of 2nd March 1975 contained this information:

Mrs. Bandaranaike herself has been hooked on the stars ever since astrologers warned her husband Solomon, when he was Prime Minister, that he was in peril of assassination – and he was killed on the date they warned him of in September 1959. She consults astrologers and palmists at moments of decision ... Mrs. Bandaranaike is also known to send trusted emissaries to read the apocalyptic 'vaccians' (ancient manuscripts) in the Hindu temples of South India.

Legends and superstitions grow easily around tombstones and there is a grave in the South Parks cemetery at Calcutta known as the 'bleeding grave'. It is a tomb to the Dennison family, father, mother and child, who died in 1806. At certain times of the year drops of red liquid appeared on the side of the tombstone, giving rise to many conjectures and hair-raising stories as to their origin. The inscription records that it is

Sacred to the memory of Mrs. M. Dennison, aged 26 years and her infant daughter who were interred on the 30th September 1806.

And of Capt. F.S. Dennison who survived his wife and child but a few days for on the 16th of October followed his decease.

He was united to them in death and buried in the same grave beneath this monument, in the 31st year of his age.

The importance attached to the mortal remains of the dead was always great, and when a close relative died in a remote area, efforts were made to have the body brought back to one of the city cemeteries where the grave could be properly cared for and maintained. The same concern was evident recently in the Americans who flew back their war-dead from Vietnam. Sometimes the body was exhumed and reburied locally, as with the wife of General Carnac, who was first buried at Surat and then reinterred in Bombay, or Mrs. Tiretta in Calcutta, whose body was moved from one cemetery to another through fear of desecration. But there were a number of remarkable cases where the body travelled long distances after reburial. The widow of Sir William Macnaghten, the ambassador assassinated at Kabul on 23rd December 1841, 'rescued his remains and brought them for Christian burial to India on 22nd April 1843' as recorded on his tombstone in the Lower Circular Road cemetery at Calcutta. Those who know the terrain from Kabul to the North-West Frontier, across the Punjab and down the Ganges to Calcutta, will understand the extent of this undertaking and appreciate the strength of the feeling for a decent Christian burial which could overcome all these hardships and hazards. General Anson, the Commander-in-Chief at the outbreak of the Mutiny, who died of cholera while collecting reinforcements on his way to Delhi, was first buried at Karnal and then reinterred in England. Another example is David Ochterlony Dyce-Sombre, the adopted heir of Begum Sumroo (see p. 142). He was brought up in her zenana at Sardhana, and at her request was later created 'Chevalier of the Order of Christ' by Pope Gregory XVI. Arriving in England in 1838 at the age of thirty, he married into the aristocracy – the Honourable Mary Anne Jervis, daughter of Edward Jervis-Jervis, Viscount St. Vincent of Meaford in the County of Stafford – became Member of Parliament for Sudbury in 1841 and was unseated the following year for corruption and bribery. He died in London in 1851, and sixteen years after his death 'his remains were conveyed to his native country ... and are deposited in the vault beneath near those of his beloved and revered benefactress, her Highness the Begum Sombre', as it says on her mausoleum at Sardhana. Many of the famous people already touched upon in this book were conveyed long distances after death to their final resting places – Francis Xavier, from off the China shores to Goa; Vasco da Gama, from Goa to Portugal; General Eyre Coote, from Madras to England; Viceroy Earl Mayo, from Andaman Islands to Calcutta and thence to Ireland; Victor Jacquemont, from Bombay to France; Frederick FitzClarence, from Bombay to the Royal vaults at Windsor – and we must not forget the

Armenian Uscan whose heart enclosed in a golden casket was conveyed to his family home in Persia (see p. 146).

The desire for a Christian burial in a consecrated European cemetery was understandably very strong in a foreign, 'heathen' land, but people had to qualify both by faith and by racial origin for these last rites. One who almost did not was Bandsman Holmes, who was killed in the Bannu uprising in 1848. Rumour about his half-caste origins and marital arrangements made it uncertain whether he could be permitted a burial in the European cemetery. He was given the benefit of the doubt, but at least some of the gossip turned out to be well-founded when claims for a pension were received 'by three mothers and two widows'.

A few young men, faced with the probability of an early death, composed wills of a somewhat bizarre nature to ensure that at least momentary notice would be taken of a common event. Charles Danvers who died in Madras in 1720, rich at 21 through three years of private trade supplementing his paltry Company salary of £5 p.a., left these unusual instructions in his will:

> My corpse to be carried from the Town Hall at 7 o'clock at night. I desire that all the free merchants of my acquaintance to attend me in their palankeens to the place of burial; and as many of the Company's servants as I have had any intimacy within my lifetime; that all that attend me may have scarves and hat-bands decent. I desire that Mr. Main and the charity boys, may go before my corpse and sing a hymn; my corpse to be carried by six Englishmen or more if occasion; the minister and the rest of the gentlemen following. I desire of the Honourable Governor that I may have as many great guns fired as I am years old, which is now almost twenty-one ... After my corpse is buried, which I desire may be done very handsomely, the remainder of my estate I desire may be laid out in rice, and be given to the poor at the burial place as long as it lasts.

The will of Thomas Saunders of Bengal, mariner, made in 1712, was not exactly bizarre but certainly down to earth:

> To a slave girl, named Clara, her liberty, with all her jewels and five hundred rupees; and if brought to bed within eight months and a half after my leaving Bengal, being the twenty-third day of January one thousand seven hundred and twelve, I bequeath unto the said child four thousand rupees and to be under the care of my executors. A slave boy named Pompey I give his liberty,

and five rupees per month during his life. A slave boy named Anthony, his freedom. If the said child that I bequeathed four thousand rupees dies afore it come to age or married, then the said four thousand rupees shall go to my son John Saunders.

An unusual 'death', announced in a black-edged edition of a local newspaper in 1819, was that of the very unpopular Governor of Madras, Hugh Elliot, when his period of office was extended for three years. The Governor was not amused by this mock obituary – his second wife had just died – and the editor was threatened with deportation back to England.

Wherever one travels in India, the cemeteries yield fascinating sidelights on history – on forgotten occasions and customs, on strange theories and beliefs. At Landour, close to the celebrated hill-station of Mussoorie, there is a bronze plaque attached to a tall deodar tree at the cemetery entrance, with an inscription telling of its planting there by His Royal Highness the Duke of Edinburgh in 1870. At Cawnpore, the Mohammedan cemetery at Kursawan contains the grave of Private Reed, 2nd Bn Rifle Brigade, and one is left to speculate whether he became a convert to Islam, and how he died on 7th December 1857. In a Madras church is an inscription to a Scot, Sir Robert H. Dick, a hero of the Peninsular War and Waterloo who was killed at the battle of Sobraon, as can be read on the battleroll-pedestal against which a sculptured 42nd Highlander in full uniform is resting. Dick is described as 'of Tullymet, N.B.'. The significance of this becomes clearer when one locates in Bareilly Cemetery the tomb of his younger brother J.C. Dick, a Judge in the Civil Service and '4th son of Dr. Dick of Tullymet, Perthshire, North Britain', who died in 1831. This again illustrates the family ramifications so often found in India: both men were born in Calcutta where their father was a Surgeon, having obtained his appointment through the patronage of Henry Dundas and Edmund Burke, and there were no less than nine Dicks in the Company's service before 1846 when Sir Robert died.

At Chunar, near Benares, that pensioners' station where so many Invalid Battalions were based, and which was consequently unusually rich in cemeteries, there lie in the picturesque and now abandoned graveyard below the fort several graves recording the year of death as 'A.M. 5794' or 'A.M. 5795'. The A.M. refers to 'Anno Mundi'; thus J. Dinigan, the Apothecary at Chunar whose tombstone gives the date 'A.M. 5794, A.D. 1794', evidently subscribed to the theory that the world began in the year 4000 B.C. The concept of 'Anno Mundi' was used by the Scottish Masons, though they dated the creation of the world at 3759 B.C. Many tombs are found throughout India with the Masonic devices of compass, set-square and sun, reflecting the strength of the movement. Some epitaphs reveal the name of a Lodge, such as that on the tomb of Sergeant William Knowles of the 11th Dragoons at Cawnpore, 'erected by the W.M. and brethren of Lodge Harmony of Cawnpore'. A few refer to another brotherhood:

> Loyal Orange Lodge No. 131 Held in His Majesty's 16th Lancers. Beneath this Tomb are deposited the mortal remains of the following Brethren of this Institution, who after a short Residence in India made their Exit as follows.

> John Marrow died 15th June 1823 aged 35 years.
> Wm. Aston died 17th June 1823 aged 28 years.
> Wm. Ferguson died 13th Jan. 1824 aged 27 years.

> Here, our mutual joys are o'er
> 　Earthly converse social bliss
> Our three Brothers are no more
> 　Till we meet in Worlds of peace.

Another example is the epitaph of Sergeant John Thomas Greenwood, of 'Loyal Orange Association No. 1242', who 'assisted in closing a Lodge Below to enter a Nobler one above'. His tomb was 'Erected by his Sorrowing Brethren of the above Lodge' in 1821, when he died aged 24. Perhaps these examples of collective solidarity illustrate the need for some form of organised social bonding and support, in a predominantly male society far from home and family.

6 Causes of Death

In this chapter I have selected some examples of the astonishing variety of causes of death, to illustrate the range of dangers external and internal to which Europeans were exposed, or to which they exposed themselves by their own reckless recreations such as tiger-shooting and pig-sticking.

Fevers and Diseases

'The Disease reign according to the Seasons ... in the extreme Heats, *Cholera Morbus*', wrote an early traveller to India in 1673. The word 'cholera' was first commonly used by Europeans in India at the beginning of the nineteenth century; previously it was called 'mort-de-chien'. The following vivid description of its symptoms was given by an early Portuguese writer in Goa:

> And this malady attacked the stomach, caused as some experts affirmed by chill; though later it was maintained that no cause whatever could be discovered. The malady was so powerful and so evil that it immediately produced the symptoms of strong poison; e.g. vomiting, constant desire for water, with drying of the stomach; and cramps that contracted the hams and the soles of the feet, with such pains that the patient seemed dead, with the eyes broken and the nails of the fingers and toes black and crumpled. And for this malady our physicians never found any

cure; and the patient was carried off in one day, or at the most a day and night; insomuch that not ten in a hundred recovered, and those who did recover were such as were healed in haste with medicines of little importance known to the natives.

The native remedy mentioned was to apply a thin red-hot rod under the heel until the patient screamed with pain, and then to slap the same part with the sole of a shoe – to drive the pain from the centre of the body to an extremity.

The disease occurred both sporadically – striking down an individual here and there – and in an epidemic form, when the scale of its devastations was almost beyond belief. There are hundreds of tombstones attesting to the speed and horror of this disease, which was known as 'the wandering Jew'. At Calcutta is an inscription to a woman who died of it aged 38:

> Jane Anne, the beloved wife of Major Henry Debude of the Bengal Engineers. Within two months after her return to India she was attacked by cholera at noon on the 27th February 1841 and died before midnight on the same day.

Rawlins wrote to his parents in 1851 about the dramatic loss of one of the few marriageable girls in his up-country station:

> I have just returned from the funeral of poor Miss Codrington ... poor girl, she was only ill six hours. On Thursday last she made me a 'favor' for the Ball, to which she came and looked as well and lovely as usual. Saturday morning she was seized with Cholera and died the same day! So much for the terrible uncertainty of life in India.

The fever was thought to be connected with the humid monsoon winds, and one medical authority in 1796 confidently asserted:

> It is occasioned, as I have said, by the winds blowing from the mountains ... the consequence is that malignant and bilious slimy matter adheres to the bowels, and occasions violent pains, vomiting, fevers and stupefaction; so that persons attacked with the disease die very often in a few hours. It sometimes happens that 30 or 40 persons die in this manner, in one place, in the course of the day.

This theory that cholera was an airborne disease persisted until the end of the nineteenth century, and the army adopted a special procedure for dealing with it, known as 'cholera-dodging'. The order used to be given to march out of barracks against the wind to higher ground and camp there, and they would move on to a fresh site if there were any more cases, and carry on marching from camp to camp until there were no more deaths. Hence the existence of 'cholera camps' outside the main Cantonment towns, with their little clumps of tombs – Beechola, Raj Baba and Mile 4 Napier Road outside Meerut; Jehangira, Pipla, Singaria and Denaria around Neemuch. Two hundred people a day died during a period following the monsoon of 1817 in Calcutta and the Governor-General's camp was decimated: 'one-tenth of its occupants perished, including many personal servants of the Governor-General and his historian.' Ferozepore had a terrible epidemic in 1856: Captain Mercer laconically records the names and numbers of the dead (see p. 10), and mentions an even worse toll at nearby Lahore 'where the Artillery lost about a third of their number out of about 450 men'. The Royal Munster Fusiliers lost 27 men in one night in 1869, and Mrs. Webber Harris, the wife of the commanding officer who nursed the sick and dying, received a gold representation of the Victoria Cross – the nearest a woman has got to receiving the award itself – from General Sir Sam Browne, himself a V.C., 'for her indomitable pluck during the cholera epidemic of 1869'. Benares, Allahabad, Cawnpore, Lucknow and Agra – each town had similar epidemics from time to time; indeed they occurred throughout India down to the beginning of the twentieth century, when the disease was traced to a waterborne virus and control measures through hygiene and inoculation became increasingly effective.

Other fevers took a heavy but less spectacular toll on the unacclimatised European. Dysentery, the 'bloody flux', was a more gradual debilitating disease which attacked the guts, again caused through ignorance of hygiene – not keeping flies from food and drink. General Havelock died of dysentery at the moment of victory at Lucknow in 1857, and the records of the military graves in Bombay and Bengal during the First World War show the frequency of this disease among troops in comparatively modern times. The primitive state of medical knowledge at the start of the nineteenth century is illustrated by the treatment recommended by a doctor who claimed to be an authority on dysentery:

as strength must be kept up, wine and solid food was the most suitable diet ... pillaos, curried fowls, peppered chicken broth *ad libitum*, with glass or two of madeira or brandy and a dessert of ripe fruits.

Another doctor, in 1792, noticing the greater resistance Indians had to tropical diseases, suggested a blood tranfusion by venesection so that the blood in Europeans became wholly Indian!

Another fever with often fatal results was typhoid or enteric, known generally in the early days of John Company as 'the putrid fever' – another fly-born bacillus attacking the intestines, not recognised and controlled until modern times. A soldier in a British Regiment records in his diary the loss of a number of men from enteric fever in 1904, and the War Grave Records list many fatal cases during the First World War among the troops based in India. As in all these fevers, there were isolated outbreaks affecting perhaps only one person, such as Private J. Wilson aged 23, of the King's Royal Rifle Corps, who contracted the fever at Dalhousie where he went for a few days leave in 189(?) and whose comrades composed this touching little incription for his tomb:

> We little thought when he left Peshawar
> His race was so near run
> But alas death called him
> Before he did return.

There were also epidemics, such as the high incidence of typhoid reported among the A.D.C.s and other members of the Viceroy's staff at Simla during the second half of the nineteenth century, which was attributed to the fact that Government House was built very close to an old graveyard. The cause of these violent fevers was the subject of the wildest speculation and superstition. In many cases, the fever was classified by the name of town or district in which it was contracted. Hence such unusual terms as 'Baumunghattee fever', inscribed even on the tombstones:

> This tomb is erected by Lt. Col. Doveton and the Officers of the 38th Regiment Native Infantry as a melancholy proof of esteem and is sacred to the memory of
>
> Surgeon James Macra, died 27th May 1832
> Lt. T.G. Mesham, died 1st June 1832
> Lt. G.S. Fullerton, died 1st June 1832
> Ensign F.S. Manningford, died 28th May 1832
> Cadet J.D. Pinder, died 3rd June 1832
>
> All of the 38th Regiment who were victims to the climate of Baumunghattee.

Or sometimes death was simply ascribed to an anonymous 'fever', as on the monument in Jumaulpore Burial Ground to the memory of three young Scots indigo planters – Gilkison, Logan and Crawford – who died within a few days of each other at the end of the 1831 monsoon: 'The above fell victims to a fever contracted during an excursion to the Garrow Hills.'

The climate itself accounted directly for a number of deaths through heat-stroke and sun-stroke, partly as a result of the unsuitable clothing and headgear worn, and ignorance of the need to take adequate quantities of salt during the hot weather. Lord Pigot, the Governor of Madras in 1777, is recorded as having died of heat-stroke. Major G.A.A. Baker, of the 6th Bengal Cavalry, 'died of apoplexy brought on by excitement over lost baggage and exposure to the sun' – a picture for the cartoonist! And on the tombstone of Sir G.Parker Bt., who died of sunstroke at Cawnpore in 1857, is inscribed this appropriate quotation from the Bible: 'Neither shall the sun light on them nor any heat.' Parades were sometimes held in the heat of the day, but generally as a result of experience they were arranged at an early hour of the morning during the hot weather. One Colonel of the old school who refused to adapt the timetable to the climate drew these comments from one of his subalterns, Cary, writing home to his parents in July 1855:

> The Colonel is maniac enough to order me to go to afternoon parades, I'll see him d—d – the insanity of going to parade on open ground with only a forage cap on!!! in the very height of the hot weather when nearly all other regiments have given up even ante-sunrise parades. If he wont give in I'll go to the Doctor's – why the Doctor who attended me says, 'Your fever arose entirely from your going to the Colonel's that day'. I should tell you I was not out 15 minutes and had a Pugree or turban round my solar topee and an umbrella, moreover the whole way was under the shade of houses or trees, and yet he wants me to go into a parade ground for an hour daily, where there is not a shadow, with a forage cap that only covers half my head. I'll see him d—d first, wouldn't you?

The marches which the troops and officers endured at the height of the hot season are almost unbelievable. They covered hundreds of miles; on one occasion, in 1778, a column actually traversed India from Calcutta to Surat, but not without a toll of lives. The Officer Commanding reported in despatches:

I have had the misfortune to lose Captain James Crawford who commanded the 4th Battalion of Sepoys by a most violent fever which carried him off in less than two hours.

He was buried near Margayan in a large masonry tomb with an inscription in Persian, erected no doubt some time after the column had moved on. Along the Grand Trunk Road and the other main arteries of communications which the Engineers and the Pioneers and later the Public Works Department had laid out and maintained – thoughtfully planting trees along the route to give shade to the soldiers and travellers – there were tiny cemeteries or clusters of graves at about 12-mile intervals, known as 'marching cemeteries', where the casualties of heat-stroke were buried when the marchers camped for the night: Dachepalle, Nadkudi, Vinokonda, Gurzala, Tumercode, Pidugaraha, or anonymous places – 'Mile 8', 'Mile 20' on such-and-such a route – the list is as long as the roads. Kipling caught the spirit of the endeavour:

> The ports ye shall not enter
> The roads ye shall not tread
> Go make them with your living
> And mark them with your dead.

Smallpox was another enemy the European had to contend with, which took many lives, though seldom in an epidemic form. Sir Robert Peel's son, the V.C. hero of Sebastopol and Lucknow, died of smallpox contracted after being wounded and carried on a litter which had previously been used for conveying a smallpox case to hospital – so little was known in those days about infections and contagious diseases. William Griffin, an Assistant at an indigo factory with the prophetic name of Doomdoomah, died of smallpox in 1849. The Burial Registers record many such isolated cases down the years, and it is interesting to note in the *Calcutta Gazette* of 4th May 1786, twelve years before Jenner published his discovery of vaccination, that there had been

a successful instance of inoculation in this climate. The managers of the Orphan Society, about two months ago, agreed that all the children under their charge, who had not already had the smallpox, should be inoculated ... 53 children who were inoculated have had the disorder, and are now perfectly recovered; but out of nine who took the disorder in the natural way, three have died.

Deaths through bacteria and viruses as yet unidentified were added to by those from the bites of insects, although cause and effect were not understood for a long time. Fleas, spread through rats, accounted for many epidemics of plague, even in comparatively recent times, such as the terrible Bombay visitation of 1896. Lice carried typhus; and, of course, the ubiquitous anopheles mosquito caused malaria, although the connection between the two was not proved until 1895 when the cure was found by British doctors working in India. A plaque is fixed at the Seth Sukhlal Karnani Memorial Hospital in Calcutta with a verse composed by Sir Ronald Ross to celebrate his triumph in finding the cause of malaria:

This day relenting God
Hath placed within my hand
A wondrous thing; and God
Be praised at his command.
Seeking his secret deeds
With tears and toiling breath,
I find thy cunning seeds
O million-murdering death.
I know this little thing
A myriad men will save.
O death where is thy sting
And victory, O grave?

Before the days of the scientific diagnosis and treatment of malaria, there were a number of traditional 'cures' for this recurring, debilitating disease, ranging from copious draughts of madeira or opiates to blood-letting, cupping and the application of leeches. Many people died of malaria, or 'jungle fever' as it was called. The Vicereine Lady Canning was one (see p. 22). Colonel Charles Parker of the Bengal Artillery was another; he contracted this fever while out on a shooting expedition near Simla in 1837. The Reverend F. Wybrow died of malaria at Gorakhpur in 1840, and the forest tracts of the lower hills were the worst-affected areas. Whole townships were decimated and made virtually uninhabitable. Ganjam was closed in 1815 and moved to Berhampore. Karnal was closed, as graphically described in the diary of Rawlins:

On the 18th January [1847] we reached Kurnal, which was, in 1842, the finest station in India and was then our frontier; but the cantonment became so susceptible of a malarious kind of fever, produced by the canal which had lately been completed, the regiments became so utterly decimated it was abandoned and transferred to Umbala [Ambala]; there was a beautiful church erected there, which bore the strongest evidence of the deadly nature of the climate, as the various monuments inside could testify; whilst outside, the cemetery was filled with graves of many a brave and gallant man who had prematurely died of this frightful fever.

The army were the worst sufferers, perhaps due to their greater exposure to risk, both in operations on the jungle fringes during the night, and in the early morning marches when mosquitoes were most active. In 1890 it was officially estimated that 20 per cent of the army suffered from malaria. The figures of malaria deaths in India mask the truth, as many people were invalided out in broken health to die on the voyage or within the first few years of returning home.

Medical confusion and ignorance over these deadly contagions continued almost to the end of the nineteenth century. There is a record of the visit of no less a medical officer than the Surgeon-General to an epidemic town in 1875:

> After some delay he arrived ... and remained in hiding for 5 days ... before he ventured forth, and at last feeling that by this position as head of the medical authorities in the division he was compelled to show himself abroad and take some action in the crisis, he at last visited my hospital and passed through its wards in the most perfunctory manner, suggested nothing, and holding a bottle of ammonia at his nostrils; and his whole visit to the 100 sick and dying [of cholera] was completed in about the space of sixty seconds.

The writer hastens to add:

> ... but thank God, such morbid nervous ? men are rare indeed and as a rule no men face death and danger with greater *sang froid* than members of this noble profession.

Quacks, however, were quick to exploit the willingness to try any remedy, and there was an astonishing variety of cures advertised. The *Calcutta Gazette* of 14th March 1822 claimed special properties for cigars, imported at one rupee per bundle: 'Real Manila Segar or Cheroots (Sovereign remedy against fevers and damps).' Rawlins, who in 1875 was one of the very lucky few to survive an attack of cholera, ascribed his survival to his two 'nurses' (an Indian bearer and a Gurkha orderly) who 'gave me a wine glass of champagne every quarter of an hour, and the repeated injection of morphia by the Hypodermic syringe tended more than anything else to allay the frightful sickness', and he observed from his Mess bill that he had consumed 'no less than 24 bottles of sparkling wine'. Another Officer, Cary, wrote home in 1858 describing how he was treated for an undiagnosed attack of fever: 'They had forty leeches on my throat and followed them up with lots of blisters and I got better.'

Considering the primitiveness of these Western attempts at cures, the traditional Eastern methods deserve attention. Fanny Parkes describes how the Hindoo women propitiated the goddess who brings cholera or plague, to drive the diseases from the bazaar:

> They go out in the evening about 7 p.m., sometimes two or three hundred at a time carrying a brass vessel filled with sugar, water, cloves etc. In the first place they make pooja; then, stripping off their chadars, and binding their sole petticoat around their waists, as high above the knee as it can be pulled up, they perform a most frantic dance, forming themselves into a circle, whilst in the centre of the circle about five or six women dance entirely naked, beating their hands together over their heads, and then applying them behind with a great smack, that keeps time with the music, and with the song they scream out all the time, accompanied by native instruments, played by men who stand at a distance; to the sound of which these women dance and sing, looking like frantic creatures.

The English Nursery Rhyme 'Ring-a-ring of roses' may have had similar origins, dating back to the Great Plague, as some authorities suggest – 'roses', from the rosy rash which was a symptom of the plague; 'pocket full of posies', from the posies of herbs carried as a protection; 'A-tishoo, A-tishoo', as sneezing was a final fatal symptom; and 'all fall down' being exactly what happened. If this frenzied dance did not succeed in frightening away the cholera, there was one other 'infallible' method of getting rid of it. A bull was symbolically impregnated with cholera and then, accompanied by prayers, the people drove the beast out of the town and into the river. When the poor animal attempted to land on the other side the local inhabitants there drove it back again until it was carried away by the current and drowned. The nature of these infections was partially understood: 'for by a wise resolution of the Hindoo religion,' writes Colonel Rawlins in his diary during the 1875 epidemic –

persons who die of cholera, small-pox and other contagious diseases, are committed to the earth, and not placed on the funeral pile for cremation, as they believe that the ashes of the deceased may be wafted by the winds to other places, and the fell disease spread in all directions.

These sudden deaths among the European inhabitants were frequently put down to eating and drinking particular substances and liquids. A General died in 1812 and the doctor put down the cause as 'eating too many radishes'. Rose Aylmer was said to have died, as already noted, of a surfeit of pineapples. Another young lady, the 'lovely Emily' Warren, mistress of Mr. Pott, a courtesan painted many times by Sir Joshua Reynolds – 'he often declared every limb of hers perfect in symmetry and altogether he had never seen so faultless and finely formed a human figure' – died in 1782 on the banks of the Ganges after drinking in rapid succession two large glasses of extremely cold water mixed with milk, when suffering from prickly heat. 'She complained of faintness and suddenly fell back dead.' Prickly heat was another scourge of the climate, described by Lord Minto:

> To give you some notion of its intensity, the placid Lord William [Bentinck] had been found sprawling on a table on his back; and Sir Henry Gwillin, one of the Madras Judges, who is a Welshman, and a fiery Briton in all senses, was discovered by a visitor rolling on his own floor, roaring like a baited bull.

Pott spared no expense in erecting two magnificent memorials to Emily – a huge mausoleum in the Calcutta cemetery for Rs30,000, no longer standing; and a strangely designed column at the place where she died, 'amongst herds of tigers', known as 'Pott's Folly' or 'the Kulpi Pagoda', a solid mass of masonry shaped like a Hindu temple and standing 35 feet high. This, and other graves along the Ganges delta, still serve as navigation marks for the Hugli pilots.

While some of these deaths may have been due to fevers, rather than drinking or eating, others seem to have been directly caused by a surfeit. A surgeon fell dead in 1780 after 'eating a hearty dinner of beef, the temperature being 98°'. Dinner in those days was a meal

> at two o'clock in the very heat of the day ... A soup, a roast fowl, curry and rice, a mutton pie, a forequarter of lamb, rice pudding, tarts, very good cheese, fresh churned butter, excellent Madeira ...

Drunkenness was a frequent cause of death – 'several Europeans pay their lives for their immoderate draughts,' remarked an early traveller – and the Emperor Akbar made a special exception for Europeans to consume intoxicating spirits in his country, for 'to prohibit them the use of it,' he said, 'is to deprive them of life'. In the same way, nearly three hundred and fifty years later, an independent India classified Europeans as 'drug addicts' to exempt them from the new prohibition laws in certain states. Drinking and riding were evidently as dangerous then as drinking and driving now, judging by the number of fatal accidents: an 1842 epitaph at Lahore records that H.F. Stanislas 'when intoxicated with liquor, died of a fall from his horse at night'. The liquor which did so much damage was variously called arrack, rack, toddy or punch, and was basically the fermented and distilled sap of the palm tree. 'Toddy' became adopted as a Scotch word, as in Burns's verse:

> The lads an' lasses blythely bent
> To mind baith saul an' body,
> Sit round the table, weel content
> An' steer about the toddy.

And 'rack-punch' was referred to in Thackeray's *Vanity Fair* as 'the cause of all this history'. Wild orgies were attributed by President Aungier to 'the usual effect of that accursed Bombay punch, to the shame and scandal and ruin of the nation and religion'. Tom Coryate (see p. 90), who had walked to India in James I's reign, quenched his thirst too frequently on arrack and died of over-indulgence. Beer and wine were imported, but it was difficult to obtain regular supplies except in the main port-towns, and in the nineteenth century attempts were made to manufacture 'country beer' in the hill-stations. This locally made beer was always regarded as very inferior, although in one particular year a specially good brew of Mussoorie beer was remarked upon. On investigation it was discovered that a coolie had fallen into the vat and drowned, adding to the fermentation.

The army often marched and fought on alcohol or some other stimulant. The Royal Irish Rifles, when covering eighty miles in four days during the monsoon of 1857, were given a double ration of 'rack'; the Scinde Camel Corps marched fifty miles a day in 1848 aided by *bhang* (cannabis) issued on the orders of Sir Charles Napier; and Officers frequently took opium. Deaths due to taking these drugs to excess are seldom recorded. It is known that a Mercer child was buried in Lucknow about 1850 after being in an opium-induced

coma, and Mrs. Sherwood wrote in her 1807 diary: 'Half the
European children who die in India, die from the habit which their
nurses have of giving them opium.' It was a recognised practice for
Indian mothers to put opium on the nipple of the breast before
suckling their baby to keep it quiet, or, in the extreme case of the
Rajputs and others who practised infanticide, an overdose would be
given to a daughter. Opium was both easy and cheap to obtain.
Taken in pellet form it was socially acceptable in Indian aristocratic
circles, particularly as a palliative for the elderly. The Moghul
Emperors indulged in it; Humayun regularly took a pellet with
rosewater and Jahangir, with unconscious historical irony, became
an addict while forbidding the smoking of tobacco, which he
considered a noxious drug. Opium was not regarded as dangerous,
and any evidence in that direction was ignored on account of the vast
profits which the East India Company made from their monopoly in
the trade.

A sense of the iniquity of the trade began to percolate through the
minds of the officers of the Company in the second quarter of the
nineteenth century, and one comes across references to the harmful
effects of the drug, usually made by men freshly arrived from
England. In 1844 Rawlins visited Patna, the town which in the
1770s had the reputation of being the biggest opium centre in the
world, exporting annually over 4,000 chests, each weighing 300
pounds, to China and the East Indies. Rawlins writes:

> Here are the famous opium godowns, that deleterious drug which
> ruins hundreds of thousands every year; but as its monopoly
> produces a revenue of nearly nine millions sterling annually, and
> is one of the chief resources of the budget, it is not probable that
> the philanthropists of Exeter Hall, or the injurious effects
> produced upon people, will be taken into consideration, and its
> manufacture discontinued.

Cary, visiting Ghazipur, another opium town, in 1856, gives a
detailed account of the manufacturing process, with horrified
comments on the scale of the profits:

> Each ball weighs two pounds of opium and is valued in the
> factory at Rs25. They give Rs3 to the cultivator for the same
> weight!! They pay their ball-makers from Rs6 to Rs8 a month,
> each man makes from 80 to 120 balls a day!!! They even strip
> every man and wash him before he leaves; my idea is that it is the
> most scandalously grasping and unjustly lucrative thing going ...

It is a most tyrannous trade too, for the cultivator is not allowed to sell his opium to any but Government or to keep it, and is obliged consequently to take what they choose to give – one of the iniquitous monopolies of India.

Life was constantly at risk, whether from fevers and unknown diseases, or the drugs amd medicines used to combat them – if not from some other unexpected danger. A sad epitaph at Guntoor records that Evan Marsh White, aged 23, died on the 17th August 1976, not from dysentery or cholera or malaria, but from 'the incautious use of castor oil nuts'.

Sporting Tragedies

The ever-present danger of death led to a reckless attitude which was reflected in the recreations, sports and pastimes in whic.` the typical Anglo-Indian male indulged – whether pig-sticking, bɛ ar-hunting, tiger-shooting or playing polo. Pig-sticking was described as follows by the late A.B. Reid, when giving a talk in 1963 on the historical perspective of the Indian Civil Service:

> ... an amazing sport in which a man armed himself with a spear, mounted his best horse and then pursued some wild boar, a pugnacious and formidable beast, over the wildest and most dangerous country imaginable, at full gallop. If you overtook the boar, which was a fast mover, as often as not the boar turned on you and charged, and then it was more or less a case of its life or yours.

At Muttra in the United Provinces is a tomb of a subaltern, Lt. Spartan of the 10th Hussars, who died pigsticking in 186(?), typical of many.

Bear-hunting sounds not much more dangerous than deer-
stalking, but there were a number of fatalities, usually the result of
extreme foolhardiness. Lieutenant Edward Percy St. Maur, second
son of Edward Adolphus, 12th Duke of Somerset, had his promising
career cut short at the age of 24 in 1865 when, as his epitaph at
Yellapur, Mysore, relates:

> Attacked by a bear he had wounded while out shooting, he
> encountered it knife in hand. He received a dangerous wound on
> the knee joint which rendered amputation necessary and sank
> under the shock.

In the Himalayas is an epitaph to Major T.W. Knowles 'who met his
death at Dharmsala by an attack from a bear on 25th October 1883,
aged 50: "in the midst of life we are in death".' A bear-hunt at
Dharmsala in 1872 is described by Rawlins:

> They turned out 200 men and had a 'hank' in the khuds below
> the Bhagsoo barracks, always a sure find in the early winter
> months; on this occasion they were very fortunate, no accidents
> occurring, no beaters shot, no coolies mauled; and when the sport
> was over, 9 huge black bears had fallen to the rifles of the
> sportsmen.

Most men shot one or two tigers in the course of their service in
India, for bagging a tiger was an accolade of manliness. Reid
mentions a man in his province – in the twentieth century – 'who
had certainly shot over 200 tigers', and Rawlins records enjoying a
little *shikar* with a Commissioner who had 'bagged upwards a
hundred tigers' and continues to describe a typical incident:

> Early in the new year [1862] a most serious accident befell
> Colonel Brownlow, the superintendent of the Jumna canal; he
> had received intimation that a tigress with three cubs had been
> lately seen hovering about his canal rest house, and he
> determined at once to proceed in quest and bring the beast to
> bay: he started in company with a young Civilian and Lieutenant
> St. John, and on arriving on the spot commenced operations for a
> beat – and did that which is always dangerous in the pursuit of
> tigers – followed her on foot; he took however all precautions
> against an accident. Brownlow marshalled his men to various
> points, when almost instantaneously the brute sprung right upon
> him and mauled him very severely. St. John lost not a moment in

proceeding to his friend's assistance – I am sorry to record the young 'Competition Wallah' bolted – and found the tigress actually upon him, knawing [sic] at his very vitals! he fired his rifle, inflicted a severe wound upon her, which made her cease her grip, and then he beat her off his victim with the butt end of his weapon! The brute skulked away and left poor Brownlow lacerated and wounded in a fearful way; he was sent ... to Mussoorie ... and his case was thought so hopeless, that I was warned to be in readiness to command his funeral party, which at that time, it was supposed, would be required on the morrow! but on this occasion he did the doctors, and after months of suffering he partially recovered.

Others were not so lucky and there are several notable tombstones to record their fate – Erskine, McMurdo, Bridges and Humphreys all killed by tigers in the early nineteenth century. Lieutenant-General the Hon. Sir James Charlemagne Dormer, the Commander-in-Chief of the Madras army, was killed by a tiger in 1893 and lies in the Roman Catholic cemetery at Ootacamund. The Hon. Henry Handcock, A.D.C. to the Governor of Madras, met a similar fate in 1858 and is buried in the Church of England cemetery in the same hill-station. Tiger-shooting became the sport of Governors, the new kings of India, and killing a tiger in some unconscious way symbolised the conquest of the mysterious forces of the East. This identification was certainly encouraged by Tippoo, the ruler of Mysore, whose name itself meant 'tiger' and who adopted the tiger as his badge of livery – on his clothes, his furniture, his throne and his weapons. A fanatical Muslim, with a deep-rooted hatred of the infidel British – stemming from the time his father was defeated and humiliated by General Sir Hector Munro – he delighted in decorating his walls with terrifying caricatures of Englishmen being torn to pieces by tigers. He even commissioned a mechanical tiger, now in the Victoria and Albert Museum, which emitted awesome shrieks and growls as it crouched over its English victim, believed to represent the only son of Sir Hector. The young Munro had in reality been killed by a tiger in 1792, and the vivid account which appeared in the *Gentleman's Magazine* a few months later illustrates the aura of dread surrounding the animal at that time:

To describe the awful, horrid and lamentable accident I have been an eye-witness of, is impossible. Mr. Downey, of the Company's troops, Lieut. Pyefinch, poor Mr. Munro and myself, went on shore on Saugor Island to shoot deer. About half-past three we sat down on the edge of the jungle to eat some cold meat sent us from the ship and had just commenced our meal ... when I heard a roar, like thunder, and saw an immense royal tiger spring on the unfortunate Munro, who was sitting down. In a moment his head was in the beast's mouth, and he rushed into the jungle with him, with as much ease as I could lift a kitten, tearing him through the thickest bushes and trees, everything yielding to his monstrous strength ... The human mind cannot form an idea of the scene; it turned my very soul within me. The beast was about four and a half feet high, and nine long. His head appeared as large as an ox's, his eyes darting fire, and his roar, when he first seized his prey, will never be out of my recollection.

A descendant of the victim, Hector Hugh Munro, who achieved literary fame as 'Saki', was obviously influenced by stories of his relative when as a small boy he wrote the limerick:

> There was a young girl called O'Brien
> Who sang Sunday-school hymns to a lion,
>   Of this lady there's some
>   In the lion's tum-tum,
> And the rest is an angel in Zion.

Leopards, or panthers as they were called, could prove as dangerous as tigers, particularly when wounded; as Lieutenant St. John Shaw of the Royal Horse Artillery found to his cost. He was killed by a leopard he had shot and injured while on *shikar* near Nagpore in 1866. The Indian beater who came to his aid killed the beast single-handed with a spear and was rewarded by a plot of land donated by public subscription, which became known as 'Shaw-gunge'.

The variety of animals included in the bag of a day's *shikar* was quite astonishing. Rawlins lists the results of three day's sport in November 1861, in a party of three, using elephants as beaters: '2 tigers, 4 leopards, 3 hyenas, 2 bears, 7 boars, 2 barasinga, 5 cheetal and 6 khakur, beside many peacock and jungle fowl.' The scale of killing seems excessive, but not so long ago many of these animals were a real menace and their destruction a blessing to the Indian peasants, as shown by this random selection of figures from the Hazaribagh District *Gazette* – a District with a population of just over one million at the time:

People killed by:

	Tigers	Leopards	Bears	Wolves	Hyenas	Snakes
1912	16	2	6	86	2	123
1915	57	7	4	3	1	114

If rhinoceros and buffalo are added to the list, as well as wild elephants, the range of beasts hunted and capable of attacking the hunter is almost complete. For instance at Palni, South India in 1875, a Mr. Linnell was killed by a buffalo – in the records as a 'bison' – and there were a number of fatalities inflicted by a charging rhino or elephant.

Another challenging sport where life was staked, often quite recklessly, in the quest for honour and glory, was mountaineering. Many of the highest peaks were just beyond the borders of India, in Nepal and Thibet, so the acts of heroism and the occasional disaster lie outside the scope of this book, but mountain climbing on a minor scale within India still contributed a crop of tragedies, such as Major George Dalhousie J. Raitt, 2nd Queen's Regiment, who died on 28th May 1843 in ascending Mount Abu, aged 35:

This tomb is erected by his brother Officers in token of their esteem and regard for one of the oldest members, whose whole service of 20 years had been in Queens in which also his ancestors had served with distinction.

And Major Minchington at Dharmsala, aged 39, 'who was killed in a climbing accident on the "Mun" on the 3rd June 1927. "And the mountains shall bring peace".'

The variety of 'harmless' sports that took place in the typical up-country town or cantonment in the nineteenth century can be deduced from the casualties in the cemeteries. In the Rajpura cemetery, Delhi, lies Captain William Clayton-Clayton, and the inscription on his monument explains that he died of an accident at polo on 26th December 1876, aged 37 years and 8 months. The imagination conjures up a picture of a particularly wild game of polo on Boxing Day after all the festivities. Mr. Weare of the 9th Regiment met his death horse-racing on the 15th November 1880, as the result of a collision in a foolhardy ride, and the epitaph on the tomb of Captain Andrew Ernest Russell of the Royal Artillery, aged 33, A.D.C. to the Commander-in-Chief, states 'killed by accident on race-course', at Ootacamund.

Hunting with hounds was a surprising recreation to find in the orient, but the British enthusiastically exported as much of their own way of life as they could, and the tradition still lives on in the India of today. The occasional hunting accident could be expected:

Captain Richard William Preston, 1st Bombay Grenadiers, born 19th February 1857, drowned in Kroormund River while out hunting with the Ootacamund hounds, 12th June 1893.

But the cemetery of St. Stephen's Ootacamund, where he lies buried, must be unique in containing the graves of a hunting casualty, an elephant casualty (David Ogilvy Wedderburn of 37th Grenadiers, aged 27, on 2nd September 1853), a tiger casualty (the Hon. Henry Handcock, mentioned earlier), and a race-course casualty (Mr. Weare).

The climate encouraged thoughtless and compulsive swimming in lakes and rivers whenever the opportunity occurred, and there are many graves dotted around India recording the fate of young men who got into difficulties in the unexpected currents; for example:

Private W. Bailey, 1st Bn Connaught Rangers, drowned while bathing at Dehra Gopipur 28th April 1855

and:

H. Prussia, accidentally drowned in the Kangra River April 11 1895, aged 18
'Out of the depths have I cried unto thee, O Lord.'

And there was the tragedy at Government House, Lahore, in one of the first indoor swimming-baths in India, when a young officer, over-enthusiastic for a swim after a hot game of tennis, dived into it empty and was killed.

Sailing was another popular sport in the rare places where it was practicable, such as on the lake at Naini-Tal. There was a legend that the lake belonged to a Hindu goddess who claimed an annual tribute of a human life from those who dared sail on her waters, and it was a sinister fact that fatal sailing accidents occurred almost every year near a rock on which stood a Hindu temple; the bodies of the victims were never recovered.

Boxing, though forbidden, was a common sport among the troops, and at Allahabad is the grave of C. Crooly who was killed in a boxing match in 1806 with a pugilist of no less a name than James Dempsey. Dempsey was charged with manslaughter, and the severity of his sentence reflects contemporary attitudes – one week's detention and a fine of one rupee.

Europeans in India pursued their sports with a desperate disregard for the customs of the country, and the local population was surprised and bewildered by their values – the needless heroism, the unnecessary activity of mind and muscle – when the climate had taught Indians for countless generations that passivity was the answer. On this point there was a real gulf between East and West.

Unusual Accidents

Soda-water was introduced as a popular drink for the hot weather in the early years of the nineteenth century. Advertisers referred to 'the medicinal qualities of this Water ... the most eminent Physicians recommend it ... particularly in calculous complaints and in habitual stranguarie; and it is besides a cool and grateful beverage, particularly adapted for this climate.' Schweppes soda water was imported, while locally prepared soda was sold fractionally cheaper, usually by chemists. It was in the manufacture of this aerated water that a fatal accident occurred at Allahabad on the 4th July 1875 when the explosion of a bottle killed the Chemist, A. Burge.

Another explosion on an altogether vaster scale occurred a short distance down-river at the Hindu religious centre of Benares, when in 1850, at the height of the hot weather, there was a shattering roar among thirty-four Company barges conveying ammunition to the army. Two barges containing gunpowder had exploded and the rest sank. Houses along the river-front were flattened and 818 people were killed. The only reminder of this horrific disaster is the epitaph on the tomb of the solitary European casualty, Mrs. G.B. Small, aged 46, the daughter of Robert 'Cat. H. Cart' (the stonemason's rendering of 'Cathcart'), 'the wife and fellow labourer of the Rev. G. Small, Baptist Minister':

> ... on the night of 1st May, her brief but luminous career on earth was suddenly terminated by a violent and instantaneous explosion of a magazine fleet at Rajghat.

Gunpowder was the cause of another accident at Benares, this time of a harmless domestic nature, as recounted by Cary to his parents in 1862:

> Yesterday, oh, unhappy day, I tried to smoke a snake out of a hollow tree intending to shoot the brute when he came out. I told

the natives to prepare some touch-paper with gunpowder IN water (as I could not get any pure salt-petre); they did and gave it to me, I put it into the hole, applied a light, and puff! my beautiful moustachios (the pride of Bundlekund) were gone, as also one eyebrow, one eyelash and a little of my hair. Oh miserable fate, and now I'm as naked as the day I was born – the brutes had put DRY gunpowder into the paper. I was not hurt but OH! if it had been one eye that I had lost I could have borne it, but my own, my BEAUTIFUL!!!!!! Well, I did not lose my temper, I only looked at them; but when I got home, I assembled my servants, explained what had happened through the careless stupidity of my bearer and chaprassie and then I punished them this way. I got a looking-glass and pair of scissors and cut off the few hairs or stumps that were not quite burnt off, divided them equally in two, wrapped each half most carefully in paper, and gave one to my bearer and one to my chaprassie, and every day they have to bring it to me, the bearer at breakfast time when the other servants are present, and then they have to tell me what they have got, how they got it, through whose carelessness it was burnt, and what their punishment is – natives hate ridicule.

When Cary was not smoking snakes out of holes, he was paying snake-charmers to lure them out with music or firing at them with his gun. His letters home have a hysterical note regarding cobras, kraits and the other venomous snakes:

We have tremendous falls of rain now [August 1860] ... it has brought the snakes out pretty thickly. I killed a most venomous one in my bedroom, one of the most venomous. Perhaps if I had not got up till my usual time, he might have managed to get into my bed.

Snakes! I'm not a fool; two large cobras have come at me when out snipe shooting and paid for it with their lives, I seldom go where I am very likely to meet them without a gun in my hand, and I wear thick what-do-you-call them, antigropelos? If a snake gets into my bed I can't help it, all I hope is, gratitude for warmth would prevent his biting me.

Cary then goes on to relate the case of an Indian who *was* bitten in his bed:

I have just had a man brought to me, dead from a snake bite in

the great toe. He was asleep at the 　ie and never opened his eyes
or moved afterwards. His house is 　ily a quarter of a mile from
mine. I wonder what snake it could 　ıve been, so rapid its effects?
It shows one thing, they do not wait ı., be attacked before biting.

However, it was very rare for a European to be bitten and there are
surprisingly few recorded fatalities. The *Bombay Calendar* mentions
the death of John Hodgson Pearson from snake-bite at Malabar on
the 11th May, 1818. The inquest on the death of Lieutenant
Montague at Colaba in 1839 records that:

> returning from Mess, [he] put his foot in a hole, received a slight
> wound which in 25 minutes carried him off. Some jurors thought
> it was from the bite of a serpent.

And, during the last few years of the British Raj, the Burial Register
at Calcutta records the death from snake-bite of F. Hughes in 1943.

While the horrors of snakes may have been exaggerated, there was
another form of bite which was invariably fatal, that from a 'pagal'
dog, a mad dog. Even to this day, and in spite of all the anti-rabies
serums, once the symptoms of rabies have appeared, there is no
known cure. At the hill-station of Dalhousie, a retreat from the
fevers and diseases of the plains, there is a sad and bitter epitaph
over the grave of wee Willie Walker, aged 2½, who was bitten by a
puppy he was fondling – it later developed hydrophobia, and so did
he (188?):

> Friends take this as a warning.

And at Benares, to show that this terrible affliction was no
discriminator of age or rank, is the tomb of a Colonel who
contracted rabies in 1945 and died in spite of all that medical science
could do.

The hill-stations with their 'khuds', precarious bridges over
raging torrents and overhanging rocks, provided the background for
a number of peculiarly Indian accidents. A casual glance through
the Burial Registers of the small Himalayan churches reveals many,
such as:

> Mr. A. Seale, at Dharmsala, killed by falling over a khud at
> Kunyara on 17th January 1904, aged 52 and 7 months.

> J. Cash, Battalion Sergeant Major, at Chakrata, fell over khud,
> aged 34, in 1904.

W. Blundell, Major, at Landour, both man and pony were killed
when the pony slipped and plunged down the khud in 1834.

And at Simla it is recorded that the Queen's Birthday celebrations
were marred one year when two officers riding one horse were killed:
the pony took fright and threw them over the khud.

Also at Simla is recorded the death of Sir Alexander Lawrence,
son of Sir Henry Lawrence the great administrator and Mutiny
hero, who fell with his horse through a bridge on the Tibet road.
Rawlins records the final leap of a young Miss Salmon, who was
also betrayed by a slender bridge:

> *June 8th 1847.* Pitched on the banks of the Nundakanee River
> where a Miss Salmon met her melancholy death in 1827. The
> bridge was of the usual construction in Kumaon ... Miss Salmon
> and Major H— were very foolishly playing some childish pranks
> when suddenly the bridge gave way.

The log bridge had broken in two and the girl with her companion
'were dashed into a boiling snow torrent from a considerable height',

according to Major John Hearsey, the 'Major H—', in his own account of the accident – the same John Hearsey who commanded Gardner's Horse, and defied the mutineer Mungul Pandy thirty years later with the scornful 'damn his musket':

> I endeavoured to save her, but in vain, and was all but drowned myself. We remained on the bank of this torrent for three days. The body of the young girl was recovered on the third day, fourteen miles lower down ... I had a case made for the body, and her mother with her own hands folded around it a cerement saturated with turpentine got from a neighbouring village. The body was then laid in a mass of pounded charcoal, and the case carried before us in funeral procession for five days until we arrived at the civil station at Hawalbagh, near Almorah, where it was buried in Mrs. Traill's garden there and a tomb erected over it.

The tomb, beneath encircling willows, mentions that Elizabeth Salmon

> was killed through the breaking of the Alpine bridge while she was crossing it on 20th September 1827 at the age of 16 years and 14 days.

The Himalayas, with their vast valleys and towering hills, were constantly reminding the human intruder of his pygmy stature. The incident of a rock falling on the party of young Italian musicians and killing all four of them has already been related (see p. 140). Another similar tragedy occurred at Nurpur in 1846, where the inscription on the tomb narrates:

> C.D.O. Bowen the only son of S. Bowen, Fife Major 56 Regiment Native Infantry ... met his death by a fall from a rock 30th December 1846 aged 14 years 4 months.

These tragedies were made more poignant by occurring in the hill-stations, the summer health-resorts where the women and children were sent to escape the heat and fevers of the Plains.

Another group of accidents was connected with the obsession for faster and faster means of communication. For some reason, incomprehensible to the Eastern mind, Europeans were always in a hurry; whether travelling by palanquin, *ticca gharry*, camel or elephant, they were constantly urging it on. 'Jaldi jao, aur jaldi,

jaldi,' was the usual exhortation for greater speed. *Jaldi* was almost
the first world a European learnt in India. Not that the time saved
was put to any useful purpose, as there was a curious custom of
breaking a long journey at regular intervals for a meal served with
all the dignity and leisure of a dinner-party, using a complete service
of silver and plate and a retinue of servants. Later, in the age of
railways – from 1850 until the Second World War – the train would
often stop at a station and, with the Indian passengers waiting
patiently, the sahibs would sup to their satisfaction.

Unfamiliarity with the methods of transport, lack of carriage
maintenance, and undue haste led to many accidents, a few of them
fatal. A palanquin pole would break, the axle of a pony cart snap –
there was always something going wrong. Stephen Popham met his
death at Conjeeveram in 1795 'by a fall from a curricle'. He was a
Solicitor of the East India Company, a Member of the Irish
Parliament, diamond-trader, cotton-planter in South India with
1,400 employees; he was an architect of the Indian Police Force, and
'Popham's Broadway' in Madras City is named after him. Almost a
century later, in 1877, a Commander of the P. and O. fleet, Captain
G.F. Henry, was thrown from his carriage in Bombay and died of
his injuries.

Steamships were well established by then, but they had had a
struggle, beginning with S.S. *Enterprise* which reached Calcutta in
1825. Disasters off the coast of India were common. The surf off
Madras was 'the greatest in the world, there scarcely passes a
monsoon without the loss of several lives', wrote an Officer on
H.M.S. Caroline in 1803. The East Indiaman *Lord William Bentinck*
went aground off Bombay in 1840 with the loss of all the women and
children and eighty troops. And, in modern times, five ships were
sunk off Bombay on German mines – laid by the cruiser *Emden* in
1917 – with the loss of many lives.

Railways were a special feature of Anglo-India. In 1846 it was
prophesied by a railway engineer that they would be the only real
contribution of the West to India and the railway network would be
the finest memorial of the British Raj. They began to be built in the
1850s, primarily for strategical reasons, for more rapid troop
movements across the sub-continent; 28,000 miles of track had been
laid by 1905. It was laid out with careful regard for religious
susceptibilities, skirting a Hindu Raja's territory so that the beef-
eating sahibs would not pollute his land. The railways were soon
taken over by the caste-conscious masses, who struggled to fill every
inch of space regardless of their orthodoxy. A train crash near
Bombay in the 1880s resulted in the death of a European passenger

and the accident was recorded by Douglas, the local historian:

> Poor Howard was killed. The gentleman next him, extricating himself (besmeared with blood) from the debris of the broken train, was confronted by his servant, weeping bitterly, and bearing in his hand the fragments of a cigar-box, the cause of all his loud lamentations.

John Pethers fell off the engine at Mirzapore and was killed; and the mother and daughter of the Standen family were run down by an engine near Allahabad in 1922. The 'husband, father, sons and brothers' had these curious words inscribed on their joint tomb – perhaps as a curse on the engine-driver:

> 'Vengeance is mine, saith the Lord, I will repay.'

The Railway Officers had their own separate cemetery, so did the Road Superintendents in the Public Works Department, and the canal officials; all spreading communications into the hinterland of India and leaving small clusters of graves behind as they advanced.

> And the end of the fight
> Is a tombstone white
> With the name of the late deceased
> And the epitaph drear
> 'A fool lies here
> Who tried to Hustle the East.'
>
> > (Kipling, *The Naulakha*)

Natural Calamities

The gigantic scale of the Himalayas, the thousands of miles of unrelieved flatness of the Plains, and the extremes of climate, with months of drought followed by a few weeks of torrential rain, make India a land prone to natural disaster. Between the 16th and 19th of September, 1880, twenty-five inches of rain had been recorded at the hill-station of Naini-Tal and the European residents at the Victoria Hotel, overlooking the lake of the vengeful goddess, were becoming bored with the unremitting rainfall which prevented any outdoor activity. Suddenly the whole building began to move down the hill. At that moment, at the height of the storm, an earthquake set off a second landslide and the hotel, Assembly Rooms, Library, Orderly Room and Mr. Bell's shop were hurtled into the lake. One hundred

and fifty-one people were killed, including 43 Europeans, and a monument was erected to their memory with the words:

> They died according to the word of the Lord and he buried them in this valley.

The local Hindus, and the superstitious among the surviving Europeans, believed that the goddess was punishing the invasion of her thousands of years privacy.

The climate, in the form of wind, was the cause of another major building collapse in 1846 when a terrific storm swept over Ludhiana and flattened the whole range of barracks, including the hospital, burying men, women and children in the ruins. Fifty men, 16 women and 17 children 'of Her Majesty's 50th Regiment ... were killed by the falling of the Barracks on 20th May, 1846', and 135 people were seriously injured. This tragedy was deepened by the fact that the men had just come through four of the most sanguinary battles of the Sikh wars, probably some of the hardest-fought battles in the history of British arms. The inscription refers to the irony of events, before listing the names of the dead:

> This tablet is erected by the comrades of the deceased Non-Commissioned Officers and men who shared with them the dangers and glories of the four victories of the campaign of the Sutledge, as a slight token of deep sorrow and commiseration they feel for the sufferers by the melancholy accident.

As well as gales, those unforgettable tropical storms held another danger: lightning accounted for a number of deaths each year, and sometimes Europeans were among the victims. G.C. Aubert, aged 26, was killed near Calcutta on 29th April 1843 when horse and rider were struck by lightning. Another victim was H. Collis, killed on the 2nd of March 1865; the inscription on his tomb at Nawadah cemetery in Darbhanga District states that

> he was travelling to his factory on an elephant, which during a stormy and rainy day was struck by lightning, and fainting away was severely burnt by the ignited trappings in which he was enveloped, as a shelter from the rain. He died a few days after at Nawadah factory.

Floods, caused by storm-waters rushing down the usually dry river beds and overflowing on to the plains, caught many of even the most experienced travellers unawares. Colonel J. Wharton was drowned with his horse and dog in 1802 and a tomb was erected at the spot, near Kanauj, which became a landmark for river traffic and was regularly whitewashed each year. Mr. St. George, a Resident Engineer, was drowned in 1859 while crossing a flooded valley.

Torrential rain, lightning, storms and floods followed by long periods of drought – these extremes of weather were to be expected in India; but occasionally there was a natural event, such as a cyclone or earthquake, of such devastating magnitude that it dwarfed everything else. The years 1737 and 1837 were memorable for cyclones which wrought tremendous damage in Calcutta and around the Bay of Bengal, with a high toll of Indian lives. Another cyclone caused enormous damage in 1854, and 1864 became the year of the 'Great Cyclone' when the town of Masulipatam was almost totally destroyed with fearful loss of life. Comparatively few Europeans died in this holocaust, which in Calcutta alone flattened 90,000 dwellings; it is ironic that the only memorial to the Indian dead should be inscribed on a European monument, dedicated to nine members of a family by one of the survivors, who, as the inscriptions says, 'caused this pillar to be erected on the very spot where his relatives perished (which for years had been their happy home) to perpetuate the remembrance of this awful event'.

> This monument commemorates the melancholy fate of Anthony and Mary Fruvall and their sons Joseph, Michael, Peter, Manuel and David, their daughter Mary Ann Honey and her children

Joseph and Georgiana and about 30,000 souls who were
unexpectedly swept into eternity by the ocean wave which
desolated this town on the night of the cyclone of 1st November
1864.

'Oh ye seas and rivers bless ye the Lord, praise and exalt him
above all for ever.'   (Daniel III 78)

Another tombstone refers more simply to:

Mrs. M. Jamieson, age 62 years, 10 months, 8 days ... and her
grand-children

Mary, aged 7 ⎫   Children of J.E. Kellie,
Jessie, aged 5 ⎬   Inspecting Postmaster
James, aged 4 ⎭

who all perished in the inundation on the night of Nov. 1st 1864.

Earthquakes added to the possibilities of unexpected death.
Moderate shocks occurred regularly and were part of the experience
of most of those who lived any length of time in India. At Cutch
between the 16th of June and the 23rd of November 1819 over 100
earthquakes of varying severity were reported. In 1905, a serious
earthquake was felt over several hundred miles of the Himalayas.
Lives were lost at Landour, Mussoorie, Chakrata and at Dharmsala
where over 200 Gurkha soldiers were killed. The tower of the
Dharmsala church of St. John's in the Wilderness was cast to the
ground, and the new church at Mussoorie which was nearing
completion was totally destroyed, killing a number of the workmen
and causing superstitious rumours that the earthquake was an
expression of their gods' anger at the building of the White Sahibs'
church. More than 20 Europeans were killed by this earthquake at
Dharmsala, including three members of the Indian Civil Service,
and this singularly appropriate quotation is inscribed on the tomb of
Captain James Muscroft of the 1st Gurkha Rifles:

'We will not fear, though the earth be moved and though the hills
be carried into the midst of the sea.'

The last great earthquake occurred in May 1935 at Quetta; one of
the victims was brought to Amritsar and lies buried in the Roman
Catholic cemetery, whose Burial Register notes:

Victor Bonta, aged 25, died in Quetta Earthquake; 3rd July 1936.

Murders, Duels and Suicides

The East provided contagions and infections, fevers and diseases, wild animals and snakes, cyclones and earthquakes on a scale outside the normal European experience; yet a large proportion of deaths were the direct result of man's own agency. As if nature were not a great enough destroyer on her own, man had to lend a hand through assassination, duelling and suicide, not to mention riots, battles and mutinies, to swell the number in the already overstocked graveyards.

Although duelling was illegal, there are records of many fatal duels in India down to the middle of the nineteenth century, often involving important public persons. Dr. Johnson defended the custom – 'its barbarous violence was more justifiable than war, in which thousands went forth, without any cause of personal quarrel, to massacre each other' – but it seems a senseless way to die. The cause was often gambling or some slight to the family honour. In 1787 a duel took place in Calcutta between 'Mr. G., an attorney-at-law, and Mr. A; the former was killed on the spot', and the newspaper report went on to comment that the quarrel originated over a gambling debt. Colonel Henry Hervey Aston, of the 12th Regiment of Foot, a friend of the Prince of Wales, was killed in a duel at Madras on the 23rd December 1798. He was a noted duellist and an unerring shot. The day before his fatal duel he had been 'called out' by Major Picton, brother of the Waterloo hero; when Picton's shot missed, the Colonel fired in the air. In his last duel he adopted the same policy of letting his antagonist, Major Allen, fire first; and as he received the fatal shot he again fired his own pistol in the air, declaring: 'My last act shall not be one of revenge.' His magnanimous action is referred to on his epitaph at Masulipatam Fort:

Lamented shade! Pupil of spotless truth
First in the ranks of honor's ardent youth
Thy generous soul, magnanimous in death,
Stamps on our hearts who caught thy latest breath
Our country's loss. But while we mourn the doom
That sinks untimely Aston to the tomb
The worth to which we consecrate this grave
Shall waft thy spirit to the good and brave.

Both the Majors were tried by Court Martial and 'admonished', and

Major Allen, the Paymaster, never held his head up again, dying of
fever three months later.

.Near Madras, at Arni, a 65-foot monument was erected by
Colonel Urban Vigors to the man he had just killed in a duel,
Colonel Robert Kelly. Vigors, in conversation with his wife, had
referred to Kelly as 'an old woman'; she repeated the words to Mrs.
Kelly, who insisted that her husband should obtain satisfaction. The
inscription describing this totally unnecessary death reads:

> Sacred to the memory of Colonel Robert Kelly, who departed this
> life in the vicinity of Arnee, September 29 A.D. 1790 aet: 52.
>   This monument was erected by Lt-Colonel Urban Vigors as a
> mark of respect for a gallant soldier.

.At times deaths from duelling were recorded as being from
'cholera' to avoid any repercussions from the legal authorities. An
example of this occurred at Poona in 1842, with all the bitter
undertones of the Irish problem. A young officer called Sarsfield, a
member of an old Catholic family, whose ancestor was a General
under James II at the siege of Londonderry, was posted as a
subaltern of nineteen to join the 27th Foot (the Inniskillings), a
regiment from the north of Ireland who were all Protestants. An
argument arose in the Officers' Mess and he was challenged to a
duel, which he at first avoided by tendering an apology. Cold-
shouldered and ostracised by his brother officers for this
'cowardice', he lived with the situation for three long months, until
his self-control snapped and he deliberately dashed the contents of
his wine glass into his original challenger's face. A duel inevitably
followed and he was killed. His family sent his brother out to
investigate the cause of death, recorded as 'cholera', but the matter
was never satisfactorily resolved.

Indians had their own more civilised, if more noisy, methods of
resolving personal disputes. The two parties joined in an insult-
hurling ceremony, a 'Kabi', either partaking themselves or hiring a
professional 'Kabi-wallah' to represent them, while a crowd
gathered round to judge which of the two was the master of abuse,
vituperation and scurrilous verses.

.Suicide seemed an unnecesary act when the climate was as likely
as not to do the work for you if given half the chance, yet there was a
definite suicidal tendency at certain times of the year. The *Calcutta
Gazette* in September 1787 commented on the unusually high rate of
suicides among cadets. 'To what cause to impute this melancholy
disposition we know not, nor can we pretend to say whether in any

respect it may be ascribed to the climate.' Whether from this cause, or from loneliness, distance from home, or the cumulative effects of endemic complaints such as hepatitis, there are a surprising number of 'suicide's graves'. A suicide's corpse was usually buried just outside the boundaries of the consecrated cemetery, and in some cases, as in Meerut, the little plot of land with a cluster of graves was even called 'the suicide's cemetery'. Near Darjeeling at Senchal is a similar small plot of land, also known as 'suicide cemetery' or 'God's acre'; here it must have been the elevation rather than the heat which affected the mind, as the Cantonment stands at a height of nearly 9,000 feet with a superb view on a clear day of the greatest Himalayan peaks including Mount Everest. Perhaps the isolated situation of the barracks, and the cold winters and months on end shrouded in cloud, had a depressing influence. Whatever the reasons, at least ten suicide victims are buried in this cemetery, several of whom committed mass-suicide on the same day. After this incident the Cantonments were moved. An inscription declares the cemetery to be

> Sacred to the memory of the Officers, N.C.O.s and men who died at Senchal during the years 1844-1865 and whose mortal remains rest in this cemetery.

> 'I know that my Redeemer liveth.'

Outside the Fort of Seringapatam is the 'Scott Bungalow', still preserved with its furniture from the time of the tragedy in 1817 when Colonel Scott, the Commandant, reputedly drowned himself on returning to find his wife and daughter dead. The incident is captured in these verses in *Lays of Ind* by 'Aliph Cheem', the *nom de plume* of Captain Yeldham:

> There stands on the isle of Seringapatam
>   By the Cauvery, eddying fast
>   A bungalow lonely
>   And tenanted only
>   By memories of the past.
> It has stood, as though under a curse and spell
> Untouched since the year that Tippoo fell.
>
> The mouldering rooms are now as they stood
>   Near eighty years ago.
>   The piano is there
>   And table and chair

And the carpet rotting slow
And the bed whereon the corpses lay
And the curtains half time-mawed away.

Murders and political assassinations punctuated the history of the
British Raj, reminding the administrators, however well-meaning
and paternalistic, that the Westerner was in India as a foreign
invader. Cherry at Benares, Ellis at Patna, two Agents of the
Governor-General, were massacred in the eighteenth century; Earl
Mayo, the Viceroy, was murdered in 1872 and a few months earlier
the Chief Justice was killed on the steps of the High Court; a
Governor-elect of Bombay and Envoy to Afghanistan, MacNaghten,
was assassinated at Kabul and also a later Envoy, Cavagnari;
attempts were made on the life of the Governor of the Punjab in 1930
– shot at and wounded – and the Governor of Bengal in 1938, the
bullets killing some of his entourage; a bomb was thrown at the
Viceroy in 1912, killing the attendant sitting immediately behind
him on the State elephant; and another bomb exploded under the
Viceroy's train in 1929. Even when enjoying retirement in England,
these high officials were not immune from such attacks; O'Dwyer, a
former Governor of the Punjab, was shot dead by an Indian in
London in 1940. Statistically these murders were not very
significant, when seen over the long period of time and the vastness
of the country administered, but they occurred suddenly, without
warning, and had a disturbing influence on the outwardly calm
Anglo-Indian scene. The District Officer and District Magistrate,
who of all officials were in closest touch with the native population,
were from their very isolation the most exposed to the danger of
sudden death at the hand of extremists. Three magistrates in
succession were murdered at Midnapore in the early 1930s. F.E.
Moore, a Deputy Commissioner at Rohtak, near Delhi, died on the
6th August 1877, as his tomb explains, 'from wounds received from
a fanatic while sleeping'. Henry Valentine Conolly, the Collector
and Magistrate of Malabar was murdered at 9 p.m. on 11th
September 1855 by members of a fanatical Muslim sect, the
'Moplahs', while he was sitting on the verandah with his wife. His
epitaph records that

his European and native friends in Malabar, loving and admiring
his public and private virtues, have united to raise this slight
memorial of his eminent worth and Christian character.

His brother, Arthur, was beheaded in prison at Bokhara in 1840·

brother Edward was killed in action at Kohistan in 1842 and another brother, John, fell at the capture of Kabul the same year – not an uncommon pattern of family tragedy for those days. Then there were the numerous murders of Political Officers on the North-West Frontier and in the sensitive Provinces, still administratively unsettled, where British power was trying to extend and consolidate its influence. A monument at Multan is typical of this kind of murder and the reaction it provoked among the tough Victorian administrators and soldiers. On it are inscribed these words:

On this, the farthest frontier of the British Empire, which their deaths extended, lie the remains of

> Peter Vans Agnew   .   William Anderson
> of the Bengal   Lieut. 1st Bombay
> Civil Service   Fusilier Regt.

Who, being deputed by the Resident at Lahore, whose assistants they were to relieve Dewan Moolraj (Viceroy of Mooltan under the Sikh Empire) ... were ... with a signal breach of national faith and private hospitality, most barbarously murdered in the Eedgah, under the walls of Mooltan.

Thus fell these two young public servants, full of youth, rare talents, high hopes, and promise of utility; even in their death doing their country honor. Covered with wounds, they could not resist, but hand-in-hand awaited the onset of a bloodthirsty rabble: calmly foretelling the day when 'thousands of Englishmen should come there to avenge their death, and destroy Moolraj, his army, and his fortress'.

History recalls how the prophecy was fulfilled. After two separate sieges, the Fort of Mooltan was surrendered to the British troops, and the bodies of the two murdered Officers (which had been treated with the most savage indignities) were, in all righteous vengeance, carried through the breach made by the British guns, and buried, with military honours, on the summit of the citadel.

'Thousands of Englishmen' stood round the grave.

Dewan Moolraj was brought to trial at Lahore, convicted of murder, and sentenced to be hanged: but was recommended to mercy, and finally ordered to be transported for life.

His rebellion was followed by an insurrection of the Sikh people, and brought on the second Sikh war; which resulted in the annexation of the Punjab ... and the restoration of peace, after many years of anarchy ...

Thus did an overruling providence bring good out of evil.

The Englishman who ventured beyond the boundaries of the Company's jurisdiction did so at his own risk. The early mercenaries were particularly vulnerable, and if they fell out of favour with their Indian masters were liable to summary execution in accordance with the prevailing standards of the time. Vickers, Ryan and Dodd were decapitated by Jaswant Rao in 1803 for refusing to lead his Mahratta troops against the Company's forces; Hamilton, a prisoner of Tippoo, was executed on the grounds that the fortifications which he had been ordered to construct were not impregnable. As no other weapon was at hand, he was beheaded with a shoe-maker's knife. A pair of compasses engraved with his initials was found in the possession of an Indian carpenter thirty years later and led to the identification of his unmarked grave. A century later in 1891 Quinton was barbarously beheaded by the public executioner of the small State in Assam to which he had been sent on a mission by the government of India. Bird, who elected to stay behind on the Andaman Islands when they were occupied by the Japanese during the Second World War, was executed with a sword.

The standards of Eastern justice and Eastern punishments had remained constant for centuries while Western standards were undergoing rapid change under the influence of humanitarianism. But there were many inconsistencies in this pattern. The *Calcutta Chronicle* of 19th February 1789 published a gruesome discription of the carrying out of a sentence on a gang of dacoits or robbers found guilty of burglary by a Native Court; one hand and one foot were amputated and the limb dipped in boiling ghee or fat. More than half of them survived. Contrast this to the sentence meted out by an English judge on a gang of five European robbers – English, Portuguese and Italian – captured after burgling a rich Indian merchant's house on the night of 18th February 1795; all were hanged. The Moghul Courts were familiar with mutilation, flogging and a variety of horrible ways of execution, including lashing to death. The Company made mutilation illegal in 1793, and temporarily abolished flogging in the Indian Army during the Governor-Generalship of William Bentinck in the 1830s – a period of enlightenment which also saw a decline in the Hindu practices of suttee and infanticide. Ironically, flogging still remained in the British Army for another forty years, and the 'civilised' Victorians were still blowing mutineers from guns in 1860.

Mutinies and Mass Memorials

Deaths arising from religious and political misunderstandings, as far as they affected large groups of 'unthinking' men under orders in battles, mutinies and revolts, are often commemorated by a monument above a mass grave, or simply by an inscription recording the heroic deeds of men whose bones lie scattered over the Indian plains.

> They braced their belts about them
> They crossed in ships the sea
> They sought and found six feet of ground
> And there they died for me.
>
> (A. E. Housman)

The first great battle the British fought in India – considered by some authorities as one of the decisive battles of the world – was at Plassey in 1757, and yet the total of British dead was under 30. A mound was built over their grave, and a monument erected on it to commemorate the fact that the fate of Bengal, and through it the rest of India, was settled here for the next two hundred years. One hundred and fifty years later, at the height of British imperialism, Lord Curzon the Viceroy erected a second memorial at Plassey to keep the event fresh in men's minds. A British regiment, the 2nd Dorsets, recorded the presence of their men – then the 39th Foot – at Plassey by the placing of a silver plaque in St. John's Church, Calcutta.

Outside this church stands a domed pavilion over fifty feet high, with twelve pillars, to commemorate the casualties of the Rohilla wars of 1774 and 1794 which consolidated the hold of the Company on Bengal. The inscription merely records the names of fourteen officers who were killed in the second campaign. An obelisk of red sandstone still stands on the site of the last battle, near Fatehganj village, Bareilly, to Colonel George Barrington, officers and men who fell in this action.

Disasters as well as successes attended British arms. A detachment of some 3,000 men under Colonel Baillie were surrounded and almost annihilated near Conjeeveram in South India in 1780. Of 86 British officers engaged, only 16 surrendered unwounded, and two lofty obelisks are all that remain to mark the deaths of the dozens of officers killed. This defeat was avenged by General Eyre Coote the following year at the battle of Porto Novo, but not without heavy casualties among the British force, which consisted of 2,000 Europeans and 6,000 sepoys. A historian has commented: 'If a moment was to be named when the existence of the British power depended upon its native troops, we should fix upon the Battle of Porto Novo.' Coote was so impressed by the courage shown by the 73rd Highlanders on the same occasion that he presented them with a sum of money to purchase a 'pipe of silver' in honour of the day.

The battle of Assaye in 1803 marked another great turning-point in the domination of India by the East India Company; its small well-drilled forces were often outnumbered by ten to one but had the advantage of inspired leadership and artillery. The Mahrattas were decisively defeated after a bitter and hard-fought struggle in which the British suffered comparatively heavy casualties, amounting to about 400. General Wellesley was in command, and when in later years after Waterloo he was asked the hardest fight he had been in, he replied without hesitation 'Assaye'. The British dead were buried north of the fort of Assaye and a memorial plaque to the officers and men of the Highland Light Infantry who fell in the battle has been erected in the low wall surrounding the burial-place. This is all that remains to be seen, apart from the one solitary grave of an Officer, Colonel Maxwell, whose personality was such that he became the patron saint of Assaye village. He was referred to as 'Ussell Sahib', and his grave was kept clean and decked with marigolds on special occasions. This cult of heroes was not confined to the local population. The British tended to erect ostentatious monuments to commemorate outstanding officers killed in battle, with scant reference to the men they commanded who fell beside them, and generals regarded the loss of a brilliant officer commanding a key unit as a major tactical disaster. For example, on the field of Assaye, when Wellesley heard that Colonel Maxwell had been killed, he declared 'I would rather have lost a Brigade than have lost Maxwell' – and meant it.

Another action against the Mahrattas fifteen years later was called by a contemporary writer 'the Indian Thermopylae'. At the small village of Koregaon a British force of 500 sepoys, 250 newly raised irregular cavalry and two six-pounder guns served by 24 European gunners, under a Sergeant and a Lieutenant, withstood odds of over forty to one after a forced march of 27 miles. An obelisk 70-feet high on the river-bank opposite the village has an inscription on the north and south sides in Mahratti and on the west side in English:

This column is erected to commemorate the defence of Coregaum by a detachment commanded by Captain Staunton of the Bombay Establishment which was surrounded on the 1st January 1818 by the Peshwa's whole army under his personal command and withstood throughout the day a series of the most obstinate and sanguinary assaults of his best troops.

Captain Staunton, under the most appalling circumstances, persevered in his desperate resistance, and seconded by the unconquerable spirit of his detachment, at length achieved the signal discomfiture of the enemy and accomplished one of the proudest triumphs of the British army in the East.

To perpetuate the memory of the brave troops to whose heroic firmness and devotion it owes the glory of that day the British Government has directed the names of their Corps and of the killed and wounded to be inscribed on this monument.

Battles took place at each corner of India as the Company's Empire extended to protect their trade in the three Presidencies of Bengal, Madras and Bombay. Plassey and Rohilla wars in Bengal; Wandewash and Seringapatam in the south, against Hyder Ali and Tippoo his son, the Tiger of Mysore; Assaye, Koregaon and the engagements of the Pindarry wars against the Mahrattas in the west; wars against the Gurkha kingdoms in the north and finally the fiercest battles of all against the Sikhs in 1845 and 1846. Obelisks were erected to mark each main encounter; at Mudki – 18th December 1845; at Ferozeshah – 21st and 22nd December 1845, when the British army lost nearly 2,500 officers and men including five aides-de-camp of the Governor-General killed and four wounded; at Aliwal on the 26th January 1846; and at Sobraon, one of the last battles, on 10th February 1846, when over 300 British troops were killed and 2,000 wounded. After hundreds of major and minor battles, skirmishes and desperate encounters against Indian troops and cavalry over the length and breadth of the continent – some commemorated in lofty monuments, many forgotten and unsung – the Company emerged as the only military power in the land. Henceforth the battles were fought on the extreme frontiers, against the tribesmen of the North-West Frontier and those on the border between Assam and Burma; while in India a new battle was being contested – over men's minds. Indians could choose between an acceptance of the Pax Brittanica with all its material benefits, bought at the price of disturbing age-old customs and beliefs, or a refusal to bow to the West and submit to a permanent feeling of cultural and racial inferiority. Out of this conflict sprang the great

Mutiny of 1857 and the nationalist revolt.

There had been many mutinies and massacres of Europeans in India before the great Mutiny. One of the earliest recorded massacres, at Onore, illustrates the cleavage between Western and Eastern culture that had developed over hundreds of years:

> In 1670 the chief of the English factory got a fine English bulldog from the captain of a ship. After the ship was gone, the factory, consisting of eighteen persons, were going a hunt and carried the bulldog with them, and passing through the town the dog seized a cow devoted to the pagoda and killed her. Upon which the priests raised a mob, who murdered the whole factory. But some natives who were friends of the English made a large grave and buried them all in it. The chief of Karwar sent a stone to be put on the grave with the inscription, 'That this is the burial-place of John Best with seventeen Englishmen who were sacrificed to the fury of a mad priesthood and an enraged mob.'

How were the English to know about the religious susceptibilities of the Hindus who set the life of a cow above a human life? And how were the Hindus to understand the enthusiasm amounting almost to fanaticism with which the English pursued their hunting activities with horses and dogs? There were many such misunderstandings, often with tragic results, springing from a mutual love-hate relationship of two incompatible cultures. Genuine friendship between individuals of the different races was rare. Admiration and loyalty were balanced against fear and superstition; a religion based on history came up against one more mystical and philosophical. The introductory handshake, instinctive to a Westerner, was contamination to the Brahmin. When anything was changed the motives were suspect: a new uniform with cross-bands was interpreted as having Christian significance; orders to travel over the seas, the *kala pani* or black water, to Burma or other dependencies, were directly contrary to their sacred creed. Mutinies of various seriousness occurred at fairly regular intervals throughout the period of British occupation for these and similar, often imagined, grievances. At Vellore in south India two European companies of 14 officers and 113 men were wiped out by sepoys one night in July 1806, the superficial cause being an order to wear a new style turban and train beards in a particular way, and prohibiting caste-marks on the forehead. There had been a number of mutinies earlier, sometimes simultaneously with white troops over pay and conditions, and it is tempting to surmise that the technique of organised disobedience was learnt from the proud and independent sons of Shakespeare. The 34th Native Infantry mutinied in 1844, the 22nd Native Infantry in 1849, the 66th in 1850, and the 38th in 1852. In the year of the Mutiny, which broke out in June 1857, there had been earlier rumblings at Dum Dum in January and at Barrackpore in March. There was therefore a long background of spasmodic outbreaks, usually put down ruthlessly with the ring-leaders being publicly executed and the regiment disbanded. The great Mutiny, however, bore the marks of a planned revolt on a national scale, although its main effect was confined to the recently-annexed province of Oudh. The churches and churchyard cemeteries of almost every town and outpost in that part of India bear evidence of the massacres that took place – Agra; Aligarh; Azamgarh; Banda; Bareilly; Benares; Cawnpore; Delhi (the key beseiged city); Fatehgarh; Ghaziabad; Jhansi (where the mutineers thoughtfully buried men and women in separate mass graves); Lucknow (of Residency defence fame); Manikpur; Meerut (where it all started); Muttra; Shahjahanpur; and so on. A few of the epitaphs are bitter and retributive – 'Vengeance is mine, I will repay, saith the Lord', at Cawnpore, and 'Awake and stand up to judge my quarrel, avenge thou my cause, my God and Lord' at Meerut. Some reflect the underlying religious tension: 'He died as a Christian hero,' at Etawah. Many show a quiet acceptance of God's will: 'Though He slays me, yet will I trust Him', to Judge Thornhill, his wife and two children at Cawnpore. Some keep a lively faith in the future, such as this to J. P. Barrett, Collector of the Toll-Bar, at Allahahbad:

I am killed here, leaving my beloved children and friends behind committed to the protection and guardianship of my Redeemer, to battle in the pilgrimage of this dark world.

Typical of the mass memorials is this one at the Well of Cawnpore:

Sacred to the perpetual memory of a great company of Christian people, chiefly women and children, who near this spot were cruelly massacred by the followers of the rebel Nana Dhoondopunt, of Bithoor, and cast, the dying with the dead into the well below on the 15th day of July, MDCCCLVII.

'Our bones are scattered at the grave's mouth as when one cutteth and cleaveth wood upon the earth. But our eyes are unto thee, O God, the Lord.'

(Psalm CXLI)

The extent to which God's hand was seen in the terrible events of 1857 is reflected in some of the official prayers which were printed to be read out to the European Christian congregations in July when the whole safety and future of Englishmen in India hung in the balance:

O most powerful and gracious Lord God ... we make our address to Thy Divine Majesty in this our present season of disquietude, when evil and misguided men have, in many places of this land, risen up against their just and lawful rulers, and have treacherously and cruelly taken away the lives of those whom they were bound to serve and to defend, drawing down upon themselves the guilt of rebellion and of blood, and spreading confusion, and distress, and fear, where Thy servants, whom Thou hadst set over them, were seeking to promote only order, and equity, and happiness.

O Lord, our eyes are up unto Thee; take Thou the cause into Thine own hand, and judge between us and these sons of violence; let not their mischievous imagination prosper; stir up Thy strength, O Lord, and come and help us, for Thou canst save by many or by few; rebuke the madness of the people, and stay the hand of the destroyer ...

Teach the natives of British India to know their mercies, and to prize those right and equal laws which by Thy good Providence Thou hast given them through the supremacy of our Christian land ...

If it be Thy good pleasure, establish our Empire in this land on a surer basis than ever heretofore; and above all, make it the blessed means of advancing every where the kingdom of Thy Son.

After 1857, there was still the occasional outbreak of violence among the civil population, and an occasional mutiny in the army, although this was not always confined to Indian troops. In 1920 there broke out what became known as the Jullundur rebellion, a mutiny among the Connaught Rangers, whose Irish nationalism was aroused when they were involved in suppressing the emergent and militant Indian nationalism. It occurred at the height of the hot weather in June, as nearly every other major mutiny in India had done, when self-control under the intense and stultifying heat of the barrack-room reached breaking point. The men refused to parade until Ireland had been given her freedom; officers trying to address their men were shouted down, jostled and threatened with violence. Ironically, it was a nearby Indian army unit that was ordered to cordon off the Connaught's barracks, such was the complete confidence in their loyalty, a confidence which was to be justified time and time again down to the last days of the Raj. Five months later, with the minimum of publicity, this terse statement was issued by Headquarters, New Delhi, as the only epitaph for Private James Daly, the ring-leader, who lay in Grave No.340 in Dagshai Cemetery, one of the last British soldiers to be executed for mutiny in peacetime:

His Excellency the Commander-in-Chief regrets to announce that serious cases of mutiny occurred in the 1st Battalion, The Connaught Rangers, between 28 June and 2 July 1920, at Jullundur and Solon in consequence of which 69 non-commissioned officers and men were brought to trial on charges of varying degrees of mutiny. Of these, 61 were found guilty and eight were acquitted. Of those found guilty, 14 were sentenced to death by being shot.

In the case of one private the sentence of death was carried into execution at daybreak on November 2 1920.

In the case of the remainder the death sentence was commuted to penal servitude for life and less.

The remoteness of India from the eyes of the world was soon to disappear under the publicity gained by the Indian nationalists, though there were fortunately few mass graves, thanks to the 'non-violent' campaigns of Mahatma Gandhi. There had been the Kuka rising in 1872, leaving behind a monument in the little church at Palampur to those Europeans killed by the fanatics; and the massacre of Quinton, the Chief Commissioner at Shillong, with his officers and escort in 1891. Then immediately after the First World War there had been the outbreak of violence at Amritsar, the Punjab rebellion, in which several Europeans had perished, followed by the tragic over-reaction in suppressing it; and in 1921 the Moplah rebellion in Malabar, the most serious since the Mutiny, in which thousands of Hindus were murdered by Muslim fanatics and over 2,000 Muslims killed by the forces of law and order, with several European casualties, including two assistant superintendents of police – W.J. Rowley and C.B. Lancaster. There had been the occasional incident in an Indian army regiment of a soldier running amuck and killing a British officer, such as the shooting in cold blood of first Major W.C.S. Haycraft and then Captain P.J.W. McClenaghan in 1929 and 1930, both of the 8th Punjab Regiment and holders of the Military Cross.

One of the last British casualties, as the curtain came down on the British Raj, was a young Lieutenant who tried to keep the peace between the Sikh and Muslim communities immediately after the formal declaration of Independence. The Burial Register at the Putligarh cemetery, Amritsar, records:

Lt. William Morley – killed by rioters on 22nd September 1947.

Another group of mass-graves which Britain was proud to leave behind was of those that died in comparatively recent times while trying to improve the living conditions of thousands of poor and hungry Indians. For instance, at Katni in central India is a monument to nine officers of the civil administration who died in 1896-97 while on famine relief duties. This was after two disastrous years of drought due to failure of the monsoon followed by a year of exceptional late rain washing out the freshly planted crops. It was estimated that one in six of the population of the Province died from malnutrition, starvation and cholera.

Death, in one form or another, was never very far away; and even the tombstones, intended to be a lasting memorial, were often damaged or destroyed – if not by the climate, then by the indigenous peepul tree, regarded by the Hindus as sacred. In the words of Colonel Sleeman:

No wonder that superstition should have consecrated this tree, beautiful and delicate as it is, to the gods. The palace, the castle, the temple, and the tomb, all those works which man is most proud to raise, to spread, and to perpetuate his name, crumble to dust beneath her withering grasp. She rises triumphant over them all in her lofty beauty, bearing, high in air, amidst her light green foliage, fragments of the wreck she has made, to show the nothingness of man's greatest efforts.

Appendix A
Funeral Customs of Mohammedans, Hindus and Parsees

The contrast between some of the funeral customs, graves and monuments of the European community in India, and those of their own kind in the Europe they had left behind, illustrates the extent to which they were influenced by the oriental conditions and circumstances. Funerals held at night, the speed of burials, commemorative lights on tombs and the massive monuments – some in Grecian style, some Saracenic, some Muslim, some Hindu – reveal a connection with Eastern burial customs which deserves closer examination.

The link with Mohammedanism through a common belief in the 'resurrection of the body' and the 'day of judgment' provided an identical motive for erecting permanent monuments of such size and ostentation – if one was rich enough – as to be proof against decay. The Rev. J. Ovington, a chaplain in His Majesty's Service who published his voyage to Surat in 1689, writes:

> The English and all the Europeans are privileged with convenient repositories for their dead within half a mile of the city. There they endeavour to outvie each other in magnificent structures and stately monuments, whose large extent and beautiful architecture and aspiring heads make them visible at a remote distance, lovely objects to the sight, and give them the title of the principal ornaments and magnificencies of the city.

Later, in the middle of the nineteenth century, an account of the Surat cemeteries was published by Bellasis which described the most important tombs in detail with their stately towers and minarets, and went on to remark:

> It would be tedious to describe the many other mausoleums which crowd the English and Dutch cemeteries of Surat. They are mostly of one type, taken from Mahommedan models, of which they are bad imitations.

Another traveller describes several monuments as

> coffin-shaped, with a place to burn incense at the head, like the
> Moors, only over it a cross: one of more eminency had an arch
> over it at the upper end.

The Muslim's tomb is traditionally an arched vault of plastered
brick, providing ease of exit for the departed on the Day of Judgment
and, as described by Richard Burton,

> large enough for a man to sit up at ease and answer the
> Questioning Angels; and the earth must not touch the corpse as it
> is supposed to cause torture. In the graves of the poorer classes a
> niche offsets from the fosse and is rudely roofed with palm fronds
> and thatch.

The tomb is usually sited under a tree, to give shade, with the head
facing towards Mecca. The body is often carried to the cemetery on
a camel; hence the superstition that to dream of a camel is an omen
of death. Many Muslim burial grounds have a place where women
may sit and weep unseen although the practice of crying for the dead
is not encouraged in Al-Islam. Regular visits to cemeteries are
made, both to burn lights and adorn the tomb with flowers, for the
Prophet said that 'whoever visiteth the grave of his parents every
Friday, he shall be written a pious son', and 'frequent the cemetery,
'twill make you think of futurity'.

The Hindus, along with the offshoots from their religion – the
Buddhists, Jains and Sikhs – cremate their dead, and there are thus
no monuments over the mortal remains, the belief in reincarnation
making such marks of the finite world unnecessary. It is interesting
to speculate how this practice evolved over the centuries before the
Hindu religion became formalised. No doubt the need for quick
disposal of corpses in the East, and the difficulty of digging
sufficiently deep graves to prevent the hyenas and other scavengers
devouring the bodies, were contributory factors. Even the British in
the nineteenth century encountered these problems, and there are
several macabre accounts of soldiers reburying remains dug up
overnight from shallow graves by these predators. There also existed
the primordial belief that any would-be sorcerer might practice
magic on a corpse and interfere with its soul's passage to the infinite.
A trace of this can be seen in the European's attitude to corpses, as
in the letter quoted on p. 14. The main observable influences of
Hinduism on Anglo-Indian customs are the occasional European

tomb designed in the shape of a Hindu temple or an umbrella-topped shrine (tomb in foreground, p. 83), such as the tombs of General Stuart (see p. 84), Augustus Cleveland (see p. 71) and Colonel Pritchard at Jaipur; and perhaps in the ceremonial surrounding funeral processions, where the customary pomp had a peculiar mixture of East and West, with torch-bearers and a general atmosphere of oriental grandeur.

There is a description by Lang of the funeral of Maharaja Hindoo Rao, a Mahratta chief, who lived at Delhi and was noted for his hospitality. The year is 1854:

> They dressed up the old gentleman's corpse in his most magnificent costume, covered his arms with jewelled bracelets of gold, with costly necklaces of pearls and diamonds hanging down to his waist, placed him in a chair of state, sat him bolt upright – just as he used to sit when alive – and thus, attended by his relations, friends and suite, he was carried through Delhi to the banks of the Jumna where the body was burnt with the usual rites and the ashes thrown into the river.

At the other extreme, there is this account in the *Calcutta Chronicle* during the famine of 1788:

> Some more decent and less shocking manner should be practised in carrying the dead bodies to the river instead of that now in use. Sometimes they are loosely flung across a bamboo, and frequently tumble off on the way. At other times, the feet and hands are tied together and in this shocking and indecent manner the bodies are carried naked through the streets.

The arrangements at that time for the cremation of Hindu dead were extremely limited, and the poorer classes generally disposed of their dead by throwing the bodies into the river after a symbolic cremation using the few faggots they could afford. The position is not very different today, as any visitor to the burning ghats on the Ganges will discovery; the body lies on a light litter by the water-side enshrouded in a cloth of a prescribed colour – red with white dots for a married woman, plain red for a maiden, white for a man and saffron for an elder. (It is strange to note the different colours signifying mourning in various religions: green for the Muslim, black for the Christian, light blue for the Armenian, greyish brown for the Ethiopian, white for the Chinese.) The body is then ritually immersed in the river two or three times by a few male relatives with the minimum of formality before being prepared for cremation in a simple and moving ceremony. There is no great feeling of finality; in their belief the body is merely the shell, and Creator and creation, death and birth are one as in the Upanishads. Their idea of God is something like Wordsworth's description:

> Something far more deeply interfused,
> Whose dwelling is the light of setting suns,
> And the round ocean, and the living air,
> And the blue sky, and in the mind of man;
> A motion and a spirit, that impels
> All thinking things, all objects of all thought,
> And rolls through all things.

The profoundness of this philosophy accounted for the unquestioning acceptance by Hindu widows of the custom of suttee which seems to us so utterly inhuman. In the 1820s over 6,000 cases of suttee were recorded around Calcutta, and with the anomalies of administration dividing certain areas under 'King's Law' and 'Native Law', it is reported in the Press that 'widows are reduced to ashes on one side of the Circular Road but not on the other; at Garden Reach but not at Chandpal Ghaut; at Howrah but not on the Esplanade'. Cases continued to be reported long after the custom had been legally abolished, and well into the twentieth century. There have even been reports of suttee since Independence, usually in a small column of the local press, such as this account from Rajasthan on 20th September, 1950, referring to three policemen who tried to stop the ritual before a crowd of 1,500 villagers:

> The police had argued with the widow, a mother of four. They threatened to lock her in her house. But the mob would not let them. Re-inforcements were called – but they were too late. The widow sat with her husband's head in her lap, reciting hymns while the fire was lit. As the flames licked her body she shook off her jewels and placed them on his body before she died.

For all Hindus, Buddhists, Jains and Sikhs there is a common epitaph given in the *Rigveda*:

> Were I thou, Agni, and wert thou I, this aspiration should be fulfilled.

The Parsees are a religious group who neither bury nor cremate their dead. Descended from Persian Zorastrians or fire-worshippers who fled to India one thousand years ago to escape Mohammedan persecution, they established themselves as merchants, ship-builders and bankers, monopolising much of the business of Bombay, Poona and Guzerat. They tended to remain a tight-knit community like the Jews and the Quakers, yet contributed to society through large charitable gifts to European and Hindu institutions. Their practice consists of exposing the corpse on a tower, the 'tower of silence', for the birds of the air to devour under the rays of the sun.

Although the various customs of Christians, Mohammedans, Hindus and Parsees seem so different, it is interesting to note the part played by the primitive elements of earth, fire and water in each, particularly earth. The Hindu on the point of death seeks to be placed on the ground to be in direct contact with the earth to which the spirit returns. The Christian recites 'earth to earth, ashes to ashes, dust to dust'. The Mohammedan in a negative sense seeks to protect the corpse from the corruption of the earth. The Parsee is wrapped in clean clothes and placed on an oblong piece of polished stone which is laid on the floor – again the contact with the earth. Then the hands are laid crosswise and joined on the chest, the feet are crossed and tied, like those of a Crusader, or kept straight, and the following ritual ensues, as described by the notable Parsee Dosabhai Framji Karaka in 1884:

> If death takes place at night, the body is kept in the house till the next morning, but if during the day – four or five hours before sunset – it is removed to its last resting place in the afternoon. Until the last funeral ceremony has been performed, a priest continues saying certain prayers before the corpse, burning sandalwood over the fire all the time. When the time for the removal of the body approaches, it is placed upon an iron bier which is brought in by the corpse-bearers ... When this recital is finished, the dead body is taken out of the house on the bier and carried on the shoulders of 'nasesalars' or corpse-bearers to the 'dokhma' or tower of silence which is generally erected in a solitary place and upon an eminence. Arriving at its resting place, the iron bier is put upon the ground, the face of the deceased is uncovered for a few minutes in order that a last look may be taken of it, and the whole assembly bow before it. After a few minutes the body is carried by the bearers into the dokhma and the vultures, which are always in the vicinity, soon denude it of flesh.

Suicide is rare in Muslim lands, for as Richard Burton sardonically points out, 'the Mohammedan has the same objection as the Christian "to rush into the presence of his Creator", as if he could do so without the Creator's permission'. The Hindu also has some curious prejudices on the subject; he will not hang himself by the neck, for fear his soul might be defiled by exiting through an impure channel, and would prefer to leap down cliffs, drown or starve to death.

The absence of deep mourning is very striking among the Hindus, particularly when an elderly relative has died; instead there is almost an atmosphere of serenity. Muslims are also discouraged from tears, for it is written: 'Verily a corpse is sprinkled with boiling water by reason of the lamentations of the living'; and the Zoroastrian Parsees believe that tears shed for the dead 'form a river in hell, black and frigid'.

Appendix B
Searching for Ancestors

Finding information on an ancestor buried in some remote Indian town in the mid-nineteenth century can take a lot of time, and these notes are added to help those with family connections in India who may wish to pursue inquiries, not only about deaths but also about births and marriages.

The starting point for the search depends on the details sought, the accuracy of existing information regarding names and dates, and on whether London is accessible. The India Office Library and Records (197, Blackfriars Road, London SE1) is the 'Somerset House' of expatriate births, deaths and marriages and for a nominal fee (75 pence in January 1976) will carry out a search for a single event within a five-year bracket. Should the search be successful, a certificate of the birth, death or marriage can be obtained for a further fee (£2:75 in January 1976). The search is conducted among the Ecclesiastical Returns which started at the beginning of the eighteenth century. It must be stressed, however, that these Returns – in common with nearly all records from the East – are only about 80 per cent complete.

Some never reached England due to shipwreck; many failed to record those who died in outlying Districts and were privately buried by the road-side or in a garden; some births were never registered, especially if there was no chaplain available, and a number of civil marriages escaped the Return. Some Returns were never sent back, but exist in India. The Returns were only intended to cover European Christians in India who owed allegiance to the British Sovereign, and hence those of other nationalities and faiths were omitted, although there were some inconsistencies. Eurasians featured little before 1820, but from then onwards many registered. The Indian common-law wife of an Englishman would generally be referred to as a 'native woman' or 'Hindoo-Briton' (up to about 1840) in the maternal column of the British Register. An Indian Christian would not normally be registered, unless a convert and adopted by an English family; and Roman Catholics, Indian or

English, were not formally registered until after 1836.

Those interested in compiling a family tree with branches extending to India may wish to conduct their own searches, and for this no fee is charged at the India Office Library and Records. Again, the Ecclesiastical Returns are the best source. These are arranged chronologically by Presidencies, Bengal from 1713, Madras from 1698, and Bombay from 1709; births, deaths and marriages are listed separately, with an alphabetical index in each to help locate the exact page, provided one has the correct year-volume. Marriages are only indexed under the husband's name until approximately the turn of the twentieth century.

If the searcher has no more information than the name, it is probably better to start elsewhere. The four privately-typed volumes on *Deaths in India* (with other volumes on *Births* and *Marriages*) are invaluable. The original volumes can be seen at the Society of Genealogists, 37, Harrington Gardens, London SW7 (where there is also a card index of names connected with India, available to non-members on payment of a small daily reading-fee). These volumes were compiled by Colonels H.K. Percy-Smith and H. Bullock between 1941 and 1946 from a great variety of Almanacs, Directories, Annual Registers, Army Lists and so on. They are arranged alphabetically, with all sources clearly set out in the Bibliography of Volume I.

If the ancestor being traced was in the Services, it is worth trying the National Army Museum, Royal Hospital Road, London, SW3, which has the *Hodson Index of Honourable East India Company Officers*. This is available in the reading room; it is complete for 'officers of the armies, maritime services and civil services of the Presidencies of Bengal, Madras and Bombay' up to 1846 and has further information to about 1860. The Miscellaneous Records section of Somerset House (now moved to St. Catherine's House, Kingsway) also has records of the births, deaths and marriages of British Army personnel in India from about 1870.

For a researcher requiring detailed bibliographies and lists of records, there is the comprehensive *Guide to the India Office Records, 1600-1858* (London, 1919), by Sir William Foster. From page 110 onwards it traces a path for the ardent genealogist through the Indian Civil, Military, Medical and Ecclesiastical Establishments; Lists of Passengers on East Indiamen; the licence-system for Europeans *not* in the Company's service (before 1833); Casualty Lists, Wills and Probates, and the Ecclesiastical Returns of births, deaths and marriages. A simplified summary by Major V.C.P. Hodson of this Guide, 'India Office Records', was published in *The Genealogist* (Vol.

VI, 1939, pp. 198-208), and a more general document on the India Office Records as a whole, by Joan C. Lancaster, 'Archives: The India Office Records', in *The Journal of the British Records Association* (Vol. IX, No. 43, April 1970). A good guide to genealogical sources is *In Search of Ancestry* by G. Hamilton-Edwards (London, 1966); Chapter 15 deals with the East India Company.

Several useful books give lists of Europeans in particular groups or professional categories, with names and details of service:

Addiscombe Cadets: *Addiscombe: Its Heroes and Men of Worth*, by Col. H.M. Vibart, 1894 (Addiscombe was the East India Company's military seminary from 1809 to 1861; 3,600 cadets passed through it into the company's armies in Bengal, Madras and Bombay).

Army: *Alphabetical List of Officers of the Indian Army, 1760-1887*, compiled by Messrs Dodwell and Miles, London; *General Military Register of the Bengal Establishment, 1760-95*, compiled by White. The *Journal of the Society of Army Historical Research* has lists of epitaphs from British graves in India under the heading 'Notes and Queries', between 1930 and 1936, compiled by H. Bullock. Two publications of the Commonwealth War Graves Commission are also useful: *The War Graves of the British Empire* (Memorial Registers of the 1914-18 war, with separate volumes for groups of cemeteries in India, Pakistan etc.), Nos 1-190; and *Their Name Liveth*, a series of books containing photographs and descriptions of cemeteries and memorials of the 1914-18 and 1939-45 wars.

Artillery: *List of Officers who have served in the Regiment of the Bengal Artillery, with Tables of Successive Establishments, Roll of the Victoria Cross and Stations of Troops and Companies from its first formation down to its absorption into the Imperial List*, by Maj.-Gen. F.W. Stubbs, 1892.

Churchmen: *Parochial Annals of Bengal, A History of the Bengal Ecclesiastical Establishment in the 17th and 18th Century*, by H.B. Hyde, Calcutta, 1901.

Civil Servants: *A General Register of the Hon. East India Company's Civil Servants of the Bengal Establishment, 1790-1842*, compiled by Doss under the direction of H.T. Prinsep, Calcutta, 1844; *Bombay Civil Servants, 1750-1858*, a compilation made by the India Office, London, c. 1880; *Alphabetical List of Hon. East India Company (Bengal Civil Servants) from 1780 to 1838, distinguishing with the dates the several high and important offices held by them during their official career ... Also dates of Retirement, Resignation and Death*, by Messrs Dodwell and Miles, London, 1839; similar volume for Madras Civil Servants.

Governors: *Bengal: Its Chiefs, Agents and Governors*, by F.C. Danvers, London, 1888.

Governor-General's Body-Guard: *Historical Records of the Governor General's Body-Guard*, by Lt. V.C.P. Hodson, 1910.

Indigo Planters: *Bengal and Agra Annual Guide, 1841: Indigo Planters in Bengal*.

Medical Officers: *Alphabetical List of the Medical Officers of the Indian Army with the date of their respective Appointment, Promotion, Retirement, Resignation or Death, whether in India or in Europe, 1764-1838*, compiled by Messrs Dodwell and Miles, London, 1839; *Roll of the Indian Medical Service, 1615-1930*, by Lt.-Col. D.G. Crawford, London, 1930; *Some Echoes of the Past* (a record of the military services of Medical Officers in India who lost their lives in the N.-W.P. and Oudh – now U.P. – from 1788-1860), by Lt.-Col. W.A. Morris, 1911.

Non-Officials: *Non-Official Europeans in India, 1780-1820*, by Lt.-Col. H. Bullock, 1941-3 (a list of Europeans or Anglo-Indians not in the Company's or King's Service, contained in various annual registers and publications); *Duplicate Notes* and *Anglo-Indian Collections*, by Lt.-Col. H. Bullock, 1947 (typed notes in India Office Records and at the Society of Genealogists).

People whose details are difficult to trace from other sources can sometimes be found in one of the Directories and Almanacs published at various times between 1780 and 1860. These include the *Bengal Directory*; *Bombay Almanac*; *Bombay Calendar and Directory*; *Calcutta Annual Register and Directory*; *East India Register* (N.B. between 1803 and 1860 this was published twice a year – the forerunner of the later Civil and Indian Army Lists – and also contained, up to about 1835, lists of non-official residents, with births, marriages and deaths); *East India United. Service Journal and Military Magazine*; *Madras New Almanac*; *Thacker's Bengal Directory*.

Those interested in epitaphs and monumental inscriptions should refer to the official volumes on them, the Provincial Series, commissioned by the government at the turn of this century in an attempt to build up a *Corpus Inscriptionum Indicae Britannicae*, although they are far from complete and very uneven in value. The individual titles are as follows:

Assam: *List of Inscriptions on Tombs and Monuments in Assam*, Shillong, 1902.

Bengal: *List of Inscriptions on Tombs and Monuments, Bengal*, compiled by C.R. Wilson, Calcutta, 1896. (The journal of the Calcutta Historical Society, *Bengal Past and Present*, also contains much detail.)

Bihar and Orissa: *List of Old Inscriptions in Christian Burial Grounds in*

Bihar and Orissa, Patna, 1926.

Bombay: *List of Old Inscriptions, Bombay*, Bombay, 1901; and *Revised List of Tombs and Monuments of Historical or Archaeological Interest in Bombay and other parts of the Presidency*, Bombay, 1912.

Central Provinces and Berar: *List of Inscriptions on Monuments or Tombs in the Central Provinces and Berar*, compiled by O.S. Crofton, Nagpur, 1932.

Hyderabad: *Inscriptions on Tombs and Monuments – H.E.H. Nizam's Dominions*, compiled by O.S. Crofton, Hyderabad, 1941.

Madras: *List of Inscriptions on Tombs or Monuments in the Madras Presidency (also French India, Travancore, Mysore and Hyderabad)*, compiled by J.J. Cotton, Madras, 1905 (revised edition 1946); *List of European Tombs etc. for Districts in the Madras Presidency (North Arcot; South Arcot; Anantpur; Tanjore)* by H. Le Fanu, 1893; S.G. Roberts, 1894; and other 'Collectors', 1894-99, Madras.

N.-W.P. and Oudh: *List of Christian Tombs and Monuments, North-West Province and Oudh*, compiled by Rev. A. Führer, Allahabad, 1896; *List of Christian Tombs and Monuments of Archaeological and Historical Interest and their Inscriptions in charge of the Public Works Department in the United Provinces*, compiled by Rev. A. Führer, Allahabad, 1896.

Punjab: *List of Inscriptions on Christian Tombs and Monuments in Punjab, North West Frontier Province, Kashmir and Afghanistan*; Part I, compiled by G.W. Rhé-Philipe, and Part II, *Biographical Notices of Military Officers and others mentioned in the Inscriptions in Part I*, compiled by Miles Irving, Lahore, 1910 and 1912.

Rajputana and Central India: *List of Inscriptions on Tombs and Monuments in Rajputana and Central India*, compiled by O.S. Crofton, Simla, 1935.

There are a number of other publications with a Provincial or District coverage, such as E.A.H. Blunt's *List of Inscriptions on Christian Tombs and Tablets of Historical Interest in United Provinces of Agra and Oudh* (Allahabad, 1911), and *The Bengal Obituary, or, A Record to Perpetuate the Memory of Departed Worth* (Calcutta, 1848 and 1851) published by Holmes & Co. The Ruinous Graves Notices issued by the Public Works Departments of the various Districts also contain useful material. Information on individual cemeteries and towns can be obtained from a wide range of reference books, some recording only the more important historical inscriptions, others giving a more comprehensive list.

Anyone fortunate enough to be touring India, and able to spare a few minutes from the splendours of the Taj and other Indian sightseeing to search among the ruins of a European cemetery for an ancestor's tomb, may be glad of some practical hints. Questions on the whereabouts of a European cemetery are apt to receive misleading answers; there is usually a number of cemeteries of varying age and size, some in the Civil Lines and some in the Military Cantonments. For instance, in towns such as Allahabad and Lucknow there are 7 and 12 cemeteries respectively, occupying acres and acres of land, often in the middle of the present-day city, some open, some closed and others abandoned. Having located the cemetery, the searcher must be prepared to find the lych-gate occupied by the nominal *chowkidar* (caretaker), his wife and children with their cattle, goats and chickens; washing and dung-cakes laid out on the near-by tombstones; and, perhaps, a mausoleum converted into a rude shelter for a squatter's family. Local experts assemble in no time to help identify the sought-for tomb – usually the same one, with the illegible inscription, for each visitor! – while a train of small children makes photography difficult. The long grass and thoughts of snakes will discourage all but the most intrepid grave-explorers, but there are still many interesting inscriptions in cemeteries all over the country which have never been recorded.

Glossary

Abdar: domestic servant in charge of water and wines.

Ango-Indian: originally used of persons of British birth having connections with India. Sometimes used of persons of mixed blood.

Arrack: distilled sap of palms etc.

Ayah: Indian nurse or lady's maid in European household.

Barasinga: red deer of Kashmir.

Beebee (bibi): woman or mistress.

Beebeeghar: apartment set aside for mistress.

Campoo: native troops under European mercenaries, serving the Mahrattas.

Cantonment: military station in India.

Chaprassie (chuprassy): official messenger.

Cheetal: a deer.

Chobdar: bearer of a silver mace.

Choga: long-sleeved robe.

Chowkidar: watchman, caretaker.

Eedgah: space for Mohammedan worship.

Fakir: mendicant, ascetic.

Farman (firmaun, firman): order, licence or passport.

Godown: warehouse or storeroom.

Griffin: newcomer to the East.

Haji (Hadjee): title given to one who has made a pilgrimage.

Hakeem: oriental physician.

Hawa khana: lit. 'to eat the air', to go for a walk or drive.

Howdah: framed seat on elephant's back.

Interloper: person trading without licence of the East India Company.

Jagir (jagheer, jaghire): assignment of land.

Jaldi jao: go quickly.

John Company: nickname of the Honourable East India Company.

Khakur (karkur): barking deer of the Himalayas.

Kharita (kareeta): brocade bag for letters.

Khud: precipitous hillside of the Himalayas.

Mahrattas: Hindu race occupying parts of central and western India.

Mofussil: country station or district outside the Presidencies.

Mohor (mohur): chief gold coin of India, once roughly equivalent to two guineas (£2.10).

Nabob (Nawab): Moghul title; colloquially, an Englishman returned from India with a fortune.

Pagoda: gold coin of Madras, current until 1818; once roughly equal to a third of a guinea (35p).

Pagri (*puggry, phuggree*): turban.

Pooja (*puja*): Hindu worship.

Peshwa: title of the last Prime Minister of the Mahratta government.

Pukka (*pucka, pucca*): top-grade first-class.

Purdah: system of secluding women.

Ranee: wife of an Indian Raja.

Sahib: deferential title.

Sanyasi (*sunyasee*): Hindu religious mendicant.

Sardar: leader, chief; used as a title.

Sepoy: native soldier in European armies in India.

Shikar: sport; shooting and hunting.

Shree (*shri, sri*): honorific title, literally saint.

Suttee: immolation on the funeral pyre of deceased husband by Hindu widow.

Thuggee: highway assassination and robbery, practised by Hindu sect.

Ticca gharry: hired carriage or pony-trap.

-Wallah: adjectival affix meaning man, doer, possessor etc.

Zenana: harem or women's apartments.

Bibliography

Andrews, W.E., *Monograph on Major-General Claude Martin*, Lucknow, 1942.

Anon., *Biography of Her Highness the Begam Samru*, Roman Catholic Press, Sardhana, 1879 and 1932.

Anon., *Catholic Calendar and Directory for the Archdiocese of Agra*, Simla, 1907 (on Indian Bourbons).

Anon., *H.M.S. Caroline; An Account of a Voyage to India, China, etc., performed in the years 1803-04-05, by an Officer of the Caroline*, London, 1806.

Anon., *Poona's Great Days*, 1786-1818, Bombay, 1945.

Anon., *Roman Catholic Burials: Rules*, Ecclesiastical Branch of Home Department, Native Archives, No. 8, 5th October, 1859, New Delhi.

Anon., *School Memorials*, Lawrence Royal Military School, Sanawar, Simla, c. 1948.

Anon., *The Story of Serampore and the College*, Calcutta, 1918 (1927 and 1961).

Anon., *Victoria Crosses and George Crosses of the Hon. East India Company and Indian Army, 1856-1945*, National Army Museum, London, 1962.

Archer, Mildred, *Tippoo's Tiger*, Monograph No.10 Victoria & Albert Museum, London, 1962.

Atkinson, G.F., *Curry and Rice*, London, 1858 and 1911.

Bamfield, Veronica, *On the Strength: The Story of the British Army Wife*, London, 1974.

Barber, N., *The Black Hole of Calcutta*, London, 1969.

Bellasis, A.F., *An Account of the Old Tombs in the Cemeteries of Surat*, Bombay, 1868.

Bence-Jones M. *Palaces of the Raj*, London, 1973.

Bhatacharya, S. *The East India Company and Economy of Bengal, 1704-1740*, Calcutta, 1969.

Bidwell, S., *Swords for Hire: European Mercenaries in 18th Century India*, London, 1971.

Bond, Ruskin, *Strange Men Strange Places*, Bombay, 1969.

Boxer, C.R., *Portugal and Brazil*, Oxford, 1958.

Brown, Hilton, *The Sahibs*, London, 1948.

Buck, Sir Edward, *Simla Past & Present*, Bombay, 1904.

Burton, Sir Richard, *Love, War and Fancy* (Chapter on 'The Couch of Earth'), edited by Dr K. Walker, London, 1964.

Busteed, H.E., *Echoes of Old Calcutta*, London, 1908.

Caine, W.S. *Picturesque India*, London, 1891.

Lady Canning's Scrap Book, compiled by Emily Bayley, India Office Records, MSS EUR D. 661.

Carey, W.H. *The Good Old Days of Hon. John Company*, Calcutta, 1906 and 1964. (See also under Wilson and Carey for *Glimpses of Olden Times*.)

Chatterton, Eyre, *History of the Church of England in India*, London, 1924.

Colburn's: United Service Magazine, 1849 (article on Indian Army, pp. 31, 342, 503), London.

Coleridge, the Hon. S., *Letters to my Grandson on the Glory of English Poetry*, London 1923.

Curl, J.S., *The Victorian Celebration of Death*, London, 1972.

Dewar, D., *Bygone Days in India*, London, 1922.

Dewar, D., *In the Days of the Company*, Calcutta, 1920.

Dodwell, H.H., *The Nabobs of Madras*, London, 1926.

Doig, D., *Calcutta: An Artist's Impression*, Calcutta, 1965.

Downes, M.P., *Ooty Preserved: A Victorian Hill Station*, London, 1967.

Douglas, J., *Bombay and Western India*, London, 1893.

Dunbar, Janet, *Golden Interlude: The Edens in India, 1836-1842*, London, 1955.

Edwardes, M., *Battles of the Indian Mutiny*, London, 1963.

Edwardes, M., *British India*, London, 1967.

Edwardes, M., *Glorious Sahibs*, London, 1968.

Edwardes, M., *Bound to Exile*, London, 1969.

Elliott, Maj.-Gen. J.G., *The Frontier, 1839-1947: The Story of the North-West Frontier of India*, London, 1968.

Gardner, B., *The East India Company*, London, 1971.

Griffiths, Sir Percival, *To Guard My People: The History of the Indian Police*, London, 1971.

Griffiths, Sir Percival, *The British in India*, London, 1946.

Halliday, J. (pseudonym of D. Symington), *A Special India*, London, 1968.

Hamilton, Capt. Alexander, *A New Account of the East Indies*, London, 1710.

Hare, Augustus, *The Story of Two Noble Lives*, London, 1893.

Hickey, William, *Memoirs*, Volume II, 1775-1782, London, 1960 (reprint).

Holtzman, J.M., *The Nabobs in England, 1760-1785*, New York, 1926.

Hunter, Sir William, *The Thackerays in India and Some Calcutta Graves*, London, 1897.

Indian Church History Review, June 1974, Mysore City.

Indian Horizons, Vol. XXIII, Nos. 2 and 3, September 1974, Delhi.

Karaka, D.F., *History of Parsis*, Vols I and II, London, 1884.

Kaye, Sir John, *Peregrine Pultuney, or Life in India*, Vols I and II, London, 1844.

Kincaid, D., *British Social Life in India, 1608-1937*, London 1938 and 1973.

Kincaid, W., article on Indian Bourbons in *Asiatic Quarterly Review*, 1887.

Kipling, Rudyard, *The City of Dreadful Night*, Allahabad, 1891.

Kipling, Rudyard, *The Naulakha*, London, 1892 (with W. Balestier).

Kipling, Rudyard, *The Day's Work*, London, 1898.

Kopf, D., *British Orientalism and the Bengal Renaissance*, Calcutta, 1969.

Love, H.D., *Vestiges of Old Madras* (3 volumes), London, 1913.

Malcolm, Sir John, *Memoirs of Central India* (2 volumes), London, 1823.

Mason, Philip, *The Founders*, London, 1953 (under the name of Woodruff).

Mason, Philip, *A Matter of Honour*, London, 1974.

Minney, R.J., *India Marches Past*, London, 1933.

Moorhouse, G., *Calcutta*, London, 1962.

Muller, Max, *India: What It Can Teach Us* (a course of lectures delivered before the University of Cambridge), London, 1883.

Ovington, Rev. T., *A Voyage to Surat in the Year 1689*, Oxford, 1929.

Parker, H.M., *Empire of the Middle Classes* (Tracts), London 1845 and 1858.

Parkes, Fanny, *Wanderings of a Pilgrim in the Search of the Picturesque*, (2 volumes), London, 1850.

'Quiz', *The Grand Master or Adventures of 'Qui Hi' in Hindostan: A Hudibrastic Poem in Eight Cantos*, illustrated by Rowlandson, London, 1816.

Rawlinson, H.G., *British Beginnings in Western India*, Oxford, 1920.

Reid, A.B. A private paper on the Indian Civil Service, 1963; and typed notes on the duties of the Superior Revenue Officer of a District, for the Land Administration Manual, 1889.

Renford, Raymond K., *Archival and Library Sources for the studies of the Activities of the Non-Official British Community in India: A Brief Survey (1880-1920)*, S.O.A.S., London, 1976.

Richards, F., *Old Soldier Sahib*, London 1936 and 1965.

Rivett-Carnac, J.H., *Many Memories*, London, 1910.

Ross, F.E., *General Josiah Harlan (1823-1841)*, Central Asian Series, 1939.

Roy, B.V., *Old Calcutta Cameos*, Calcutta, 1946.

Sen, S.P., *The French in India (1736-1816)*, Calcutta, 1946.

Seth, M.J., *History of the Armenians in India*, Calcutta, 1895.

Shellim, M., *Patchwork to the Great Pagoda: India and British Painters*, Calcutta, 1973.

Sheppard, E.W., *Coote Bahadur*, London, 1956.

Sheppard, S.T., *Bombay*, London, 1932.

Short, Bertie, *Between the Indian Flags* (on horse racing), Allahabad, 1887 and 1894.

Smith, Vincent, *The Oxford History of India: From the Earliest Times to the End of 1911*, Oxford, 1921.

Spear, Percival, *The Nabobs*, Oxford, 1963.

Standford, J.K., *Ladies in the Sun: The Memsahibs' India, 1709-1860*, London, 1962.

Stocqueler, J.H., *The Oriental Interpreter and Treasury of E. India Knowledge*, London, c.1840.

Symington, D. (see Halliday, J.).

Trevelyan, Lord Humphrey, *The India We Left*, London, 1972.

Talboys-Wheeler, J., *Madras in the Olden Times, 1639-1748* (Vols I-III), Madras, 1882.

Wilson, C.R. & Carey, W.H., *Glimpses of Olden Times: India under the East India Company*, Calcutta, 1968 (re-print).

Woodruff (see Mason, Philip).

Wright, A., *Bengal, Assam, Behar & Orissa: Their History, Commerce, and Industrial Resources*, compiled by Somerset Playne, London, 1917.

Young, D., *Fountain of the Elephants* (about Count De Boigne), London, 1959.

Yule, Col. H. and Burnell, A.C. (editors), *Hobson-Jobson: A Glossary of Anglo-Indian Colloquial Words & Phrases, and of Kindred Terms, Etymological, Historical, Geographical and Discursive*, London 1886 (re-printed 1903 and 1968).

Index